STATES AND THE MASTERS OF CAPITAL

COLUMBIA STUDIES IN INTERNATIONAL ORDER AND POLITICS

COLUMBIA STUDIES IN INTERNATIONAL ORDER AND POLITICS

Stacie E. Goddard, Daniel H. Nexon, and Joseph M. Parent, series editors

The Columbia Studies in International Order and Politics series builds on the press's long tradition in classic international relations publishing while highlighting important new work. The series is founded on three commitments: to serve as an outlet for innovative theoretical work, especially that work which stretches beyond "mainstream" international relations and cuts across disciplinary boundaries; to highlight original qualitative and historical work in international relations theory, international security, and international political economy; and to focus on creating a selective, prominent list dedicated to international relations.

Making War on the World: How Transnational Violence Reshapes Global Order,
Mark Shirk

States and the Masters of Capital

SOVEREIGN LENDING, OLD AND NEW

Quentin Bruneau

Columbia University Press
New York

Columbia University Press
Publishers Since 1893
New York   Chichester, West Sussex
cup.columbia.edu
Copyright © 2023 Columbia University Press
All rights reserved

Library of Congress Cataloging-in-Publication Data
Names: Bruneau, Quentin, 1989– author.
Title: States and the masters of capital : sovereign lending,
old and new / Quentin Bruneau.
Description: New York : Columbia University Press, [2023] |
Includes bibliographical references and index.
Identifiers: LCCN 2022013969 (print) | LCCN 2022013970 (ebook) |
ISBN 9780231204682 (hardback) | ISBN 9780231204699 (trade paperback) |
ISBN 9780231555647 (ebook)
Subjects: LCSH: Debts, Public—History. | Finance, Public—History. |
Merchant banks—History. | International finance—History.
Classification: LCC HJ8011 .B77 2023 (print) | LCC HJ8011 (ebook) |
DDC 336.3/4—dc23/eng/20220727
LC record available at https://lccn.loc.gov/2022013969
LC ebook record available at https://lccn.loc.gov/2022013970

Cover design: Noah Arlow
Cover image: Moritz Daniel Oppenheim, *Mayer Amschel Returning
the Inventory of the Elector of Hesse.*
The Anthony de Rothschild Collection, National Trust Photographic Library.
John Hammond/Bridgeman Images.

À mes parents, Robin et Nathalie

CONTENTS

viii

ACKNOWLEDGMENTS

I have spent a little over ten years—roughly one-third of my life—mulling over the argument of this book. This kind of time commitment means that any proper acknowledgement would include pretty much all the individuals with whom I have had a sustained relationship during my late undergraduate and postgraduate education, as well as in my early professional career. I want to begin by thanking all these people, who, I hope, will recognize themselves here. That being said, there is a smaller group of individuals that has been absolutely central to the development of my work and thought, and to whom I want to express my deep gratitude in a more direct fashion.

I conducted most of the research for this book during a DPhil completed at the University of Oxford, generously funded by both the Fond de Recherche du Québec–Société et Culture (FRQSC) and the Department of Politics and International Relations. My greatest intellectual debt is to the person who supervised this work, Edward Keene. His scholarship has been a model of rigor and originality, reconciling me with the study of international relations by putting windows where there were once walls. But it is primarily Eddie's qualities as a supervisor that I want to acknowledge here. Throughout these many years, I never felt daunted by a task I faced alone because Eddie always gave the impression that we were on a team, and that his only goal was to help me address the questions I had set for myself as well as he could. He has a unique ability to inhabit each of his students' intellectual world and to work from within it. Today, even as I have gone on to pursue my academic career thousands of kilometers away, Eddie's incisive questions have remained with me as I think and write.

During my undergraduate years in Montreal, Frédéric Mérand and André-J. Bélanger nurtured my interest in international relations and social theory. Together, they motivated my decision to pursue an academic career and gave me a sense of vocation.

Beyond these mentors, many scholars generously offered their time to help me work through various points in this book. In the Department of Politics and International Relations at Oxford, I benefited hugely from the support of Andrew Hurrell, Walter Mattli, and Duncan Snidal. In the History Department, Patricia Clavin generously read and commented on some of my early work. During visiting fellowships at Sciences Po and Helsinki University, Jan Klabbers, Martti Koskenniemi, Heikki Patomäki, and Karoline Postel-Vinay read a few early chapters and provided very helpful comments. Finally, Iver Neumann, then at the London School of Economics, kindly agreed to examine my doctoral thesis, offering suggestions I have been pondering ever since.

I would really only be telling half the story if I omitted the many fellow graduate students I met and engaged with in Paris, Helsinki, and back in Oxford. Many of them diligently listened to my early ramblings about various bits of the thesis I was writing. In Paris, I want to thank Samuel Faure and Guillaume Sauvé for welcoming me at the CERI. For many conversations over what can only be described as uniquely Finnish lunches in the cafeteria of the Helsinki Law Faculty, I thank Nana Klabbers, Sahib Singh, and Ukri Soirila. I have very fond memories of them and of the larger community of scholars of the Erik Castrén Institute. Back in Oxford, I worked among a wonderful group of students who made the process of completing a doctorate a truly enjoyable experience. For their highly stimulating company and friendship, I thank Julia Costa-Lopez, Puneet Dhaliwal, Julian Gruin, Eric Haney, Arthur Learoyd, Bruno Leipold, Pete Millwood, Sam Rowan, Mike Sampson, Jack Seddon, Omar Shweiki, Mara Tchalakov, Marion Vannier, Claire Vergerio, Tomas Wallenius, and Alexa Zeitz.

Having finished my doctorate, I still needed to turn the thesis into something that would perform a more useful task than collecting dust in the Bodleian Library. To that end, I was able to count on the support of my new colleagues in the Politics Department at the New School. I am grateful to them all for the chance they took on a young, freshly minted PhD, as well as for the freedom they have given me to pursue my own teaching interests, and the sabbatical term they granted me to complete this manuscript. Each in their own way, Nancy Fraser, Mark Frazier, Vicky Hattam, Andreas Kalyvas, Jim Miller, Jessica Pisano, David Plotke, Sanjay Ruparelia, and Deva Woodly made the transition to New York an invigorating experience. Our ongoing conversations were somewhat stopped in their tracks by the pandemic, but I very much look forward to picking them up where we left off in the near future. Anne McNevin and Rafi Youatt deserve a special mention because they welcomed me into the global politics "subfield" and have genuinely strived to include me as they created an eclectic intellectual space for our graduate students and ourselves. For their kindness, I cannot thank them enough. At the New School for Social Research, I was fortunate to start my career with a small group of junior scholars interested in economic and financial history. Aaron Jakes, Clara Mattei, and Emma Park have made my transition to a new city and a new job a delight. Moreover, their penetrating analysis of my manuscript undeniably helped to improve it. My students at the New School have also been a constant source of intellectual stimulation, and I specifically want to thank those who took my Global Political Economy course in the last few years.

At this point, I want to acknowledge the editors of the Studies in International Order and Politics at Columbia University Press: Joe Parent, whose enthusiasm gave me a second wind as I was revising the book manuscript, as well as Stacie Goddard, and Daniel Nexon. Their series is a perfect home for a book that sits at the intersection of international political economy and historical international relations. I also want to thank my editor at Columbia, Caelyn Cobb, who provided much needed guidance and encouragement during the publishing process. I have no idea who my reviewers were, but I would like to thank them too for being both demanding and constructive in their reviews.

Over the last two years, my greatest source of intellectual support has been a small network of colleagues scattered across Europe. Julia Costa-Lopez, Arthur Duhé, Eric Haney, Claire Vergerio, and Tomas Wallenius have been the equivalent of an intellectual lifeline in the rather isolated existence imposed by the pandemic. Meeting almost monthly, we have shared our work in progress, future projects, hopes, and anxieties. To this small group, I should add Alexa Zeitz and Sam Rowan, both of whom have always been very generous with their time, responding positively to my requests for their thoughts and comments on any number of chapters and articles.

Claire Vergerio deserves special praise because she read countless chapter drafts and diligently attempted to make sense of many incomprehensible diagrams and scribbles on napkins. Pursuing a doctorate was a project that we undertook together and, as a result, from our early twenties through to about the age of thirty, we have discussed the theses that would become our books countless times. Almost every page of the thesis that underpins this book was improved because of her input.

When I moved to New York, Sarah Aoun, Mark Burwick Mora, Manon Vergerio, and Alex Zimmer provided a home away from home. Since then, they have often dragged me to nights out, pushing me not to forget the world around me and helping me through some hard times. Meanwhile, from Berlin, Theresa Bergmann has been one of the steadiest pillars in my life as we both navigated our twenties. *À vous tous, merci du fond du cœur.* To BC: thank you for being a wonderful therapist.

None of this and much else would have been possible without my close family. For his cheerful friendship and constant encouragement, I want to thank Kerry Wilson. My uncles Bruno Metzger, Eric-Emmanuel Schmitt, and Yann Le Cam have done more to help me make my way in the world than many people's own parents. I have been profoundly moved by their generosity. My sister Sibylle has been an unfailing source of support and I want to acknowledge how lucky I am to have her.

Finishing this book was an arduous task, but I cannot even begin to imagine what it would have been like without the presence of Lizzie Presser in my life. She has commented on most of this book and helped me sharpen its arguments in critical ways, though I can only aspire to write as well as she does. Without her irrepressible joie de vivre, the entire experience of the last three years would have been a disaster. I feel incredibly lucky to have met someone with such capacity for love and intelligence.

Finally, I want to dedicate this book to those who taught me what it means to hope: my parents, Robin Bruneau and Nathalie Metzger. For all they have done, I owe them a debt that can never be repaid.

INTRODUCTION

The classic short story "L'Arlésienne," written by Alphonse Daudet and published in 1866, centers around a young woman from Arles. Only a few pages long, its contemporary fame is largely due to a well-crafted literary device. The woman at the heart of the tale never appears in the story; neither the reader nor the narrator or the characters encounter her during the time frame in which the story is set. Her deeds are only ever mentioned secondhand, and her intentions merely presumed. Yet, they drive the plot, even spurring her fiancé to suicide. Since Daudet wrote the story, the notion of the *arlésienne* has entered French parlance, referring to someone or something that is both pivotal to a situation and also conspicuously absent.

This book is not about Alphonse Daudet's short story, nor is it about French literature or French linguistic expressions. Rather, it is about the transformation of sovereign lending—the practice of lending capital to sovereign states—over the past two centuries. However, anyone interested in this topic will find shelves full of books and articles with an arlésienne-like figure: financiers. Whether the existing scholarship explores the determinants of sovereign borrowing or the extent of the constraints that financial markets impose on states by controlling their access to capital, it places financial markets at the heart of the history of sovereign lending. Still, financiers remain elusive characters. Insofar as they make an appearance, scholars project onto them the characteristics of timeless, profit-maximizing agents.[1] From this perspective, the only changes that can be identified pertain to the world within which lenders operate. The structure of sovereign debt markets might change, along with the political and legal framework governing sovereign debt and international finance more broadly—as for instance it did during the short-lived Bretton Woods era—but the financiers themselves never change.[2] Very few analyses have managed to break free from this conventional view, and I think it has severely limited our ability to identify profound transformations in sovereign lending over the past two centuries. More importantly, it has prevented us from grasping one of the unique features of the contemporary relationship between states and financial markets, as well as from envisioning different possibilities for the future.

My intention is to explore the transformation of sovereign lending by taking a different approach, focusing primarily on the nature of lenders and the way they think about the sovereigns to whom they lend capital. To be clear, I am not interested in identifying what specific criteria determine financiers' lending decisions. Instead, my aim is to approach financiers in the same way one might study a prominent international jurist's or a famous philosopher's conception of states—or whatever else the dominant polities of the international system may be in the epoch she inhabits.[3] The principal obstacle one encounters in this context is that, unlike great political and legal thinkers, groups of practitioners such as financiers rarely lay out their thoughts about states in systematic treatises.[4] And even if a few did do so, how could they possibly be taken as representatives of the entire group? My starting point will therefore consist in clearing a path to recover this specific dimension of financiers' thought. The basic claim is that, even if they produce no easily perusable treatises on the subject, international practitioners such as diplomats, military strategists, and indeed financiers need to know the polities of the international system to perform some of their core tasks; a financier lending capital to states must in one way or another "know" them. She must accordingly rely on what I will call a "form of knowledge," that is, a stable and relatively enduring way of knowing and representing the polities of the international system.[5] These forms of knowledge, examples of which include modern cartography or statistics, constitute key tools for groups of international practitioners in any given epoch. They allow them, quite literally, to know polities. The acquisition and transmission of these forms of knowledge can take place in a variety of settings, though education is a particularly important one. It offers an excellent vantage point to observe their adoption and internalization by specific groups of practitioners before they are eventually put in practice, leaving different sorts of material traces in the process.[6]

This concept leads to what is really the central argument of the book: that over the last two centuries, there was a profound shift between two worlds of sovereign lending, each of which was characterized by a different type of financier and form of knowledge. What I will refer to as the "old" sovereign lending dominated the long nineteenth century and the interwar period. The financiers that defined it were transnational families of merchant bankers such as the Rothschilds, the Barings, and the Morgans, who possessed several distinctive characteristics, of which I will highlight two. The first characteristic is that these actors were as much status-seekers as they were profit-seekers. This fact has been unduly neglected, indeed almost erased by the assumption that financiers are rational, profit-maximizing actors, and it is central to grasping the nature of merchant bankers' relationship to sovereigns. It was linked to their identity as recent migrants (sometimes from persecuted religions), to their earlier and ongoing role as courtly bankers, and to the fact that they were essentially families.

The second key characteristic I want to stress here is that merchant banks' business—whether it related to the financing of international trade, central banking, or global finance—hinged to an astonishing degree on the reputation of their families. The investing public treated the name of the merchant bank that underwrote sovereign bonds as the equivalent of a credit rating. It was in part for this reason that merchant banks continued to be structured as private partnerships with complete liability into the twentieth century, as if to signal that men of their moral character had no need for the limited liability that incorporation would provide. When these financiers engaged in sovereign lending, they pursued business as well as family aims—indeed, these were always inextricably intertwined. Naturally, social status was useful to enhance their bank's reputation, but it was also an end in its own right. Merchant bankers longed for higher social standing in what remained a highly status-conscious world; by becoming acquainted with sovereigns, they could acquire both profit and status. To depict their interactions as ones in which the latter simply evaluated the former's creditworthiness is to miss half the story. These were multidimensional relationships in which something other than money was at stake.

In their quest for profit and status, merchant bankers relied on a form of knowledge I will refer to as gentility, though it was also known as "courtesy"—a type of knowledge developed for courts—in earlier periods.[7] This form of knowledge had been relatively common for international practitioners such as early modern diplomats, who had no real alternative means of knowing states. Before they could use maps or began using statistical data about population, national income and the like, diplomats knew states in person, at the court, or through their ambassadors at other courts. Having risen in a world in which few economic statistics of any kind were available, merchant bankers were and remained in many respects men of this ancien régime. They acquired gentility through a variety of means, not least of which education—for instance, by attending Oxford and Cambridge, where they seemingly learned nothing of immediate value for banking. A key rationale for the reliance on gentility is that it served the merchant bankers in their simultaneous pursuit of profit and status. After all, nineteenth-century Britain, at the center of the global financial system, was a society where access to power, wealth and status rested on conforming to "gentlemanly" ideals.[8] Thus, even as the quantity of available statistical data increased in the late nineteenth century, merchant bankers appear to have made little to no systematic use of it. In their eyes, states remained sets of people to be known in person, rather than a series of statistical data points to be compared. I am certainly not suggesting that merchant bankers were numerically illiterate; my claim is that statistics was simply not the primary means they used to know states—in other words, their primary form of knowledge.

The world of the new sovereign lending differed both in terms of the financiers that characterized it and the form of knowledge that underpinned it. The key actors were joint stock banks, though many more later joined their ranks. These types of financial institutions originated in a set of legal innovations in the period from 1850 to 1870, which enshrined principles of limited liability, unlimited life, numbers of shareholders and capital, and simple registration procedures that did not require high-level political approval.[9] Not only were they very different from merchant bankers' small private partnerships with unlimited liability, but they were also composed of very different individuals. Joint stock banks were not families. They therefore did not pursue status in any meaningful sense, other than to enhance their position on the market and *in fine*, their profits. They were typically created by individuals from a single country, who possessed nothing resembling the strong transnational family bonds of their venerable competitors. In short, they were highly "national." As a result, they were outsiders within the world of sovereign lending, at best enjoying connections to the political elites of the country where they had been created. While this began to change in the late nineteenth century in the secondary financial centers of France and Germany, in the world's financial center, the United Kingdom, and in its successor in that capacity after World War I, the United States, joint stock banks remained comparative outsiders in the business of sovereign lending. Here, the merchant bankers truly were dominant.

As they sought to invest in and, eventually, issue sovereign debt, joint stock banks found themselves at a loss to assess the creditworthiness of different states. Indeed, as "national" banks with few personal contacts with sovereigns across the world, they were in a disadvantaged position. The solution to this conundrum came in the form of a new type of employee, trained in the business schools that had been created in the late nineteenth and early twentieth century, and that had begun producing swathes of graduates. These graduates were trained to think of states through statistics, a form of knowledge that was then only a century old. The use of numbers to systematically represent and compare states, a practice initially called *Statistik* in Germany, had slowly spread throughout the world, by means of publications and statistical bureaux, as well as, crucially, educational institutions.[10] The men hired by joint stock banks eventually produced the first systematic rankings of sovereign creditworthiness, as illustrated by the Crédit Lyonnais' path-breaking experience. Thus, while merchant bankers were operating on the basis of their personal knowledge of sovereigns, joint stock banks developed systematic assessments and rankings of sovereigns largely based on statistics.

By the interwar period, the new sovereign lending had not yet triumphed. Merchant bankers still dominated the business. Two key developments took place that finally gave shape to the world we now inhabit. First, new players joined in the fray during the interwar years: credit rating agencies and the League of Nations. What defined these newcomers was that they relied on the same form of knowledge as joint stock banks. Credit rating agencies became active players in the business of sovereign lending just after World War I. Though not directly engaged in lending capital to states, credit rating agencies' role in assessing borrowers within American financial markets meant that their sovereign credit ratings came to exercise a powerful influence on this practice—all the more so since the United States had become the world's financial center. Like joint stock banks before them, they hired specialists trained in statistics, though these individuals often came from American economics departments instead of European business schools. The same is true for the League of Nations, itself deeply implicated in the large scale production of standardized country statistics.[11] Engaged in sovereign lending by way of its Economic and Financial Organisation (EFO), the league granted its "seal of approval" to a series of sovereign bond issues in the 1920s, playing a similar role to rating agencies in the business of sovereign lending and relying on the same form of knowledge to do so.

The second development, the resumption of private international capital flows after the hiatus that characterized the period from the late 1930s to the late Bretton Woods era, led to the triumph of the new sovereign lending over the old. As early as the 1960s, European merchant bankers such as Siegmund Warburg sought to circumvent the capital controls that formed a central part of postwar "embedded liberalism."[12] Their goal was to resuscitate the international financial business on which they so depended. Eventually giving rise to the Euromarkets and the return of significant international capital flows, their actions turned out to be most beneficial for actors that had completely outflanked them within domestic financial markets. In an ironic twist of fate, American and continental European joint stock banks were the major players to capitalize on this development, engaging in increasingly large sovereign lending operations in the 1970s and further developing their statistical assessments of sovereigns.[13] By the 1980s, as banks came to play a growing role in the recycling of petrodollars, private capital overtook public sources of finance for sovereigns worldwide. The world of the new sovereign lending stood triumphant, gradually expanding to include many other kinds of joint stock companies, such as insurance firms, pension funds, asset management companies, and the like. States now faced strictly profit-seeking financial actors continually evaluating their creditworthiness on the basis of statistical data—a condition that uniquely defines our epoch.

Therein lies one of the most distinctive features of contemporary sovereign lending. Because traditional studies put overwhelming emphasis on analysing the structures within which financiers operate, and because they generally assume that financiers are profit-maximizing actors, this condition appears almost timeless. Furthermore, although the practice of ranking and evaluating countries on the basis of statistical indicators has received growing attention because of its influence on state behavior, the rankings produced by financiers have largely escaped scrutiny.[14] Occasionally, scholars have glimpsed the change revealed here by examining the rise of credit rating agencies.[15] However, the emphasis on this specific type of actor has led them to ignore both the deeper transformation of sovereign lending and the singular novelty of the fact that states are subject to the continual statistical assessments of primarily profit-seeking financial actors.

These blind spots in turn affect how we think about the changing relationship between states and financial markets more generally. Much work in political economy emphasizes how statespersons, economists, and policymakers have been rethinking society's place in relation to the market since the 1980s, drawing parallels with earlier periods, such as the interwar or the pre-1914 era. To describe the present, they reach for concepts that signal similarity with these periods, such as the "re-emergence" or "resurgence" of international finance, the "second" great transformation, or yet still the "dis-embedding" of previously embedded markets.[16] These accounts give pride of place to the structure within which global finance operates, to the detriment of financiers themselves. Global finance, along with the constraints it imposes on sovereign borrowers, is accordingly depicted as something that can either be enabled, as in most of the last two centuries, or, with great difficulty, mitigated, as in the brief Bretton Woods era. But it never changes. This view not only fails to capture the profound transformation in sovereign lending and global finance identified here; it impoverishes our political imagination by preventing us from thinking in a genuinely novel way about the distinct nature of the condition we find ourselves in today.

By contrast, my interpretation of the changing relationship between states and financial markets begins with market actors and their thinking about states. Over a period of two centuries, it was not only policymakers' ideas about finance and markets that changed; financiers' own ideas about states also underwent a radical transformation. From a set of individuals to be known in person, states became numbers on a page. The 1980s did not simply witness the reemergence of global finance or its disembedding, but rather the triumph of an entirely new kind of global finance, made up of financiers who think about states in a radically new way. Symptomatic of this new world of sovereign lending are recurring questions about how exactly financiers assess sovereigns. They infuse numerous political arguments and have come to profoundly shape the horizon of political possibilities we allow ourselves to imagine individually and collectively, as societies. Precisely for this reason, the last four decades have seen specialist institutions such as the Basel Committee on Banking Supervision debate how the new lenders' statistical models can be governed and, through them, the assets they hold on their balance sheets, not least of which is sovereign debt.[17] These discussions raise questions that are unique to the new world of sovereign lending while also offering historically specific possibilities to govern the relationship between states and financial markets. I should like to confess, before anyone wanders through the chapters that contain my arguments, that I provide no answers as to how we should grapple with these thorny issues. However, recognizing their origins and historically distinctive character is a necessary first step to thinking clearly and creatively about the future, and I hope that my analysis can help us in pursuit of this goal.

Before I begin, two very brief points regarding the scope of this study are worth mentioning. The first is that I will not investigate the consequences of the rise of statistical thinking for the distribution of capital among states. My aim is to reconstruct two worlds of sovereign lending dominated by different private actors, who think about states in radically different ways, in order to reinterpret the specificity of the current relationship between states and financial markets and shed new light on the present. The second caveat is that this book focuses on *sovereign* lending. It therefore excludes lending to entities that would have been considered "semi-sovereign," such as Egypt, or nonsovereign, as in the case of many colonies throughout the long nineteenth century.[18] Some states such as the Ottoman Empire and China, while not necessarily considered "semi-sovereign," had a precarious position in the international legal order; they were subjected to capitulations and often excluded from full political and legal recognition as members of the family of "civilized" nations.[19] As a result, it was not uncommon for parts of their fiscal administrations to be controlled by Western Powers, as the case of the Ottoman Public Debt Administration and the Chinese Imperial Maritime Customs Service illustrate. Such cases are set aside in light of my exclusive focus on sovereign lending.[20] Though this choice excludes lending to a number of polities throughout the long nineteenth century, one of the key justifications for it is that sovereign lending as I have described it here has come to apply to the entire world since decolonization, with the extension of the system of sovereign states to all parts of the globe.[21]

My starting point is the question of how to study the ways in which financiers think about states. It is here that I develop the concept of forms of knowledge that allows me to construct the two worlds of the old sovereign lending and of the new. I then move on to examine the old world of sovereign lending, first presenting its main actors, merchant bankers, and the form of knowledge they used to know states, gentility. The second empirical section of the book delves into the world of the new sovereign lending and follows the same structure. It first examines the new actors of sovereign lending, joint stock banks, and then moves on to their new form of knowledge, statistics. Finally, I examine the development and triumph of this world in our time.

Chapter One

HOW INTERNATIONAL PRACTITIONERS
THINK ABOUT STATES

The purpose of this chapter is to explain how I will study the ways in which a specific group of international practitioners—financiers—think about states. This question is more unusual than one might think. Traditionally, studies of sovereign lending (many of which I referred to in the introduction) have sought to identify the specific criteria that determine states' access to capital, using bond yield data to compare the explanatory power of different variables. Some scholars have criticized this type of work, explaining that it projects "modern theories . . . onto past data," and called instead for an approach that would recover historical theories about sovereign creditworthiness.[1] In this chapter, instead of explaining how we might recover such theories, my purpose is to deal with the question of how financiers and other practitioners think about states in a larger sense, much in the same way one studies how famous political and legal figures think about these entities.

To begin, I will turn to a field for which the issue of how we think about the nature of polities has traditionally been central: the history of international political thought. My first claim is that we should locate the study of financiers' thought regarding states as a specific subset of this field. Nonetheless, the methods of international political thought need to be modified, as they are primarily geared toward the study of what one might call "great thinkers" and their famous treatises containing clearly stated ideas about the polities of the international system, rather than to practically oriented individuals such as financiers, and their more inchoate ideas on this front. The task that ensues thus revolves around two questions. First, what exactly should we be looking for if financiers—and practically inclined individuals more generally—do not produce clear statements laying out their ideas about the nature of the polities that make up the international system? The claim I will develop is that one particularly promising path consists in studying the knowledge that practitioners use to know these entities. More specifically, we ought to focus on the *stable and enduring ways of knowing and representing polities* they rely on, which, for the sake of brevity, I call "forms of knowledge," examples of which include gentility and statistics as well as modern cartography, heraldry and many others. They are key epistemic tools that international practitioners rely on to know and represent polities in the conduct of their professional activities. The second question pertains to "where" one ought to look for the thought of practically inclined individuals who do not write great treatises about the constituent units of the international system. Drawing on the insights of a number of social theorists and historians, my second claim is that the study of practitioners' education is a particularly promising starting point because of the critical role it plays in the transmission of knowledge.

Though this method is developed with regard to this specific inquiry into financiers lending capital to sovereigns, it could in fact be applied to a host of other international practitioners, such as diplomats, military strategists, economists, and the like, all of whom possess specific conceptions of the polities of the international system, even if they are not always spelled out. In this sense, this chapter outlines a novel approach to examine a significant aspect of international political thought.

INTERNATIONAL POLITICAL THOUGHT AND ITS LIMITS

The question of how people think about the polities that constitute the international system has been central to a key strand of work in International Relations (IR) concerned with systemic shifts. This body of scholarship is concerned with moments when the political units that constitute the international system undergo a radical transformation;[2] these transformations are thought to alter the "basic texture of international relations," constituting "fundamental discontinuities" or, even more unequivocally, "the most fundamental type of change" in international relations.[3] A classic example of this kind of systemic shift is the stylized transition from the medieval conception of sovereigns as persons to the modern idea of states as abstract entities, out of which a system of sovereign states emerged.[4] Studies that examine these systemic transformations must often engage at some level with the question of how contemporaries in any given period themselves thought about the polities that populated their world, as this offers a useful yardstick to identify the moment when change takes place. This issue has attracted growing attention, particularly among students of international political thought.[5] By and large, these researchers often focus on great thinkers whose thoughts about the polities that constitute the international system can be excavated in treatises and official documents. And, even if recent years have seen a broadening of the kinds of individuals whose international political thought is studied, including an increasing number of non-European figures and women, the vast majority of this scholarship has continued to focus on individual great thinkers.[6] I am interested in a similar topic, but I want to focus on *groups* of individuals, and specifically on *a* group of individuals, financiers, who have received basically no attention from these scholars.[7]

The immediate question to ask is why one might not simply apply the methods relied on by existing studies to analyze the way financiers think about international actors. One objection consists in pointing to the fact that existing work deals with very specific types of people—great thinkers— and not with practically oriented individuals.[8] But the problem with this argument is that many of these great thinkers (e.g., Hugo Grotius or Emer de Vattel) in fact served as diplomats at one point in their career. They were therefore also practitioners. Opposing great thinkers to practitioners in this specific sense is accordingly not an entirely tenable position (though it may be in other respects).

There are nonetheless two reasons why one cannot straightforwardly adopt the methods that existing studies use. The first pertains to the format in which one finds people's thinking about international actors. In the case of famous jurists and philosophers, researchers can and almost always do turn to their great treatises. This is in fact so common that even when these thinkers produce more practically oriented pieces of writing, their more "intellectual" works tend to be privileged. For instance, scholars have mined John Locke's classic *Two Treatises of Government*, when the international dimension of his thought might arguably be better understood by reading a document such as the *Fundamental Constitutions of Carolina*.[9] If I were to apply this method to financiers, I would be looking for their statements about the "ontology" of the international system, that is, the nature of the units found in it, their key properties, and the like. The problem is that, in the case of financiers, as well as for many other types of international practitioners, no easily perusable treatises are available. Financiers, like most diplomats or lawyers, perform their tasks without necessarily stating their precise thoughts about the nature of the units of the international system in a methodical fashion.[10]

The second reason why existing methods do not provide us with a sufficiently strong starting point is that they are overwhelmingly tailored toward the understanding of the thought of a single thinker. The subject of this book is how groups of financiers think about states, not how a single financial institution—let alone a single banker—thinks about the constituent units of the international system. And just as there is no good reason to think that by reading Vattel's *Droit des gens* we can obtain an accurate picture of eighteenth-century diplomats' understanding of the nature of international actors, there is no good reason to think that by examining how one financier thinks about states, we can get an accurate picture of the whole set of institutions' thought about this matter.[11]

And yet, engaging in an analysis of the entirety of financial institutions' archives over a period of almost two hundred years to squeeze out how financiers have thought about states appears to be an elusive endeavor. What is needed here is a realistic but relatively systematic method to tease out this dimension of financiers' *mentalités*. Only after having achieved this will it be possible to rescue financiers (and practitioners more broadly) from the remarkable condescension of posterity, which has put such a premium on how great political and legal figures think about polities, and such a discount on practitioners' ruminations.

FORMS OF KNOWLEDGE AND HOW PRACTITIONERS THINK ABOUT POLITIES

To chart a way out of this impasse, the first task consists in defining what it is that we ought to be looking for. The most obvious option would be to seek out practitioners' ideas about the constituent units of the international system. As alluded to earlier, the problem with this approach is that, in the case of financiers and international practitioners more broadly, one would encounter significant difficulties in finding a source where they laid out how they think about the nature of the polities that constitute the international system. The solution I propose is to direct our attention toward the practical knowledge that international practitioners use to deal with these entities.

The idea that knowledge plays an important role in international politics is relatively uncontentious. Scholars have devoted much attention to the role that knowledge and groups of experts, particularly epistemic communities, play in identifying and articulating state interests.[12] They have further emphasized the pervasive influence of knowledge in shaping our basic representations of reality and, quite literally, creating new objects of global governance.[13] A key point to draw from these studies is that new knowledge allows policymakers to see things that were previously invisible, and that, in the words of one scholar, "what exists is," to an extent, "a function of what is knowable."[14] In this sense, studying the tools people use to know various things can reveal a great deal about what they think actually exists in the world, and what specific characteristics these objects have. For social scientists, these tools are what we call "methods," defined in turn as "concrete tools of inquiry,"[15] or "tools that can be used for a variety of tasks."[16] We believe we can know certain types of things by using certain methods, and we develop certain methods because we believe they are necessary to know certain things.[17] This allows us to deal with specific questions and to produce certain kinds of answers.

To take a concrete example, the development of statistical tables to represent economic activity in a country was intrinsically linked to the idea that there was such a thing as an "economy" that could be known and governed, provided one had the right tools to know and describe it. The development of these practical tools (i.e., statistical tables) is a good indicator of when statesmen and academics began thinking about such a thing as a national economy.[18] This basic point is critical because it provides a clue as to how one might approach the task of understanding the way practitioners think about the nature of international actors by focusing on knowledge, rather than by trying to find their explicit statements on the matter, as one would with a great jurist, for instance.

All practitioners use some set of methods. Practitioners' knowledge is precisely the stock of methods they possess to deal with specific questions, fulfill tasks, and go about their professional lives. When I speak of practitioners' knowledge I am not exclusively referring to what Emanuel Adler and Vincent Pouliot have recently called "background knowledge." In their formulation, background knowledge is "inarticulate,"[19] and "resembles skill much more than the type of knowledge that can be brandished or represented."[20] Pouliot himself once recognized that his own work aimed "to theorize a more specific dimension of social action" than Pierre Bourdieu's, "namely, nonrepresentational practices."[21] Like James Scott's 'mētis,' on this account, background knowledge is so intuitive and practical that any knowledge that is remotely representational is often held to fall outside its purview.[22] By contrast, practitioners' knowledge as I am referring to it here is not just background knowledge; it is the stock of methods used by practitioners to deal with any and all types of tasks they must accomplish. This includes knowledge of both the inarticulate and clearly articulated type. In this sense, it is much closer to Pierre Bourdieu's notion of habitus, "always oriented towards practical functions" but comprising "common schemes of perception,"[23] which can be, among other things, linguistic.[24]

But my core claim is not simply that we should examine the knowledge used by international practitioners, for it is unclear how that would shed light on the more specific question of how they think about the polities of the international system, be they states or otherwise. To understand how international practitioners, such as financiers, think about the polities of the international system, we ought to focus on the *stable and relatively enduring ways of knowing and representing these entities* that they use. These methods are akin to what Bernard Cohn has called "forms of knowledge"—a term I shall also adopt—in the sense that they are "investigative modalities" that involve "the definition of a body of information that is needed" and "the procedures by which appropriate knowledge is gathered," though the extent of their formalization can vary greatly.[25] The main peculiarity of the concept of "forms of knowledge" as I will be using it here is that it only refers to investigative modalities used to know and represent the polities that constitute the international system, rather than any and all types of knowledge that practitioners use.[26] So understood, these forms of knowledge are the key to excavating the thought of people who do not lay down their ideas about polities in clear treatises. Examples of forms of knowledge include those examined in-depth in this book, gentility and statistics, as well as modern cartography, heraldry—to which I will return in a moment—and many more.

Forms of knowledge constitute key tools for international practitioners in any given epoch. Indeed, while many practitioners involved in international relations did not write long treatises about the international system, they surely drew on some kind of tacit knowledge to know its units. Whether one is a diplomat or a military strategist, one needs to be able to know the units of the international system to perform one's tasks. Even a banker must in one way or another "know" the polities to which she wishes to lend. She must accordingly rely on one or many of the stable and enduring ways of knowing and representing these polities (i.e., forms of knowledge) available to her. For this simple reason, practitioners routinely use forms of knowledge. Because of their widespread use among international practitioners, the study of forms of knowledge can allow researchers to tease out how practitioners think about the polities of the international system.

In order to illustrate what a form of knowledge is with more precision, I would like to consider two brief examples: modern cartography and heraldry. In a recent monograph, Jordan Branch has examined the development of modern cartography and its role in the advent of an international system of territorially defined states.[27] As it developed, modern cartography came to constitute a new way of knowing and representing international actors, as territorial entities with clear geographical boundaries. At a basic level, the use of modern cartography implied that in order to understand the international system and its constitutive units, one would turn to maps outlining precise geographical entities delimited by clear borders, over which unfettered sovereign authority was exercised. By tracking the adoption of modern cartography as a form of knowledge, Branch convincingly argues that this territorial representation of the units of the international system was a practice that only took root in the late eighteenth century among European diplomats.[28] Analyzing peace treaties across the early modern era up to the early nineteenth century, he shows that cartographic references only appear at the very end of this timeframe. The Treaties of Paris (1814–1815) concluded after the defeat of imperial France constitute the real watershed moment when "territory was divided linearly, with those lines of division described in careful geographic and cartographic terms."[29] As one other scholar puts it, "The preparation of maps as part of treaty-making had been exceptional before 1715; it became routine by 1789."[30] While some individual European states, particularly France, were beginning to map their own territory earlier on, European diplomats did not share this practice and accept it as a legitimate way of knowing and representing polities before the late eighteenth century.[31] This is why "the careful delineation of boundaries in 1815 was," truly, "revolutionary."[32]

Another less-well-known form of knowledge originating in the late Middle Ages is heraldry. In the "highly visual culture" of the late medieval and early modern era, heraldry represented the constituent units of the international system with ensigns of various shapes, colors, fabrics, and metals.[33] Heraldic markers allowed various people to estimate the standing of a given polity, its claims to prestige, right to bear arms, respect, authority, lineage, and the like. Aside from being extremely practical to situate combatants on a battlefield, heraldry also served as a key tool in late medieval and early modern courtly ceremonial.[34] This is in part because transport and communication were much slower than they are nowadays, and literacy much less common. Polities were therefore known through representations, and heraldry was a crucial one. The question of heraldry was so central that it received extensive attention from Bartolus of Sassoferrato, "one of the most important figures in the legal history of the concept of sovereignty," in his *Tractatus de Insigniis et Armis* (1355).[35] Later on, institutions regulating heraldry received royal recognition and rose in importance. For instance, in England, the College of Arms received a royal charter from Richard III in 1484 and became a repository of heraldic knowledge.[36] Ultimately, this form of knowledge was well suited to a world structured around courts, dynasties, and individual sovereigns whose political authority frequently overlapped in a variety of ways.

In this book, I will seek to excavate the primary forms of knowledge on which specific groups of financiers that dominated sovereign lending relied. Before I do this, however, I want to turn to one last question, namely, where we might look to observe the forms of knowledge that different groups of international practitioners adopt.

WHERE SHOULD WE LOOK FOR PRACTITIONERS' FORMS OF KNOWLEDGE?

My central claim in this section is that the key place to look for such thought is international practitioners' education.[37] I want to stress that the importance of education for understanding how people think in a given epoch is precisely one of the unspoken reasons why scholars examine great thinkers' ideas: because these great thinkers' ideas are assumed to be widely taught, that is, transmitted through education. My basic intuition here is related to this proposition. The main difference is that I believe there is no prima facie reason to suppose that a few great thinkers capture the political thought of an age.[38] Thus, my suggestion is to focus on education more broadly. This entails examining not what one scholar or even a few famous scholars said, but rather analyzing educational curricula to observe what forms of knowledge are transmitted to which groups of practitioners. While the historian of political or economic thought might be interested in single thinkers because of their clarity or originality, the point of studying curricula is to uncover the taken-for-granted knowledge, the seemingly most mundane aspects of a given epoch's thought, among specific social groups.

The study of education remains surprisingly marginal, not to say almost inconsequential, among scholars of international relations.[39] This is truly remarkable given the now well-established interest in practice and practitioners that has taken over various bits of the discipline of IR, under the heading of the "practice turn."[40] Inspired by the writings of a number of philosophers and social theorists,[41] as well as by social and cultural turns in diplomatic and international legal history,[42] these works have sought to analyze the historical development of international relations through a history "not of international law and diplomacy, but of international lawyers and diplomats."[43] However, one of these scholars' main lights has remained hidden under a bushel. Indeed, some of the key figures on which the turn to practice has drawn were in fact eminently preoccupied with education.

Pierre Bourdieu, one of the main sources of inspiration for the practice turn, may be the best such example, not least because one of his first institutional moves as an academic was to create a Centre for the Sociology of Education.[44] In addition, Bourdieu's sociological theory was forged in large part with education in mind, whether it was to draw attention to the role of educational institutions in creating an artificial scholarly gaze,[45] or to reveal the centrality of education in the process of social reproduction and stratification.[46] This interest was further developed in the work of what one might call "second-generation" Bourdieusians. Perhaps the most emblematic is the work of Yves Dezalay and Bryant Garth, which puts enormous emphasis on professional educational change to explain the differentiated developmental paths of South American countries.[47] Similarly, the classic text on "communities of practice" identifies education as a core factor in the formation and maintenance of these communities, an observation that seems to have fallen off the radar after the import of the concept into IR.[48]

But beyond figures of sociological inspiration, many historians concerned with matters international have also pointed to the key role of education. International historian Donald Cameron Watt, alarmed by a tendency to transform historical actors into "coat-hangers or clothes horses" for attributes and worldviews projected back onto them from the present, considered the study of education to be one of the crucial ways of avoiding the "systematic repopulation" of the past "with the mental furniture of the present."[49] This was because it could provide insight into groups of individuals' actual perceptions and dispositions.[50] Contemporary social and cultural historians of international practitioners stress the role of education as well, with some explicitly framing their work against Norbert Elias's understanding of the relation between education and international relations, as outlined in the *Civilizing Process*. Instead of emphasizing the impact of social structures (e.g., courts) on the development of education, individual behavior and affects,[51] they have sought to flip Elias's argument around, recasting the "system of education and its curriculum as the most important element in the process of civilizing."[52] In some cases, educational change is seen as a process that not only transforms international practitioners but also produces and empowers new groups of practitioners.[53] In sum, the study of education appears as a particularly useful—and puzzlingly overlooked—dimension of the study of international practitioners.[54]

But what does it mean, at a methodological level, to study education? Two prominent historians define the key concerns of a history of education as centering on the question of "who, at different times, was being educated, by whom, how, and to what ends?"[55] For them, education can, at its broadest, be understood as including schools and univerisities, but also "informal networks of learning and activity."[56] Therefore, in principle, studying the education of international practitioners is a fairly open endeavor, including both professional and quasi-professional types of education. It need not be exclusively concerned with highly formalized training and could range anywhere from a structured university curriculum to practical manuals, or even to a looser form of teaching by competent individuals.

In terms of the sources that allow one to access this education, the most obvious stems from the fact that education implies some type of transmission and will therefore often leave material traces. Thomas Kuhn, for instance, notes that the emergence of new paradigms can be observed with the "the formation of specialized journals, the foundation of specialists' societies, and the claim for a special place in the curriculum."[57] Because I am not concerned with scientists, but with the people receiving an education, the sources of interest in my case are such things as manuals, educational curricula and, sometimes, entire institutions. Consider two examples. Across the eighteenth and nineteenth centuries, diplomats' education began slowly shifting from practical manuals toward newly created diplomatic institutes.[58] Understanding the content of the curricula in both these sources would be crucial to grasping how diplomats thought and how this changed over time. Likewise, early modern international lawyers were initially trained in universities all across Europe, their legal training being recognized across the continent. This system was later replaced by national legal institutes, fragmenting the international legal space of early modern Europe.[59] Again, studying the changing curricula in these institutions would give us a valuable insight into the shifting underpinnings of international law as a profession and practice.

To be clear, education is of course not the only means through which individuals learn and acquire forms of knowledge. It therefore does not constitute the only site one might investigate. Furthermore, the regular use of a specific form of knowledge by international practitioners sometimes leaves material traces, which offer yet another site to examine which ones practitioners use. For instance, at major international congresses, diplomats are bound to refer to the units of the international system and thus to rely on specific forms of knowledge to know and represent them. If diplomats regularly use modern cartography to know and represent the units of the international system, it is likely that we will find maps in the records of peace conferences and as appendix to treaties. Though I will rely on such traces throughout this inquiry, I shall nevertheless for the purposes of systematicity put quite some emphasis on practitioners' education (for a summary

TABLE 1.1
Forms of Knowledge

---

1. Forms of knowledge are stable and relatively enduring ways of knowing and representing the polities of the international system.
2. Forms of knowledge constitute crucial tools for groups of international practitioners.
3. Forms of knowledge are transmitted through professional or quasi-professional education, frequently leaving material traces.
4. The use of forms of knowledge often leaves material traces.

---

of the properties of forms of knowledge as I described them in this chapter, see table 1.1).

In this chapter I sought to provide an answer to the question of how we could study the ways in which financiers and international practitioners more broadly think about states. My preliminary claim was that the study of financiers' thought about the polities of the international system should be understood as a subset of the history of international political thought. This transposition is less straightforward than it seems, however. The main issue is that the methods of this field are mostly calibrated toward the study of individual great thinkers who produce relatively clear treatises, laying down their ideas about the units of the international system and their characteristics. I thus addressed two key questions that arise directly from this discrepancy. The first was what exactly one should look for to understand how international practitioners think about polities, insofar as they do not publish clear statements on this matter. The answer I put forward was that we ought to seek out the practical tools they use to know and represent these entities, which I referred to as "forms of knowledge." I then briefly illustrated what these tools were, using the example of modern cartography and heraldry.

Second, I addressed the question of where one might look to find the forms of knowledge that international practitioners acquire and use regularly. Here, I pointed to education as a key site to investigate what forms of knowledge different groups of practitioners acquire at different points in time. More specifically, I suggested that we could examine the manuals, curricula, and institutions with which these different groups are educated and observe what forms of knolwedge are transmitted therein. Conveniently, this provides a number of obvious sources for empirical research, which I will rely on in the two substantive sections of this book ("the old sovereign lending" and "the new sovereign lending"). Beyond education, I also explained that the use of forms of knowledge could at times leave material traces, thus providing another potential site for empirical investigation.

One of the key points to take away here is that the method I outlined is not specifically tailored for financiers. It could be applied to a host of other kinds of international practitioners who, despite not writing great treatises about international relations and the international system, nonetheless think about those issues, if only tacitly. The inaccessibility of their thought by contrast with that of great thinkers is almost proportional to its importance for the conduct of international relations. The present inquiry will focus on the individuals who lend capital to sovereigns, but there are a vast number of social groups to which one might apply this approach in order to recover their distinct, though not always clearly spelled out, thought about the "international."

The remainder of this inquiry is structured following the method outlined in this chapter. In each section, I present the relevant group of international practitioners and move on to an analysis of their main form of knowledge. The section on the old sovereign lending first presents the dominant financiers of the period from 1815 to the 1930s, merchant bankers, before laying out their key form of knowledge, gentility. The section on the new sovereign lending begins with an account of the rise and nature of the new sovereign lenders from the late nineteenth century onward, joint stock banks, and proceeds with an analysis of their main form of knowledge, statistics. A penultimate chapter on the triumph of the new sovereign lending, followed by a conclusion, close the analysis.

PART I

The Old Sovereign Lending

Chapter Two

THE INSIDERS—MERCHANT BANKERS

"Money is the God of our time, and Rothschild is his prophet."[1] The importance of merchant bankers to international finance was obvious for
nineteenth-century writers such as Heinrich Heine. Numerous others wrote
about this group of financiers. Lord Byron famously explained in *Don Juan*
that every one of the merchant bankers' loans "seats a nation or upsets a
throne," telling his readers that "Jew Rothschild, and his fellow Christian,
Baring" were the "true lords of Europe."[2] In his novel *Coningsby*, nineteenth-
century British prime minister Benjamin Disraeli speaks of a certain Sidonia
who "established a brother, or a near relative, in whom he could confide, in
most of the principal capitals," claiming that Sidonia was "lord and master
of the money-market of the world, and of course virtually lord and master of
everything else."[3] This character, it has been widely recognized, bore strong
resemblance to Nathan Rothschild. Finally, Honoré de Balzac took the
House of Rothschild as a model for the House of Nucingen, a rich banking
family in his *Comédie Humaine*.[4] The crucial role of these merchant banks
within nineteenth-century international finance was thus eminently clear
to popular writers, and it has interested people to this day.

Unsurprisingly, many scholars have also noted that merchant bankers
were indeed central to nineteenth-century sovereign lending.[5] Layna Mosley, for instance, identifies merchant bankers as the key actors.[6] Economic
historian Stanley Chapman concurs and identifies 1914 as the turning point

for their decline.[7] Vinod Aggarwal claims that this decline took place between the 1860s and 1914,[8] when bondholders managed to eliminate "middlemen who did not always keep bondholders' best interests in mind."[9] And while this identification of decline as early as the 1860s is a surprising assessment in light of the existing historiography, there is some truth to the claim, insofar as new actors were beginning to challenge merchant bankers' domination in banking more generally. Nonetheless, while merchant bankers were certainly on the decline, sovereign lending was an area of business to which they clung with great success until the interwar period.[10]

One of the contributions of studies of this type is to expose the fact that financial markets, and specifically markets for sovereign debt, were highly intermediated throughout the nineteenth and early twentieth centuries. In other words, these markets did not consist of diffuse investors acting in an uncoordinated fashion; instead, they were structured around middlemen on whose financial judgement investors relied. This is an observation about the structure of markets. What this chapter seeks to do is to build on this insight and develop it further. If these middlemen (i.e., merchant bankers) were indeed critical to international finance until the interwar period, then it is necessary to understand who they were, what they sought, and how they pursued their goals. Put differently, the aim is to examine the agents that other scholars have revealed to be pivotal in their structural analysis of sovereign debt markets.

This chapter makes two key points regarding the identity of merchant bankers and their goals. First, merchant bankers were not only profit-seekers, but also status-seekers. This was linked to their identity as migrants (sometimes from persecuted religions), to their origins as courtly bankers in Germanic Europe, and to the fact that banks were essentially families, whose longing for social standing was impossible to dissociate from the business aims of the banks they ran. The relationship that bankers had with sovereigns must be understood in this light; contrary to what conventional studies tacitly assume, sovereign lending was not an exclusively economic relationship. Second, merchant bankers' business hinged to an astonishing degree on their personal reputation and social networks. This was true for their activities in trade, as it was for the business of lending capital to sovereigns. Hence, the social status that merchant banking families acquired and the acquaintances they made served them both in their business endeavors and in terms of the broader social goals they were seeking to achieve.

To make these points, the chapter proceeds in three steps. The first section examines the identity of merchant bankers and their goals. The second section of the chapter demonstrates that merchant banks were the cornerstone of the international financial system and argues that their activities depended heavily on reputation and social networks. They played a critical role in trade, in the management of central banks, and, crucially, in sovereign lending, a business they dominated until the 1930s. Finally, this chapter asks what information was available to merchant bankers as sovereign lenders and shows that, until the late nineteenth century, merchant bankers lived in a world where they had no reliable information about sovereigns' finances. The chapter thus ends with a puzzle: How did merchant bankers know and evaluate the sovereigns to whom they lent capital?

FAMILIES, MIGRANTS, AND THE PURSUIT OF STATUS

The merchant bankers at the heart of the old world of sovereign lending had two important characteristics. First, they were for the most part immigrant families from Germanic Europe and were thus accustomed to operating as financiers in a world of princely courts. Second, the structure of merchant banks was family based, which meant that the goals of families were not fully distinct from those of these banks. As families, migrants, and people used to operating in courts, merchant bankers were after more than money: they sought social status. This observation is absolutely critical to understanding how merchant bankers knew sovereigns and related to them (more on this in chapter 3). The next paragraphs unpack in more detail these social characteristics and their implications.

The first key characteristic of merchant bankers was their origin. Toward the end of the eighteenth century, a number of families established themselves in what would become the leading financial centers of the nineteenth century: London and Paris.[11] These families would become the great merchant banks that dominated international finance until the interwar period.[12] They were often Protestant or Jewish and came from German-speaking Europe, be it the Holy Roman Empire or Switzerland, though they did also include some French Huguenots. This is illustrated by R. H.

Tawney's claim that "behind Prince and Pope alike . . . stood in the last resort a little German banker."[13] Some evoke the idea of "international Huguenots," a network of "family dynasties that linked Geneva, Berne, Frankfurt, Amsterdam and Paris, with London."[14] Though the Dutch themselves had substantially developed financial operations in the eighteenth century,[15] it appears that "ethnic trading groups that had been dispersed by religious persecution were more tenacious in holding to it as it had become a way of life for them."[16]

In the British case, the late eighteenth century witnessed the arrival of a number of merchants from the continent in London and in the country more broadly. It was these continental merchant banks that eventually settled in London who came to monopolize the business of sovereign lending until the interwar period. Many initially came to profit from the industrial revolution that was taking place.[17] Indeed, the individuals who immigrated were often engaged in the import of textiles from England to their own towns and regions on the Continent. The Rothschilds and the Barings, for instance, who were to become great nineteenth-century merchant bankers, settled in England during the second half of the eighteenth century. John Baring moved to England from North Germany and resided in Exeter as a merchant of various textiles. One of his children, Francis, opened a branch in London with his brother John in 1762 and gradually established himself as a merchant banker. As for the House of Rothschild, Goethe rightly noted that it "is rich but it has required more than one generation to attain such wealth."[18] The Rothschilds indeed arrived in England in about 1798, when Nathan came to take advantage of the new opportunities in the booming textile industry.[19] In the early nineteenth century, another group of merchant banking families settled in London, including the Bensons, Dobrées, Erlangers, Frühlings, Goschens, Hambros, Huths, Kleinworts, Schröders and Seligmans.[20] There were other merchants, not from the Continent, but from other parts of the Atlantic world, such as Brown, Shipley & Co., a family firm of Irish descent who had first immigrated to the United States and then come to London. J. S. Morgan & Co. also pursued a similar path through North America. Morton Rose & Co. was another Anglo-American house, while Morrison & Co. was a family firm of Scottish descent. The period following World War I saw the brief dominance of a few Anglo-American houses, particularly the House of Morgan, but also the continued preeminence of many houses who originally came from German lands.[21]

As for Paris, the city was also an important financial center during the nineteenth century, though it certainly became secondary to London after the Franco-Prussian War.[22] A number of key families settled there from the late eighteenth century onward. These included a great number of French Protestant families who, due to persecutions, had been forced to live in Switzerland.[23] The Delesserts, Foulds, Hottinguers, Mallet, Périer, and Seillières all established themselves before the nineteenth century while the Rothschilds, d'Eichtal, Mirabaud, and de Neuflize emerged for their part in the nineteenth century. In any case, according to French business historians, the banks composing what is generally referred to as the *haute banque* had all been established by 1850, with the main thrust of the debate being about where to set the date between 1815 and 1850.[24] The Hottinguers provide a good example of the way merchant banks established themselves. The head of the family, Jean Conrad Hottinguer, arrived in Paris from Zürich in 1784 to further his training as a merchant at Lecouteulx de Canteleu's firm.[25] He then founded his own bank in 1786 and later became a Baron of the French Empire in 1810. He also served as regent of the Banque de France from 1803 to 1833, a position that was then passed on to his son.[26] Again, as in London, major merchant banking families came from Germanic Europe and settled in Paris during the last third of the eighteenth century.

Many of these migrant merchant bankers stood in the long tradition of court bankers—the Jewish ones having long been referred to as "court Jews."[27] Merchant bankers indeed "began almost as servants of the princes in whose employ they were able to accumulate great wealth"—in other words, as servants to a court.[28] This was particularly true in the German context where minor German states and princes remained important until 1866.[29] In these circumstances, merchants often lent capital to their local sovereign. For instance, the Rothschilds, who were based in Frankfurt, started lending to the Landgrave of Hesse-Cassel. Coincidentally, the German confederation often met in Frankfurt, so it was easy for the Rothschilds to make contacts there, or even to lend to the confederation itself.[30] As a result, in the first half of the nineteenth century, the Rothschilds lent to many minor German princes such as the Grand Duke of Hesse-Darmstadt, the Prince of Wied, the Duke of Bentheim-Tëcklenburg, Prince Victor of Isenburg, the Duke of Saxe-Coburg-Gotha, the Duke of Anhalt-Cöthen, and the Duke of Nassau.[31] In addition to sovereign loans, their interests often pertained to such things as bullion, mercury, diamonds, and the like.[32]

Ultimately, though not all merchant bankers were originally court bankers, most reproduced their modus operandi.[33]

Merchant bankers' practice was largely based around the idea that connections with princes, and with the court more broadly, always led to a range of other profitable activities. In this sense, they were very much men of the eighteenth and early nineteenth century, though it is interesting to note that the tradition of "court Jews" continued far into the nineteenth century, with such characters as Gerson Bleichröder, banker to Bismarck. The centrality of courts to merchant bankers' thinking is nicely illustrated by Salomon Rothschild's advice to his brothers in 1816, when, in a letter to Nathan and James, he claimed that "[a] court is always a court and it always leads to something."[34] In a similar vein, writing to his brothers, Amschel Rothschild made clear that "business transactions with royalties always end in a profitable way," and he thus subsequently asked them not to "let the smallest business go by."[35] This second quote also suggests that it might in fact not be a bad idea to take on unprofitable loans to sovereigns, as they may eventually pay off in a myriad other ways, whether in monetary terms or otherwise. One historian of the House of Morgan similarly explains that sovereign lending was "occasionally a loss-making activity," using the example of J. S. Morgan's 1869 loan to Spain.[36] Lending to sovereigns was indeed to some extent a rite of passage to becoming a great merchant banker. While all merchant bankers were not initially court bankers in the literal sense, they became court bankers in the broader sense. Put simply, they made their way into social circles in which they could meet the sovereign, or her representatives (e.g., ministers), because "it remained true that as always one thing could lead to another."[37]

In addition to their origins as German courtly bankers, merchant banks possessed a second key characteristic: they were families. Though underresearched, the familial nature of nineteenth-century financial firms is key to grasping their behavior.[38] The bank *was* the family, and its credit was passed on from father to son, as noted by Walter Bagehot, erstwhile editor of the *Economist*.[39] Being an eminent merchant bank "was a way of life as much as a way of business."[40] In fact, most business histories concerning merchant banks emphasize this point, notably by using the language of "dynasties" to describe them (e.g., House of Rothschild, House of Morgan, House of Baring). A corollary of this fact is that the goals of merchant banks were intertwined with those of families, in the same way that the goals of early modern states cannot properly be disentangled from those of the dynasties at their head. This specific social feature was reinforced by the legal structure of merchant banks. To take a key case, in England, banks were composed of six partners or less, as English law did not permit any more.[41] They also had unlimited liability. In this context, it was desirable to have partners that were family members whom one could trust and who had a stake in the maintenance of the family's reputation.

Crucially, as families, these banks were not only profit-seekers, but also status-seekers, and here I do not simply mean that they sought status simply to improve their position on the market: they sought it as an end in itself.[42] Histories of early modern bankers often present similar arguments. For instance, writing about the Fuggers of Augsburg from the late medieval period to the seventeenth century, one scholar states that researchers should be sensitive to the "social norms that were of fundamental importance" to the estate society of the time, further adding that "unbridled striving for profit most certainly was not one of these norms."[43] Indeed, Anton Fugger remarked that his acquisition of real-estate was not "for profit's sake, but for honour's sake."[44] The honor of the family's "name and lineage" was the key preoccupation of these early modern bankers, and while accumulating wealth could certainly help, it was not the end goal.[45] In the case at hand, merchant bankers who were first- or second-generation immigrants or, alternatively, members of discriminated religious minorities, were not only looking to make money, but to acquire prestige and social recognition. Here one is reminded of the words of the lead partner at Hope & Co., who wrote in a letter from 1806, "I wish that the house might always have as its motto 'honour and profit'; but if either of these words must be erased, I would that it be the latter."[46] The same comment can be made about later bankers such as Gerson Bleichröder, famous banker to Bismarck, about whom a prominent historian astutely notes that he "thirsted after power and profits—and after what both were to give him: respectability and acceptance."[47]

With regard to nineteenth-century merchant bankers, one interesting indicator of this pursuit of status is their willingness to become members of Parliament. Between 1832 and 1918, the Barings produced twelve MPs, the Rothschilds six, the Grenfells four, the Hambros three, the Gibbs three, and the Samuels four.[48] At first, such a pursuit may seem to be purely self-interested, but, in nineteenth-century Britain, "a seat in the House of

Commons . . . was only of limited value," and, indeed, people like the Roth-schilds made little use of its facilities.[49] In fact, it was not only of limited value, but could be financially damaging. For instance, as an historian of Barings Bank explains, Francis Baring's political activity "took him away from his occupation as a merchant and to that extent was detrimental to his financial well-being."[50] But such activities were part and parcel of what it was to be a gentleman, a status that required practicing arts such as "lead-ership, light administration and competitive sports."[51] Despite its financial costs, having an MP within one's family served to raise the family's status.

Though many business histories touch here and there on the theme of status-seeking, the fact has been insufficiently recognized. This is partly due to the widespread assumption that bankers are utility-maximizing actors who seek profit. And, indeed, as I will show in the next section, while mer-chant banking families did pursue status for its own sake, it was also critical for their business endeavors. My point here is not to reject the assumption that merchant bankers pursued profit, but to qualify it by saying that they had another important set of goals, of a different nature, and that we should keep this in mind in order to understand how they operated.

MERCHANT BANKERS IN INTERNATIONAL FINANCE: NETWORKS AND REPUTATION

Merchant bankers were the cornerstone of the emerging international finan-cial system of the nineteenth century. From the funding of international trade to the operation of central banks and the financing of sovereign debt, they were present in all key areas of international finance. For all these types of work, merchant bankers were dependent on two crucial features: their networks and their reputation. The importance of merchant bankers' net-works has been noted in a number of business histories dealing with spe-cific banks, as well as by works in economic history. As for reputation, recent work in financial history has drawn attention to its role in the business of sovereign lending, but overlooks the way in which it suffused all aspects of merchant bankers' business model.

Merchant bankers relied on two key types of networks: those within the banking world, and those beyond it. One useful way of establishing net-works among banks across Europe was marriage, as it strengthened ties either within or between banking houses.[52] The Rothschilds famously married within their own family. Though in the late eighteenth and first quarter of the nineteenth century Rothschilds married the members of "other, similarly Jewish families" with whom they did business, thereafter they tended to marry other Rothschilds. As a result, out of twenty-one marriages between 1824 and 1877, fifteen were between direct descendants of Frankfurt-based Mayer Amschel Rothschild.[53] This was one of the features that the Rothschilds had in common with royal families, whom they regarded as models to an extent, though even these families were not as "closely inbred."[54] These marriages made for a tight-knit family and strong ties across the European continent. A direct consequence was the presence of multiple family members in various European capitals. One alternative to intrafamily marriages was marital alliances between banking houses. For instance, the great Amsterdam house of Hope & Co. "probably . . . the richest and most powerful in Europe" in the late eighteenth century,[55] had sealed its fate with the London house of Barings when one of its partners married Dorothy Baring, Francis Baring's daughter.[56] The Hopes and Barings had been in contact long before this (at least since 1766), but the marriage sealed their destinies. Fortuitously, this event took place a little more than a decade before Hope & Co. became an empty shell, at the end of the Napoleonic period.[57] Yet another type of network-building consisted in informal alliances. In France, because the Rothschilds acquired uncontested supremacy within high finance, competitors such as the Hottinguers tried to countenance them through alliances with the Hopes of Amsterdam and the Barings in London.[58] These marriages and the connections they created often gave merchant banks a critical advantage in international finance. Moreover, they created a financial world the international nature of which was deeply embedded in the social structure of European society. As networks of families, merchant banks were not strictly organized along national lines. Though the British spoke of "merchant banks," the French of the haute banque, the Germans of the *Handelsbanken*, and the Americans of "private banks," none of these institutions were purely national, because of the social structures that underpinned them.[59]

It was on the back of this first type of network built by merchant bankers that the international financial system of the nineteenth and early twentieth century rested. This is perhaps nowhere clearer than in the case of central bank cooperation. It is difficult to think of central banking as an activity that was in any way independent of these families until World

War I. Merchant bankers were extremely well represented in the central banks of France and Britain. In fact, this trend began as early as the late seventeenth century, when the Bank of England was created, and merchants of foreign extraction (many Germans, but also French Protestants) made "substantial contributions to the capital raised to establish the Bank of England.[60] The practice of drawing directors from the merchants (and later merchant bankers) was thoroughly enshrined by the nineteenth century.

At the Bank of England, merchant bankers represented just under half of the Court of Directors. The other half were merchants. Some merchant banks were represented for over a century, while others provided directors that served for three or more decades.[61] Between 1890 and 1914, one finds familiar names on the court, including members of Baring Brothers & Co. Ltd.; Brown, Shipley & Co.; Antony Gibbs & Sons; Frühling & Goschen; C. J. Hambro & Co.; and J. Henry Schröder.[62] A number of representatives of private banks and overseas institutions (e.g., the Hongkong and Shanghai Bank) were also represented among the group of twenty-six men, but British joint stock banks (e.g., Midland Bank) were formally excluded from representation.[63] For this reason, the Bank of England's Court of Directors "operated with a world view that above all was sympathetic to the needs and risks of merchant banking," though some researchers display an incredible degree of faith in their probity, claiming that they never "took advantage of the hot tips and financial secrets" they heard.[64] Lord Revelstoke, erstwhile lead partner of Barings, expressed in what can only sound comical terms to the contemporary observer that "he saw no reason to depart from the principle that members of the clearing banks and of the discount houses should not become directors."[65] Michael Lisle-Williams has convincingly argued that this situation of dominance of the Bank of England by the merchant bankers lasted well into the interwar period.[66]

French central banking followed the same pattern. Jean-Conrad, the head of the Hottinguers, a prominent French banking family, was one of the fifteen regents of the Banque de France from 1803 to 1833.[67] After his time in post, his son Jean-Henri succeeded him until 1848, while Rodolphe Hottinguer held the same position from 1869 to 1920.[68] The Mallets established an even more impressive track record. Guillaume Mallet was a regent of the Banque de France from 1800 to 1826 and was succeeded by his son Adolphe-Jacques, who held the post from 1827 to 1860, himself succeeded by his own son, Alphonse, from 1860 to 1905.[69] The Rothschilds entered the

Banque only in 1855, when Alphonse de Rothschild obtained a seat as regent and held it until 1905. Edouard Rothschild took over and remained a regent until 1936.[70] The Rothschilds had been integrated quite late despite being by far the richest merchant bank. This was not least due to the fact that the Rothschilds were the first Jews to become regents, and that James de Rothschild had always technically remained a foreigner, though he had lived in Paris for most of his life.[71]

This domination of central banks by merchant banking families facilitated international cooperation between these institutions. In a fairly obvious sense, the presence of a Rothschild on the Court of Directors of the Bank of England and of another one on the Council of the Banque de France as regent meant that cooperation and communication between the two institutions was likely to be smooth and effective. For instance, during the crisis of 1890, when Barings nearly went bankrupt after the default of Argentina, the different Rothschilds in London and Paris coordinated the transfer of £3 million in gold from the Banque de France to the Bank of England.[72] It is no overstatement to say that merchant bankers' international networks were a crucial hinge facilitating international financial cooperation, notably among central banks.

Beyond the international networks that were developed both within and between merchant banking families, these families were dependent on international networks of a second type to conduct their business: those with wealthy families at large. They were useful in the first instance because it was these "webs of personal connections" that provided "means sufficient to mount armies and assemble the capital for large industrial projects."[73] In other words, merchant banks' networks were useful, as they allowed them to mobilize large amounts of capital. Indeed, in a context where "direct contacts between investors and borrowers were infrequent," and where investors were "diffuse, elusive and removed from borrowers," these intermediaries were of the utmost importance.[74] Merchant banks did not solely use their own capital in order to fund companies and sovereigns; they relied on the money of their wealthy clients. Networks of clients were established over time, particularly by penetrating the upper strata of European society, and in this respect the "social characteristics of merchant banking dynasties" were a major asset.[75] These wealthy clients could be members of the political establishment, the bourgeoisie, and the aristocracy. Ignoring the importance of these networks and of the funds merchant bankers could tap into has led some scholars to identify the decline of merchant banks relative to "newer" banks much too early, as they ignored the dormant money to which merchant bankers had access and only examined their personal wealth.

This is particularly apparent in the case of sovereign debt. Here, networks—both between merchant bankers themselves, and between bankers and wealthy elites—played a pivotal role in the creation of an international sovereign bond market. In the early nineteenth century, the finances of Britain were put under serious strain in their fight against Napoleonic France. Whether it was to fund their own troops or those of continental allies, their demand for credit grew by leaps and bounds, creating a surge in business for merchant bankers. From 1799 onward, for "twelve out of the next fifteen years [Barings] headed the list of successful contractors for public loans."[76] Though Barings did come out of the French Wars as the leading merchant bank, others rose during this period, too—for instance, N. M. Rothschild & Sons, J. Henry Schröder, William Brandt & Sons, and Brown, Shipley & Co. After its defeat, France owed an enormous indemnity to its former enemies, which created a renewed and substantial demand for credit. In order to pay, the French government obtained a loan totalling over 450 million francs. This loan, separated in multiple tranches, came from a syndicate led by Barings and Hope & Co—banks that as I noted earlier, had intermarried to strengthen their ties.[77] Relying on their far-reaching network, Barings sold part of the loan in the form of bonds to wealthy British investors, a move that foreshadowed the direct introduction of the first foreign loan to Britain.[78] This latter innovation took place in 1818, when N. M. Rothschild & Sons issued £5 million worth of sovereign bonds for Prussia, in London. N. M. Rothschild, who was already banker to the Prussian ambassador Wilhelm von Humboldt, had negotiated with the envoy from the Prussian treasury, Rother.[79]

In this second decade of the nineteenth century, a truly international sovereign bond market emerged based on the incredible networks weaved by merchant bankers among themselves and with the wealthy elites of Europe.[80] Sovereign lending became, in a very clear sense, merchant bankers' specific *chasse-gardée*, and it remained so until the interwar period (see table 2.1).[81] As I shall show in the next chapter, this club of eminent merchant banking houses came to organize a great deal of its lifestyle around the business of

TABLE 2.1
Top Underwiters of Government Debt in Main Financial Centers, 1818–1930

Period	Number of underwriters	Name of top underwriter
1818–1825: London	12	N. M. Rothschild & Sons
1845–1876: London	45	N. M. Rothschild & Sons
1877–1895: London	34	N. M. Rothschild & Sons
1896–1913: London	33	N. M. Rothschild & Sons
1896–1914: Paris	14	Rothschild Frères
1920–1930: New York	20	J. P. Morgan & Co.

Source: Marc Flandreau, Juan H. Flores, Norbert Gaillard, and Sebastiàn Nieto-Parra, "The End of Gatekeeping," NBER Working Paper 15128, 2010, 29.

sovereign lending.[82] For now, however, I wish to examine a second critical feature on which merchant bankers' business was based: reputation.

As I argued earlier, merchant banking families sought status as an end in itself. But the social status they acquired also had a direct impact on their businesses, because banks were entirely intertwined with families. The high status a family might acquire would thus conveniently serve both personal and business goals, because reputation was crucial to merchant banking, particularly in international trade and sovereign lending,

Merchant banks were initially active in the trade of various goods, including precious metals, metallic moneys, raw materials, produce of colonial origin, and textiles.[83] As one observer puts it, "Leading merchant banks grew up precisely in the same manner"; they "gradually changed from being primarily a merchant to acting primarily as a merchant banker."[84] As time passed, merchant bankers realized that the greatest need in international trade was for "someone to fill the gap between the buyer and seller."[85] In other words, if two individuals in different geographical areas were ready to buy and sell goods to each other, there was always an issue of trust; the seller would not send his goods without a guarantee of obtaining payment, and the buyer would not send money prior to receiving goods. What was required was a middleman in whom both parties had confidence. This problem was the basis for the business of acceptances.

As they did more and more business, merchant bankers realized "they could borrow more cheaply than could other merchants," and with this newfound ability, they started guaranteeing transactions between buyers and sellers. The way in which they did this was by accepting one merchant's bill of exchange for a small commission, and insuring the payment of goods upon arrival at their destination.[86] The key to doing this was to have a good name, a very clearly understood requirement among merchant bankers who realised that "it was easier to sell one's signature than a bale of silk."[87] By putting their name on a bill and thus guaranteeing it, they gave it credibility.[88] If things went wrong—for instance, if the buyer decided not to pay for the goods received or went bankrupt—the merchant banker had to pay the bill himself, so that the individual selling his goods would still receive the money owed. The value of these acceptance bills, and the trust that people had in them, was ultimately based on merchant bankers' reputation. These bills were a form of short-term finance for international trade that constituted a "vital function of merchant banks in international finance from the late eighteenth to the early twentieth century."[89]

As honest brokers between two parties, the role of reputation was obvious to merchant bankers themselves. It was evident to them that, as a historian of the House of Baring puts it, "he who stole his purse stole not trash perhaps, but certainly something of secondary importance," because the true foundations of his wealth rested on his reputation, which he would have preserved by sacrificing "the whole of his house's profit."[90] This was perhaps particularly true in London, the world's financial center, as the custom of verbal contracts was "one of the planks of [the City's] reputation."[91] But even in New York, the Morgans knew that trust and reputation were the fundamental basis of their business. As late as 1932, Jack Morgan explained in the Pecora Hearings that "any power which [the private banker] has comes, not from the possession of large means, but from the confidence of the people in his character and credit . . . not financial credit, but that which comes from the respect and esteem of the community."[92]

Beyond trade, reputation played a pivotal role in the business of lending capital to sovereigns as well. Merchant bankers were indispensable because the ones with good reputations acted as seals of quality for sovereign loans (and other loans as well). While today credit rating agencies provide letter grades (e.g., AAA) to certify the finances of states and inform investors on the market, there was no such thing in the nineteenth century. Until the interwar period, sovereign lending functioned with what Marc Flandreau has aptly called a "regime of certification by prestigious intermediaries."[93] To put it simply, prestigious merchant banks associated their names to what they thought constituted safe sovereign debt. This was a world in which a "few prestigious banks" wielded considerable influence, and were constrained "by their need to secure and protect prestige."[94] The number of banks at the top of the reputational hierarchy was small, and bankers themselves had a sense of this hierarchy, nicely captured when James de Rothschild, speaking to Duff Green, an American agent, described himself as "the man who is at the head of the finances of Europe."[95] This phrase illustrates, with some exaggeration, the pyramidal conception and nature of nineteenth-century international finance. Some, at the top of the social hierarchy, were extremely reputable, while others, lower down, were of questionable character. Investors used the names of merchant bankers underwriting specific sovereign bonds as an indication of sovereigns' creditworthiness.[96] In fact, they generally did not react to news of a country's behavior about which they did not know a great deal, "but rather to the presence (or absence) of a prestigious underwriter."[97] Even when they formed loan syndicates (ad hoc groups of merchant banks constituted for specific sovereign debt issues), there was always a prestigious merchant banking house that would lead it, thus putting its stamp of approval on the loan.[98]

In order to maintain the reputation that was so central to their role as sovereign lenders, merchant bankers needed to lend to good borrowers who would not default. Becoming banker to a sovereign thus required a certain amount of trust and gaining an appropriate acquaintance of the sovereign borrower in question. Long-lasting relations with borrowers were accordingly very useful.[99] It was indeed not uncommon for merchant bankers to have spheres of influence, as they tried to establish strong business relations in order to build trust. The Rothschilds had a famously long-lasting relation with Brazil, which developed out of the political ties between Britain and Portugal.[100] Likewise, Barings handled numerous debt issues for the government of Argentina. Some merchant bankers went as far as supporting sovereign borrowers when their bond yields were rising, in order to keep their own good name intact. Indeed, when they underwrote bonds, they would sometimes commit to maintaining the value of a bond at a certain price.[101]

The implication of merchant bankers' role as seals of quality for investors in sovereign debt is that one cannot think of nineteenth-century sovereign lending as something which an amorphous group of "investors" did.[102] On the contrary, merchant banks' centrality to the functioning of sovereign debt markets means that in order to understand how sovereign lending functioned, one must examine merchant bankers and their modus operandi. Now, the question remains as to how merchant bankers themselves knew the states to which they were lending.

THE PUZZLE OF INFORMATION

Merchant bankers arose and lived in a world in which quantitative information about sovereigns was indeed largely absent.[103] Of course, they knew how much money sovereigns owed them and could share this information with others. But, on the whole, from the late eighteenth century to the second half of the nineteenth, merchant bankers had to make judgments to lend to sovereigns based on something other than precise statistical information about states' finances.[104] In this sense, there is a great deal of continuity with Renaissance finance, when "even the largest Italian or South German company was unable to find out with certainty the true value" of the security a prince might offer on a loan, and when "the task of estimating the real value of different [princely] loans was too much even for the largest isolated firms."[105]

This situation also resembles the state of affairs in the eighteenth-century Amsterdam market, where "much vital information remained unavailable" to merchant bankers and investors.[106] In fact, it appears that "neither the political nor the commercial news available in Dutch periodicals was sufficient to evaluate creditworthiness among debtor states."[107] The sources of information that did exist, such as the *Amsterdamsche courant, Maandelijkse nederlandsche mercurius, Nederlandsche jaarboeken* (later *Nieuwe nederlandsche jaarboeken*), and the *Prijs-Courant der effecten*, contained information about the price of securities, but not about the sovereigns that borrowed. In addition, the rare political economy tracts and traveler accounts of foreign kingdoms that circulated at the time contained "no trustworthy information," and there is no evidence that bankers or investors actually consulted them.[108] As noted by James Riley, this led to rather curious situations—for instance, when Britain was considered to be a weaker debtor than France during the 1770s and 1780s, though it was the only country in Europe using procedures that "permitted accurate annual budget statements."[109] More broadly, sovereign bond yields of the time show the relatively rule-of-thumb approach that the Dutch investing public had to estimating creditworthiness. In 1783, a first group of established borrowers (Austria, Denmark, France) hovered around a 4 percent interest rate, while another set of more recent borrowers stood at about 5 percent (Poland, the United States).[110]

The early nineteenth century was similar: a financial environment with very little statistical information about the health of sovereigns' finances and other indicators that might allow one to estimate their creditworthiness. A recent study describes the content of the two leading stock market compendia of the early nineteenth century, *Every Man His Broker* and *Fortune's Epitome of the Stocks and Public Funds*, as "shockingly thin" as far as foreign bonds were concerned.[111] For instance, in bond prospectuses found in an 1825 issue of *Every Man*, the most information one can obtain about sovereigns is a vague number representing the total debt ("the whole debt is about . . .").[112] Most of the statements on foreign bonds in this specific issue of *Every Man* actually contain no information on sovereigns' level of indebtedness. A similar case can be made regarding *Fortune's Epitome*. In the 1833 edition, one columnist's evaluation of Spain's financial situation consists of a long lament worth quoting at length:

> Oh, Spain! who hast bartered thy former heroic valour and chivalric prowess for beads, relics, and pilgrimage, where are now thy gains? Where is the noble Castilian blood that once flowed in thy veins? A prey to factions, distracted by wavering counsels, intolerance and persecution guiding thy steps, where are thy hopes of peace? Why didst thou forsake the improvement and working of thy fleece to run after the gold and silver of the New World? Why didst thou neglect the valuable productions with which an all-bountiful Being had blessed thy own soil, for the luxurious exotics of the Indies and the uncertain tenure of a distant land? Why, even now, dost thou not gather thy sons around thee, and re-establish harmony and happiness in the bosom of thy family.[113]

This was the information available about Spain—not some "exotic and distant states" that had recently appeared on the financial markets of Europe—in one of the two best stock market compendia of the time, the title of which includes the words "containing every necessary information."[114]

It is therefore safe to conclude that, in the early nineteenth century, "investors could not tell how governments were doing," at least not in any systematic way based on numerical evidence.[115]

This was apparently even truer for lay investors than it was for bankers, the proof being the infamous case of Poyaìs, a fictitious country that was able to borrow on the London market in the early nineteenth century.[116] It succeeded in borrowing at rates that were similar to the very real countries of Chile or Colombia. The story starts in 1820, when a Scottish adventurer by the name of Gregor MacGregor claimed to have been granted a concession of eight million acres by the Mosquito King, in what today would be Honduras and Nicaragua. In *Sketch of the Mosquito Shore, Including the Territory of Poyais*, published by a certain Thomas Strangeways to build up the financial hype leading to the bond issue of Poyaìs, MacGregor was given the title "Cazique of Poyaìs." In October 1822, MacGregor raised £200,000 on the London market at 6 percent interest. It was only in August 1823 that the fraud was exposed. Though, as we saw in the last chapter, investors often used respected bankers as a sign of creditworthiness, in the early days of the international capital market centered on London, some did not, and the scarce and inadequate information they had sometimes made their gambles disastrous.

The quality of the information available to bankers in the early nineteenth century casts heavy doubts on the idea that merchant banks had easy access to good data on the financial position of states and that they demanded it.[117] Indeed, most if not all states would have been hard pressed to answer these requests. None of them, in fact, possessed estimates of their national income prior to the interwar period (see table 2.2). In chapter 5, we will see that the availability of quantitative information concerning states increased slowly from the 1840s onward, but that it was still of poor quality, and that it was not merchant bankers who made systematic use of it.

The twin questions of how merchant bankers operated in a world with almost no reliable quantitative information about sovereigns, and of why they paid so little attention to such information when it became available, are only truly puzzling if one accepts two contentious assumptions. First, one needs to think of merchant bankers as relatively "modern" actors trying to maximize their profit, and, second, one needs to conceptualize sovereign lending as a purely economic relation. However, if merchant bankers were indeed status-seeking migrant families whose goals were intertwined

TABLE 2.2
Date of First Publication of Official Estimate of National Income

Year	Country
1925	Soviet Union & Canada
1929	Germany
1931	The Netherlands & New Zealand
1934	United States
1935	Turkey
1937	Yugoslavia
1939	Switzerland & Mexico
1941	United Kingdom
1944	Sweden & Norway
1947	France

Source: Adam Tooze, Statistics and the German State: The Making of Modern Economic Knowledge, 1900–1945 (Cambridge: Cambridge University Press, 2001), 8.

with their banks, these assumptions ought to be abandoned. Through the relations they established with various sovereigns, merchant bankers were pursuing both an economic activity whose goal was profit, and a social endeavor whose endpoint was the acquisition of status. But what form of knowledge did merchant bankers rely on to know these sovereigns in both cases?

The nineteenth century witnessed the rise of merchant bankers in international finance. This much was obvious to contemporaries who wrote profusely about a group of financiers they deemed central to the dynamics of their world. A number of studies in economic history and international political economy have previously noted their importance to the practice of sovereign lending and international finance more broadly. In this chapter, I have sought to examine in more depth this remarkably influential group of financiers, in particular with regard to their relation to sovereigns. I have made three key points.

The first part of the chapter examined the identity of merchant bankers. Drawing on economic and business histories, it noted two of their key characteristics. First, they were migrants from Germanic Europe who were used to operating in a setting defined by princely courts. Second, merchant banks were families. The legal structure of banks, composed of very few partners with unlimited liability, was a strong incentive for building the bank around trusted family members. I then argued that merchant bankers pursued a goal widely underestimated by literature in economic history and international political economy: the acquisition of social status. As migrants, former courtly bankers, and families—and sometimes as part of persecuted religious minorities—they sought to acquire social status for its own sake, rather than as a purely instrumental tool to further their business. In other words, merchant bankers were not simply utility-maximizing profit-seekers; they were status-seekers as well.

The second part of the chapter then delved into merchant bankers' activities, arguing that networks and reputation were at the heart of their business model. The former characteristic has already been noted in a number of business and economic histories, but the role it played for the entire financial system—even for the operation of central banks—has been insufficiently emphasized. As for reputation, one might object that it has of course been crucial to most companies' business throughout history. However, the peculiarity of merchant banking is that it hinged almost exclusively on reputation. It was their reputation that made these bankers central to international trade as they constituted trustworthy intermediaries between buyers and sellers across the globe. Likewise, their reputation made them critical players in sovereign lending, the reputable ones acting like a seal of approval for the debt of sovereigns about which the public knew next to nothing.

The final section set up a puzzle. It argued that from the late eighteenth to the mid-nineteenth century, merchant bankers did not have access to reliable quantitative data concerning the states to which they lent capital. From vague estimates of debt to long diatribes against a specific country, investment manuals certainly did not contain "every necessary information" presumably required for investment. They contained very little valuable information, and the available information was of questionable accuracy. In fact, states themselves did not have access to good information, as they produced no official national income estimates until the interwar period. One can only conclude, along with the rest of the literature, that investors and bankers could not tell how sovereigns were doing in financial terms. In this sense, merchant bankers emerged in a world that resembled the Renaissance and early modern period in terms of their lack of information about sovereigns. This claim inevitably raises the obvious question of how merchant bankers knew sovereigns, if not primarily through numbers.

Chapter Three

GENTILITY AS A FORM OF KNOWLEDGE

Merchant bankers emerged and lived in a world with initially no available information about states' finances. This situation only gradually changed in the second half of the nineteenth century. In order to make decisions to lend, merchant bankers had to know sovereigns in one way or another. The question before us is, therefore, how did they know sovereigns, at all, to make these decisions? What form of knowledge did they use? In this chapter, my core claim will be that merchant bankers mostly relied on gentility. Gentility was both a form of knowledge—in the sense outlined in chapter 1—and a social quality that endowed one with high status. As a form of knowledge, gentility allowed merchant bankers to know states in person and to assess their good character, so that they might grant them their trust or withhold it. Beyond its use as a form of knowledge, gentility was also part and parcel of merchant bankers' acquisition of status. It allowed them to maintain a good reputation, which was crucial for their role as seals of approval for sovereigns on financial markets, and it was equally central to their pursuit of social status as an end in itself—recall that merchant bankers' relation with sovereigns was also one in which they enhanced their family's social standing for its own sake.

Before I begin, I wish to address one concern. For a number of readers, gentility may appear to be a rather unusual starting point for a discussion about merchant bankers and sovereign lending. And yet Peter J. Cain and Antony G. Hopkins's seminal work on British imperialism revisited the entire history of the British Empire through the concept of gentlemanly capitalism.[1] This was based on the idea that the landed gentry had fused with financial elites in Britain, first occupying the senior position in the duo and then losing it. In this movement, Britain developed what the authors term "gentlemanly capitalism," a capitalism imbued with distinctly aristocratic values, which enabled the preeminence of the financial sector over industry during the long nineteenth century. Crucially, the entire argument relies on an in-depth discussion of gentility and of its revival in the nineteenth century. The vast majority of the book is a titanic inquiry into the export of this gentlemanly capitalist model to the settler and crown colonies, as well as to Britain's "informal empire," through financiers' lending activities. Though concerned with different questions pertaining to the British Empire, the work of Cain and Hopkins is very close to the topic under scrutiny. This suggests that gentility is not an outlandish starting point to deal with questions of international finance and sovereign lending, but a potentially very fruitful angle.[2] To this famous example, one might add a work of much more recent vintage by Marc Flandreau, which explores the links between anthropology and finance in the third quarter of the nineteenth century, focusing on a small group of individuals involved in both activities. In this book, Flandreau notably highlights the pivotal role of the notion of "bona fide," which as he explains, partly overlaps with that of gentlemanliness.[3]

Having said this, I want to clarify two points regarding my claims in this chapter. First, I am adamantly *not* claiming that gentility was a tool in the sense of a scale, with which bankers evaluated sovereigns' creditworthiness.[4] To clarify this caveat, let me use an analogy. Saying that modern cartography became a key form of knowledge for diplomats does not directly tell us anything about what cartographic feature they will hold in high regard; at its core, this claim only tells us that diplomats began using a new method to know sovereigns. Gentility was, in this sense, the main form of knowledge that merchant bankers used to know sovereigns—at all. There were quite literally no alternatives when they started out. In this sense, knowing a state was about knowing a set of individuals, rather than a set of numbers representing an abstract entity. The second point to make at this stage is that my claim that gentility was the main form of knowledge on which merchant bankers relied does not imply that merchant bankers were entirely oblivious to numerical information once it appeared, just that it was not central to their knowledge and—to the extent that their relationship with states can be described in this way—evaluation.

In order to substantiate my claim that gentility was the key form of knowledge on which merchant bankers relied, I proceed in three steps. To begin with, I give a historical overview of what gentility was and in what way it constituted a critical form of knowledge for diplomats from the Renaissance to the eighteenth century. The reason for choosing this starting point is that it marks the moment when gentility emerged as a way of knowing polities. Secondly, I explain how nineteenth-century merchant bankers acquired gentility to know sovereigns, maintain their reputation, and gain social status for their family. Third, I briefly explain how and to what extent this continued among American merchant bankers of the interwar period.

GENTILITY AS A FORM OF KNOWLEDGE

Before the modern era, engaging with sovereigns generally meant engaging with a person: *the* sovereign herself. Court societies had emerged around sovereigns in the late medieval and early modern period,[5] and in order to know sovereigns one had to be where the sovereign resided— namely, at the court.[6] In this context, there was a specific form of knowledge one had to acquire to be part of those courts and to interact with the sovereigns who were their loci. The required form of knowledge was gentility, also called "courtesy" and "civility" at different points in history. This comprised manners, bodily conduct, and specific ways of speaking. In this book, I use the term "gentility" for the sake of clarity, except when I am discussing the history of this form of knowledge in the next few pages. Norbert Elias famously underlined the link between the word "courtesy" (*courtoisie* in French and *Hövescheit* or *Höflichkeit* in German), which emerged in the late medieval era, and the court (*cour* in French, and *Hof* in German).[7] Courtesy was, quite simply, the knowledge of courts. It allowed diplomats to access courts, to observe who the members of the international system were, as well as to evaluate and defend their sovereign's place within it.[8] Knowing polities in person or through their many diplomatic representatives in various European courts was thus standard practice.

It was during this early modern period that ambassadors began producing manuals for the education of future diplomats, explaining what qualities an ambassador should possess. In the words of one scholar, the "great majority of works discussing diplomacy . . . provide a behavioural guide for the statesman, the courtier and the diplomat."[9] These manuals addressed recurring questions, specifically pertaining to the attributes, education and knowledge that an ambassador should possess, but also regarding how he should conduct himself at foreign courts.[10] At their core, most manuals essentially suggested that a good ambassador was essentially a local courtier, sent to a foreign court. Ambassadors had to emulate the behavior of the "cortegiano," and "noble education and socialisation at court" were central to their making.[11] An extremely popular work in this genre was Baldassare Castiglione's early sixteenth-century *Il cortegiano*.[12] Until the mid-seventeenth century and, arguably, even later, his manual had a tremendous impact on European courts.[13] An ambassador himself, Castiglione was translated by other ambassadors, an indication of the relevance of his work for this group of international practitioners.[14]

Over the course of the seventeenth and eighteenth centuries, the title of manuals of this type gradually changed from *Parfait ambassadeur* to *Art de négocier* or *Ministre public*, but they remained deeply concerned with courtesy and the question of how ambassadors ought to represent their sovereign and behave in foreign courts.[15] For instance, Abraham de Wicquefort's late seventeenth-century manual, *The Ambassador and His Functions*, clearly states that the ambassador must not only be "skilful, but also a gentleman, or at least . . . appear one," a task that, in his own words, simply required following Castiglione's rules.[16] He even argued that "the civilities and ceremonies were one of the (and perhaps even the most) essential roles of an embassy."[17] Surprisingly, this was written by a man who had lived through the Peace of Westphalia and contributed to the great seventeenth-century ascent of Brandenburg-Prussia, the predecessor of the Kingdom of Prussia. In other words, this was a man whom one might expect to be more concerned with questions of power, balancing, and cold calculation than with courtly ceremonial and manners.[18] Similarly, a large number of the chapters in François de Callières's highly popular *De la manière de négocier avec les souverains* concern courtly behavior.[19] All these manuals were widely read and considered essential reading by diplomats in Europe and beyond.[20]

Within Europe and beyond it, European diplomats primarily used courtesy to identify polities, classify them, and insert themselves into local hierarchies.[21] Transport and communication were slower than they are now, making it fairly rare for two sovereigns to be in the same location at the same time, but, above all, in an age without statistics and other such means of knowing international actors, gentility was one—if not *the*—crucial form of knowledge on which practitioners of international relations relied.[22] To begin with, diplomats knew who could even be considered a member of the international system by taking note of who was represented at court. Indeed, before they could even enter into treaty relations with a given polity, they had to assess whether that entity had this capacity or not—that is, whether the polity in question possessed something akin to international personhood. Second, the way these sovereigns were represented at court provided another layer of more detailed information. In Asia, for instance, Europeans observed "the treatment accorded to the diplomatic envoys of other Sovereigns in which the latter's status was the decisive factor."[23] As one scholar puts it, the fact that "diplomacy connected the ranking at all major . . . courts" meant that "hierarchical conflict at one court could disrupt the hierarchies elsewhere."[24] Thus, within Europe as well as beyond it, Europeans relied on courtesy to know polities and to figure out how they ought to treat the new ones they encountered.

For this reason, toward the end of the seventeenth century and in the early eighteenth, some European manuals on courtly ceremonial began making reference to both European and non-European courts. For instance, Johann Christian Lünig's highly influential *Theatrum Ceremoniale* was very preoccupied with the classification of international actors, including non-European ones such as the Sublime Porte, the king of Persia, and the king of Siam.[25] In a different vein, Simon de la Loubère's work on the Kingdom of Siam, dedicated to the founder of the first school for ambassadors in Europe (the Marquis de Torcy) explores in depth the diplomatic usages of the court of this kingdom, and of "oriental" courts more generally.[26] As a European form of knowledge, courtesy sometimes yielded limited and even erroneous understandings of who the members of the international system were, where they ranked, and thus, how they ought to be treated.[27]

The focus on courtesy in diplomatic manuals only began fading slowly during the second half of the eighteenth century, when diplomats increasingly began relying on new forms of knowledge such as modern cartography and statistics, which quickly displaced courtesy.[28] This gradual shift can be attributed in great part to the rise of the "service nobility," middle- and low- ranking nobles who worked directly for the sovereign.[29] This noblesse *de robe* had accessed nobility through service to the sovereign, and it thus pushed for more specialized, or what one might call "professional," diplomatic training. Of course, courtesy never fully disappeared; it simply became a more minor form of knowledge, outflanked by a host of other ways of knowing and representing sovereigns.

Before I move on to discuss how merchant bankers used this form of knowledge, precisely at a time when diplomats were turning away from it, I want to pause for an instant to consider the implications of the account of gentility given previously. If one were to analyze the early modern period through accounts from historians of political thought, one of the most important conclusions would surely be that, as Quentin Skinner puts it, by the mid-seventeenth century "the concept of the State—its nature, its powers, its right to command obedience—had come to be regarded as the most important object of analysis in European political thought."[30] The account of courtesy provided in the previous paragraphs exposes an important gap between political thought's growing concern with the state, which had presumably become overwhelming by the seventeenth century, and the fact that, a century later, diplomats were still mostly relying on courtesy to know polities. In other words, it would seem that, despite the popularity of the idea of "the state" among political thinkers, in practice, ambassadors, through the forms of knowledge they used, were still sustaining a conception of the international system as being made up of individuals. Put simply, they knew international actors almost exclusively as persons at the court. This echoes the words of one scholar of historical international relations who explains that, until the "late eighteenth century, the equivalent of what present-day IR theory calls 'international actors,' were still, on the whole, persons wearing a crown."[31]

As I shall show in the following section, nineteenth-century merchant bankers were in many ways similar to early modern diplomats relying on gentility. Merchant bankers depended on a form of knowledge developed for a world in which the units were individual sovereigns, rather than abstract entities called states.

MERCHANT BANKERS, EDUCATION, AND
THE MAKING OF GENTLEMEN

As we saw in chapter 2, following the defeat of imperial France, a community of merchant bankers centered on London became the hinge of international finance. The question left unanswered at the close of the preceding chapter was how these merchant bankers thought about—or, more accurately, knew—states. Following the method outlined in chapter 1, I now turn to their education.

According to one source, before the 1880s, bankers had "no formal arrangements for tuition."[32] All that existed were a few handbooks on banking practice, among which one finds James Gilbart's *Practical Treatise*, first published in 1827, and John Dalton's *Banker's Clerk*, from 1843.[33] But it appears that even these treatises were written for clerks working in the newly created joint stock banks (more on those in chapter 4), not merchant bankers.[34] Similar manuals existed in other European languages such as French, Jacques Peuchet's *Manuel du banquier* published in 1829 being an excellent example, but they were hardly directed at members of the haute banque.[35] On first inspection, then, it appears as though there was indeed no specific training for merchant bankers. It is worth noting, however, that some practical education did take place within the family business. It consisted mostly in acquiring "a command of foreign languages and clear handwriting," as well as undergoing a clerkship and, finally, spending time "abroad visiting the bank's correspondents and agents."[36] This training, however, tells us relatively little about how merchant bankers knew sovereigns, and in fact one might be led to believe that merchant bankers' approach to knowing sovereigns was simply unsystematic.

The idea that their evaluations were ad hoc is perhaps true, but that still does not tell us about the form of knowledge that merchant bankers used to conduct their business of lending to sovereigns. One first clue is the somewhat common—yet unsystematically explored—theme in many historical studies about the shift from personal to impersonal relations in financial markets.[37] Business and imperial history also reveals that bankers knew many states "in person," through their representatives. Their business was indeed "intensely personal" because personal connections allowed one to know "what a man could do and how he would do it."[38] And yet, this still does not quite tell us the type of knowledge that bankers had to use to know sovereigns and their representatives. The key to unravel this puzzle is to understand why merchant bankers, in addition to their in-family training, attended educational institutions where they thought they could learn nothing of immediate use for banking. I am here referring to the public schools, as well as to the universities of Oxford and Cambridge.

The classic path for a merchant banker was to go to a public school (generally Eton or Harrow) and then to attend Oxford or Cambridge.[39] In his seminal study of city bankers from 1890 to 1914, Youssef Cassis estimates that 50 percent of merchant bankers received a public school and/or Oxbridge education.[40] By comparison, and as a point of reference, only 16 percent of iron and steel manufacturers active between 1875 and 1895 attended public schools, and only 9 percent attended Oxford or Cambridge in the same period.[41] The trend over the nineteenth century was one of rapid increase with each generation, the average going from zero for the generation born between 1800 and 1820, to 69 percent for the generation born between 1861 and 1880.[42]

Fifty percent may seem like a rather low figure. Out of his sample, thirty-three percent of the merchant bankers' education is unknown, but Cassis infers from this that they were not educated and that they were only trained in the family bank. However, a closer look at the figures exposes how some merchant banks were much better "educated" than others. Unsurprisingly, the partners in the firms that were at the very top of the banking hierarchy (and also the most active in loans to foreign sovereigns) scored high on the educational ladder. For instance, one hunded percent of the partners at N. M. Rothschild & Sons attended a public school, Oxford, or Cambridge, while eighty-three percent of the partners at Baring Brothers & Co. and seventy-five percent of those at Morgan, Grenfell & Co. did so (see table 3.1).[43] As Cassis remarks, the merchant bankers represented at the Court of Directors of the Bank of England, a clear sign of distinction, were also often the ones with the best education.[44] The cohesion of these top merchant bankers can be further established with the following fact: among those who attended British universities, an astonishing thirty-five percent attended Trinity College at Cambridge.[45]

Interestingly, in Oxford and Cambridge, students mostly read classics, but, seemingly, next to no knowledge having "practical" applications was dispensed. As Niall Ferguson puts it in his history of the Rothschilds, "For

TABLE 3.1
Percentage of Attendance at Public School, Oxford, or Cambridge in
Each of the Leading Banks, 1890–1914

Banks	Public school and/or Oxbridge (%)
Antony Gibbs & Sons	100
C. J. Hambro & Son	100
N. M. Rothschild & Sons	100
Baring Brothers & Co.	83
Morgan, Grenfell & Co.	75

Source: Youssef Cassis, *City Bankers, 1890–1914* (Cambridge: Cambridge University Press, 1994), 104.

learning about banking, the only way to do that was in a bank; if Cambridge offered anything, it was a distraction from the priorities of the family business."[46] Moral sciences—which Nathaniel Rothschild read at Cambridge from 1859—included moral philosophy, political economy, modern history, general jurisprudence, and the laws of England. Moral sciences were a rather new subject, only introduced in 1850 as a "tripos" at Cambridge.[47] The political economy component of the course was still mostly theoretical, and there was nothing as applied as financial accounting. It was "very different from economics as taught today,"[48] and was "largely based on Adam Smith's *Wealth of Nations*, to which was later added John Stuart Mill's *Principles of Political Economy*."[49] It dealt with "unemployment and poverty, tariffs and taxation" and seems not to have had "a significant place in the curricula," in Oxford and Cambridge alike.[50] Indeed, it took until 1905 for a tripos in economics to be created,[51] a course of study that would have resembled the French commercial schools' (as we will see in chapter 5).[52] At the University of Oxford, a report from as late as 1931 underlined the necessity to create two posts immediately, one of which was a readership in statistics and another a chair of finance and currency.[53]

And yet, in spite of their apparently useless practical training, the top reaches of the merchant banking community were very clear on the importance of attending these institutions. Indeed, this is obvious when one observes the great trouble to which those who were excluded from such institutions went to make it in. Consider the case of Jewish merchant bankers: while Jews were initially denied the right to take degrees at the ancient universities, this changed over the course of the nineteenth century, with the Rothschilds playing a pioneering role in this matter.[54] As Ferguson argues, this question of matriculation and graduation at Oxford and Cambridge must be considered alongside the restrictions imposed on Jews to sit as members of Parliament in the House of Commons, in that it bore similar significance.[55] The importance of this question alone should tell us about the critical nature of gentlemanly education at the time. In order to obtain the right for Jews to study at Cambridge, the Rothschilds—along with Moses Montefiore—turned to Prince Albert, the then chancellor of Cambridge.[56] In fact, this move was triggered by the refusal of the master of Christ's College to bend the rule of chapel for Arthur Cohen, a Rothschild cousin. This eventually led to the Oxford and Cambridge University Reform Acts of 1854 and 1856, which allowed Jews to take degrees (except in theology).[57] In a letter from 1862, Nathaniel Rothschild complained to his parents that he could not "see why a national institution like this which is the stepping stone to legal and political preferments as well as ecclesiastical ones should be ruled by priests as if it were a Jesuit's seminary or a Talmud school."[58] This passage goes to show how well merchant bankers like the Rothschilds perceived the role of universities as springboards for important positions in society. In the world of Nathaniel Rothschild's mother, Charlotte, "a man who has taken a good degree at Cambridge or Oxford is more highly thought of, and this good opinion acts as an encouragement to every useful exertion throughout life."[59] And, indeed, accession to Cambridge was considered a "real social breakthrough."[60] There, the Duke of St Albans introduced Nathaniel Rothschild to the Prince of Wales (the future Edward VII), with whom he shared a passion for hunting and horse racing.[61] These early ties were strengthened, and the bonds lasted for their lifetimes. Beyond useful acquaintances, passage through the ancient universities was meant to efface the social origins of individuals, specifically within the upper strata of society—a great equalizer of sorts, among the elite. Hence Charlotte Rothschild's anger at her son Nathaniel when he lent £500 to a fellow student, thus betraying his social origins.[62]

What is it, then, that merchant bankers learned in these institutions? The answer is that they acquired gentility. As I mentioned earlier in the chapter, the gentlemanly nature of nineteenth-century high finance and its aristocratic lifestyle is a common trope in a number of historical studies. Cain and Hopkins's seminal work discusses gentlemanly capitalism and the key role of merchant bankers therein, while David Landes's classic *Bankers and Pashas* speaks of "the gentle calling of high finance," and Youssef Cassis's equally groundbreaking work dwells on merchant bankers' "aristocratic way of life."[63] The ideal of gentlemanliness was absolutely central to shaping nineteenth-century international finance, particularly in Britain, the world's financial center.[64] After the Glorious Revolution of 1688, the aristocracy managed to remain the most "successful element within emergent capitalism" by entwining its fate with the City's.[65] The revolution of 1688 entrenched the power of the landed interest in the countryside "and consolidated its hold on the polity,"[66] but this group was only able to hang on to power from the nineteenth century onward by integrating the upper stratum of the service sector and, particularly, finance.[67] Those adamantly not included within this charmed circle were the captains of industry and manufacturing. As a result, British political life and imperialism were shaped largely by financial interests and not, as in many accounts, by industrial magnates.

The peculiarity of high-ranking service professions and finance in particular was that they were "suitable occupations for gentlemen."[68] They allowed one to earn money from a distance and to avoid the proximity to labor that was "associated to dependence and cultural inferiority."[69] The attitudes valued by nineteenth-century gentlemanly capitalists included an "ambivalent attitude towards capitalism" and a contempt for "the everyday world of wealth creation and of the profit motive as the chief goal of activity."[70] These cultural traits explain why bankers sometimes behaved in what appears to be an "economically irrational" manner.[71] This was a world in which economic relations "based upon personal loyalties and family connections" were the rule, superseding immediate economic interests.[72] There, the relations between high politicians and great financiers were rooted in direct personal contact, and not in any form of market competition.[73] The gentlemen that formed the very core of this economic order were produced through the reformed and expanded public schools, as well as in the ancient universities.[74]

Beyond education, there were two supplementary means of acquiring gentility. One of them was marriage into the aristocracy and landed nobility. While for the generation born between 1800 and 1820 this only happened once, the next generation's experience was utterly different, and by the end of the century marriage with aristocrats was even more widespread.[75] As always, the most prominent banking families also happened to be front-runners in this movement.[76] Some bankers acquired titles of nobility outside marriage—for instance, Lord Rothschild, Lord Revelstoke (a Baring), and Viscount Goschen. And those who did could afford to marry foreigners who were not noble, a specifically important issue for Jewish merchant bankers.[77] But perhaps the most interesting fact is "that 74 percent of bankers who married daughters of aristocrats attended public schools and Oxford or Cambridge."[78] This goes to show the interrelatedness of the various strategies to acquire gentility, and that they were obviously seen as a bundle of necessary practices.

Merchant bankers also acquired the adequate social status to reach sovereigns by buying large country estates—another key sign of gentility. The Rothschilds' estates at Ferrières, Suresnes, Boulogne (France), Gunnersbury, Waddesdon, Mentmore (Britain), Schillersdorf (Austria), and Grüneburg (Germany) are the clearest expressions of this trend. A striking feature is that many of these palaces look like eighteenth-century French châteaux, which says something about what the Rothschilds looked to as their model: the French aristocracy, which had been a reference point for genteel behavior throughout eighteenth-century Europe.[79] Merchant bankers bought these palaces not only because they could afford them and liked to spend time in the country; for Ferguson, with these houses the Rothschilds did nothing less than to stake "a claim to aristocratic status."[80] In Britain, many of the most important political decisions were taken in "those complex circuits of aristocratic country houses where the political elite spent such a large proportion of the year."[81] Some families such as the Kleinworts did not have a university education, but nonetheless established themselves as country gentlemen "like other City bankers," a move "through which they became known to the Prince of Wales's set."[82] For merchant bankers in France, the acquisition of large estates outside Paris was also a matter of course, though "the country" was certainly less important politically than in Britain. The châteaux French bankers built often served to store paintings and various objets d'arts, which prestigious guests could admire when they were invited at one of the lavish balls. Through all of these means—education, political office, the acquisition of titles of nobility (sometimes through marriage), and estates—merchant bankers displayed their gentility and cemented their place in society.[83]

After World War I, New York became the world's financial center, and the United States the world's banker. One question that looms large, therefore, is the extent to which interwar American bankers relied on gentility as form of knowledge. However, before I turn to them, I want to say a few words about the French case, as Paris was the world's secondary financial center until World War I, although it is clear that it declined markedly after the Franco-Prussian War, leaving London far ahead.

As explained in the previous chapter, it is difficult to entirely dissociate Parisian merchant bankers from those of other countries (particularly British ones), as they were either part of alliances or of the same families. While Barings was allied with the Hottinguers, N. M. Rothschild of London were linked to Rothschild Frères & Cie in Paris, and Morgan, Grenfell & Co. to Morgan, Harjes, et Cie. Beyond these links that integrated Paris into the wider network of merchant bankers, France remained a very court-centric country until 1870. Though it is often eclipsed by the French Revolution, the Restoration of the early nineteenth century, which also affected European countries beyond France, meant that landed wealth and aristocratic titles remained key markers of status and insured that aristocrats occupied key positions in the upper offices of the national administration—though this largely ceased to be the case under the July Monarchy.[84] In France as in Britain, the "*aristocratie financière* merged with the *grande bourgeoisie de robe* to form the *classe dominante*, from which the old aristocracy was not absent, even though it was more in the position of the 'junior partner' than in Britain."[85] I do not want to overstate these similarities, though, as the position of the French aristocracy was far more precarious and complex than the British aristocracy's. Nonetheless, while it was briefly interrupted with the Second Republic, France's political regime kept many "courtly" characteristics with Napoleon III's Second Empire. For instance, in 1853, when James de Rothschild found himself encountering obstacles to access the new emperor, he found his way "into the new court" by "wearing his scarlet uniform to remind anyone who had forgotten his diplomatic status" as Austrian consul-general.[86] Hence, in addition to their integration into the orbit of British gentlemen bankers, the French political setup presented a number of structural similarities with Britain.[87]

The crucial point here is that, equipped with gentility, merchant bankers could know "Europe prince by prince," as historian Jules Michelet puts it. They knew states as sets of persons and could easily tell a prince or head of government that their accounts would go in the red if they appointed "such a minister."[88] James de Rothschild's intimation to his nephews in a letter from 1839 "that one of you . . . should go to Brussels to make the acquaintance of the new Minister in order to establish a close relationship with him" was as typical as his attempt to repair the family's relationship with a Belgian minister by asking Lionel "to go to Windsor on Sunday to see the King of the Belgians."[89] This was the world of the old sovereign lending, based on gentility, and centered on London, with Paris and Berlin as satellites.

This account may go some way in explaining why, for instance, in one study of seventy sovereign loans in the period from 1880 to 1914, a little under half of the negotiations between bankers and sovereigns contained literally *no* discussion of debts and deficits—a mind-boggling fact.[90] That this sample concerns loans from the very end of the nineteenth century and early twentieth century is even more troubling; it implies that even at a time when information was becoming more widely available, it was not being systematically discussed by merchant bankers. As I have said, merchant bankers were certainly not numerically illiterate, but they did not make consistent use of numerical information about sovereign borrowers the way contemporary financial actors do.[91] Indeed, even by the interwar period, Guy de Rothschild described the financial training of the Paris branch of Rothschilds as "learning to quote interest rates in fractions instead of decimals, which he was taught by a clerk whose other function was to read him selections from the newspapers in the morning."[92] The old lenders were still characterized by an outlook and education in which quantifiable data was far from the be-all and end-all of valuable knowledge about sovereigns.

THE UNITED STATES AND THE PERSISTENCE OF GENTLEMEN BANKERS

The United States only really became crucial for foreign sovereign lending during World War I. Prior to this, as the largest capital importer in the period from 1870 to 1914, it relied intensely on private bankers to channel the inflow of foreign money.[93] Many of the private houses engaged in this business were European or linked through family to British and European bankers (e.g., the Morgans, Barings, Browns, Kleinworts, Lazards, Kuhns, Rothschilds and Speyers).[94] They were, therefore, invariably well integrated into London's orbit.

People like John Pierpont Morgan thought of themselves as part of this British-centered world, frequently referring to his New York firm as "merchant bankers" rather than using the American term "investment bankers."[95] In fact, he generally spent at least three months a year working in (or enjoying) London, while his son Jack Morgan, who took over the bank leadership when his father died in 1913, completed an eight-year apprenticeship in the London branch that began in 1898.[96] Like his British counterparts imbued with a gentlemanly ethic, J. P. Morgan showed a marked disdain for the pursuit of profit and competition, explaining that he did "not compete for deposits," that he did "not care whether they ever come," but that they did come.[97] Like all merchant bankers, he also "understood how a bank's reputation was enhanced by its proximity to a sovereign power."[98] Finally, J. P. Morgan had, as a matter of course, been sent to Switzerland and Germany to improve his French and German as a young man. Based on these characteristics, it would be almost impossible to differentiate him from a British merchant banker, save for the education—he attended neither Oxford nor Cambridge. This was why the London branch of the firm was so important.

For the House of Morgan, London remained the leading bank for all that was related to foreign corporate finance and government issues, even though by 1900 the London branch was twelve times smaller than the New York one in terms of capital.[99] Thus, even when the New York branch of the House of Morgan was asked to lead an American syndicate to make a loan to a foreign state, it designated its London partners as the main negotiators to discuss loan terms with other leading international houses. Consider the example of the 1909 (failed) loan to China. The American president at the time, William Howard Taft, and his secretary of state, Philander C. Knox, wanted to secure a place similar to other great powers' in China.[100] In order to participate in the discussions for a Chinese loan with the British, French, and Germans, Knox gathered a group of American banks, with Morgan at their head. The group itself then decided to appoint Morgan Grenfell (the British branch of the House of Morgan) "to conduct all negotiations for the American group" with the other European groups.[101] Recall that 75 percent of the partners at Morgan, Grenfell & Co. were Oxbridge graduates; they were undoubtedly gentlemen, able to engage ministers representing states from the entire world.

Beyond the importance of the London branch, which possessed all the characteristics of a British merchant bank, it is clear that the New York head of the House of Morgan thought and operated in the same manner as

British merchant bankers. For instance, during the 1912 Money Trust Investigation, also known as the Pujo hearings, John Pierpont Morgan claimed that the banking system was built on trust, and that this was itself based on individuals' honor and character, not on money or property. Thus, when asked by the investigator at the hearings about the conditions of access to credit, the following exchange, worth quoting at length, ensued:

MR. MORGAN: I know lots of men, business men, too, who can borrow any amount, whose credit is unquestioned.

MR. UNTERMYER (COUNSEL FOR THE CONGRESSIONAL COMMITTEE): Is that not because it is believed that they have the money to back them?

MR. MORGAN: No, sir; it is because people believe in the man.

MR. UNTERMYER: And it is regardless of whether he has any financial backing at all, is it?

MR. MORGAN: It is very often.

MR. UNTERMYER: And he might not be worth anything?

MR. MORGAN: He might not have anything. I have known a man to come into my office, and I have given him a check for a million dollars when I knew he had not a cent in the world.

MR. UNTERMYER: There are not many of them?

MR. MORGAN: Yes; a good many.

. . .

MR. UNTERMYER: Is not commercial credit based primarily upon money or property?

MR. MORGAN: No sir; the first thing is character.

. . .

MR. UNTERMYER: So that a man with character, without anything at all behind it, can get all the credit he wants, and a man with the property can not get it?

MR. MORGAN: That is very often the case.[102]

Put simply, and in his own words, a man that J. P. Morgan did not trust "could not get money from [him] on all the bonds in Christendom."[103] Personal trust was, for him, the "fundamental basis of business."[104] In practice, this was translated into frequent refusals to enter into business with countries with whom the firm did not have a good connection. For instance, after being solicited for a loan by the Ottomans in 1872, Morgan refused to enter into business with them, as the firm had "no business connection with

Turkey."[105] The absence of a business connection implied the lack of proper means for evaluating this country. Though it may sound rather odd to modern ears, this was not uncommon in a world where sovereign lending was primarily based on gentility. The premium put on trust and the feature that underlay it, personal character, was a defining feature of merchant bankers and of the old world of sovereign lending.[106] In this specific sense, there was not much difference between a Morgan and a Rothschild.[107]

In this chapter I sought to provide an answer to the puzzle raised at the end of the preceding chapter—namely, the question of what kind of knowledge merchant bankers relied on to know states in the absence of numerical information. The claim I put forth was that they largely relied on a form of knowledge that one might call "gentility." To support this argument, I made three points.

The first point is that, during the early modern period, gentility—understood as a set of manners and practices required to be at court—became a crucial form of knowledge for diplomats. At this time, one of the only ways to know sovereigns was in person, at the court. In the absence of maps, treaty compilations, or data about other polities, being at the court was how one "knew" sovereigns. The required form of knowledge to read courts, understand who qualified as an international actor, and infer these actors' attributes was gentility (as explained earlier, then more commonly known as "courtesy"). Diplomats could acquire it through manuals and a looser form of education at the court. Gentility was also a key tool for sovereigns themselves, so as to express their standing in international society correctly. This was a concern of the first order not only for new sovereigns, such as the Dutch Republic, but also for those who sought to improve or maintain their position in the international system.[108] Thus, while it is commonly thought that the early modern period is characterized by the development of a system of states, when one examines the forms of knowledge that were available, it would seem that diplomats had no means of "seeing states." Gentility, the main form of knowledge on which they relied, allowed them to see individual princes, not abstract entities called states.

The second point I made in this chapter is that merchant bankers were part of this old world, that they too relied on gentility to know sovereigns. The families that dominated the business of sovereign lending emerged in the late eighteenth and very early nineteenth century, sometimes as court bankers. It is thus rather unsurprising that they knew sovereigns in this relatively conventional way. Particularly indicative of their reliance on gentility is the fact that merchant bankers involved in high finance and sovereign lending overwhelmingly sought to be educated in public schools and the ancient universities. Though nothing of immediate value could be learned about banking in these institutions, this was where gentlemen were made in nineteenth-century Britain, the center of world finance. Apart from actually meeting those who might later provide the connections to sovereign borrowers in university, merchant bankers learnt how to behave in high society. As a result, they were not simple money-dealers, but could appear as courtly gentlemen. They also acquired gentility through other means, such as titles of nobility, marriage with aristocrats, and the construction of country estates that looked like eighteenth-century French châteaux. Crucially, the acquisition of gentility was also of the highest importance for merchant banking families' pursuit of social status, a point raised in the previous chapter. Gentility was both perfectly suited to the way in which they engaged in sovereign lending and to their aims as status-seeking families.

The third section of this chapter briefly probed the continuity of this old, British-centered world into the interwar United States. The claim I advanced here was that American merchant bankers such as the Morgans were indeed very similar to British merchant bankers; they thought of themselves as British merchant bankers, pursued the same lifestyle, showed a similar indifference to whatever hard data might be available about individuals' creditworthiness, preferring to grant them trust based on an assessment of their character, and privileging personal relations in their business dealings.

I do not presume to think that the argument I have put forward in this chapter is as simple, as familiar, or as neat as those of existing studies which depict ahistorical, rational, profit-oriented merchant bankers systematically seeking out numerical information about sovereigns. But it is, at the very least, a start; after all, the alternative is to ignore empirical evidence and to pretend that merchant bankers used information that they either did not have, or that they obviously did not collect and systematically analyse.

My argument in this chapter implies a substantial dimension of continuity between the old tradition of court bankers and the merchant bankers of the nineteenth and early twentieth century. The merchant banker is not in a literal sense at the court anymore, and it is perhaps in some sense the court that comes to him, but the terms on which they meet are still those of gentility. The persistent domination of sovereign lending by these seemingly outdated merchant bankers until World War II is in many ways striking. One of the keys for understanding this old world of sovereign lending and its reliance on gentility is the familial structure of merchant banks, which implied a complete intertwining of the profit-seeking goals of the bank with the status-seeking of the families at their heart. This economic structure is, as I will show, entirely foreign to the new world of sovereign lending to which I now turn.

PART II

The New Sovereign Lending

THE OUTSIDERS—JOINT STOCK BANKS

By the early twentieth century, international finance was undergoing major transformations. Powerful new actors were making inroads into all sorts of business. Most important were joint stock banks like Deutsche Bank, Crédit Lyonnais, and Midland Bank. These actors would eventually become the hinge of international finance and, more specifically, of the new world of sovereign lending. But their success was by no means immediate. Indeed, one of the striking aspects of the business of sovereign lending, by contrast with other areas of international finance, was the continued dominance of small merchant banks until the interwar period. However, because of the challenge that joint stock banks eventually came to pose to merchant bankers in sovereign lending, this chapter examines them closely.

The key question I address here is how these new actors differed from merchant banks. In the first section of the book, we saw that merchant bankers were status-seeking transnational families who relied heavily on networks and reputation to conduct their business. Based on these attributes, these actors penetrated the political elites of many countries; they were in a very clear sense political "insiders." How did the new sovereign lenders differ?

In this chapter, I will argue that, by and large, joint stock banks were "outsiders" in relation to sovereigns across the world. This was due to the fact that they were primarily national institutions in terms of their social composition, a feature that distinguished them quite radically from merchant bankers. In other words, while merchant bankers were made up of families spread out across many countries, joint stock banks were mostly made up of businessmen from a single country. A somewhat counterintuitive consequence of the rise of these new joint stock banks was thus the relative "nationalization" of international finance in the years leading up to the interwar period. As international capital flows reached unprecedented levels, the largest and wealthiest financial actors became less and less international.

Beginning with a brief account of the legal changes that enabled the creation of modern joint stock banks, the chapter then moves on to dissect the social characteristics of these actors. By contrast with the old merchant banks, what all joint stock banks shared was a lack of international networks and connections to foreign sovereigns. Beyond this commonality, I outline two stories: one Anglo-American and the other Franco-German. In the former case, joint stock banks developed in great isolation from the merchant bankers. Thus, they differed from them vastly and were far less involved in international business. There was a strong division of labor between the two sets of actors, one focusing heavily on domestic banking and the collection of deposits among the population at large, and the other on international banking and services to wealthy persons. In the Franco-German case, joint stock banks also evolved in large part independently from the most prestigious merchant banks, though some second-tier merchant bankers were involved in a few of them. The ones who first became involved in international finance were invariably the latter. Those unconnected to merchant banks faced important hurdles to penetrating international finance, particularly the business of sovereign lending.

MODERN JOINT STOCK BANKS AND THE LAW

The word "corporate" is frequently used to define our economic times. Surprisingly, however, the emergence of joint stock companies and banks—one of the key developments in the making of a corporate world—has received little attention from scholars of international political economy. The origins of this second financial revolution constitute the beginning of the story told in this chapter.[1] At the core of this tale lies, as two pundits have recently called it, a "revolutionary idea": the joint stock company.[2] The joint stock company had of course been embodied in the past by the likes of the Dutch East India Company or the Bank of England. However, across the world, the creation of such entities had long required a royal charter, or, in the absence of monarchy, some high-level political approval. It was an exceptional privilege granted with the expectation that it would serve the financial interests of the Crown or the state.[3] While joint stock companies slowly became more common, particularly with the development of canals and railways, the granting of joint stock company charters remained a jealously guarded privilege deep into the nineteenth century.

It was only in the second half of the nineteenth century that governments fully liberalized this new legal structure for business and eventually extended it to banks—hence the term "joint stock bank." In the 1860s and early 1870s, joint stock banks came to possess all of their recognizably modern qualities: an unrestricted number of shareholders, limited liability, indefinite life, and a simple registration procedure rather than a requirement for a royal charter or political authorization. So emblematic was this development that it even became the subject of an opera, *Utopia, Limited*, in which the characters actually explain the structure of a joint stock company.[4] By 1913, joint stock banks were far larger and wealthier than any of the old merchant banks (see table 4.1).

There is still, to my knowledge, no global history of the profound legal changes that took place across Europe and, to some extent, the United States, in these few years of the second third of the nineteenth century.[5] I therefore give a very brief overview of these legal changes in Britain, France, Germany, and the United States (see table 4.2).

In Britain, early nineteenth-century banking legislation was peculiar in the sense that it was parceled out between England, Scotland, and Ireland. The latter two countries had joint stock banks, such as the Royal Bank of Scotland, before England.[6] Consequently, the English could observe the results of joint stock banking experiments in some constituent parts of the realm and take note. Thus, when in 1826 England introduced joint stock banking in a sixty-five-mile radius outside the City of London (a limitation dropped in 1833), it did not really move into uncharted territory.[7] At that point, joint stock banks in England retained full liability for their debts, and they were regulated differently from joint stock companies more broadly. The Letter Patents Act of 1834 empowered the Crown to grant joint stock

TABLE 4.1
The Twenty Largest Joint Stock Banks, 1913

Bank	Total assets (in £millions)
Crédit Lyonnais (France-F)	113
Deutsche Bank (Germany-G)	112
Midland Bank (United Kingdom-UK)	109
Lloyds Bank (UK)	107
Westminster Bank (UK)	104
Société Générale (F)	95
Comptoir Nat. d'Escompte de Paris (F)	75
National Provincial Bank (UK)	74
Dresdner Bank (G)	72
Société Générale de Belgique (Belgium)	72
Barclays Bank (UK)	66
Disconto-Gesellschaft (G)	58
National City Bank (United States)	57
Parr's Bank (UK)	52
Credit-Anstalt (Austria)	50
Union of London and Smiths Bank (UK)	49
Guaranty Trust Co. of New York (US)	47
Bank für Handel und Industrie (G)	44
Capital and Counties Bank (UK)	43
London Joint Stock Bank (UK)	41
For comparison:	
N. M. Rothschild & Sons (UK)	25

Sources: Youssef Cassis, *Capitals of Capital* (Cambridge: Cambridge University Press, 2010), 92; Youssef Cassis, "Private Banks and the Onset of the Corporate Economy," in *The World of Private Banking*, ed. Youssef Cassis and Phillip Cottrell (Farnham: Ashgate, 2009), 47.

TABLE 4.2
Key Laws Introducing Modern Joint Stock Banks

Country	Year
England	1862 *English Companies Act*
France	1863/1867 *Loi sur les sociétés à responsabilité limitée* *Loi sur les sociétés commerciales*
Germany	1870 *Gesetz betreffend die Kommanditgesellschaften auf Aktien und die Aktiengesellschaften*
United States	1863/1864 *National Bank Acts*

privilege previously given with royal charters through the simpler means of letters patent.[8] However, even then, the Crown retained the privilege of qualifying the limited liability of companies. With the Joint Stock Companies Act of 1844 pushed forward by William Gladstone, then president of the Board of Trade, companies were finally given incorporation rights through a registration procedure. This is what opened up the process of registration and put it at arm's length from political decision-making. It was only in 1858 that Parliament passed "An Act to Enable Joint Stock Banking Companies to Be Formed on the Principle of Limited Liability," which defined the modern joint stock bank.[9] The privilege of limited liability had already been granted to companies (excluding banks) with the Limited Liability Act of 1855 in part because of competition from France and the United States. The legislation on joint stock banks and on joint stock companies was brought under a single regime with the Companies Act of 1862, which clarified the nature of shareholder liability and liberalized the price of shares for banks (previously at least £100).[10] The act made it mandatory for banks of more than ten shareholders to incorporate under this law.[11] Thenceforth, joint stock banks could be freely registered, rely on a wide number of shareholders, and enjoy limited liability, a situation to be contrasted with merchant banks' private partnerships, with up to ten partners retaining unlimited liability.

In France, the key period for the rise of joint stock banks was under Napoleon III's rule (1852–1871), generally referred to as the Second Empire. Until the 1860s, joint stock banks were a highly political affair in France. State consent was necessary to form this type of business. Indeed, all the banks that were created from the early nineteenth century to the 1860s had political connections and support. For instance, after the fall of the First French Empire in 1815 and the Restoration of the Bourbon dynasty, the banker Jacques Laffitte made proposals twice to create a Caisse Générale du Commerce et de l'Industrie that would fund nascent French industries, specifically ironworks and railways. The first one was supposed to have a capital of 240 million francs, while the second was for 100 million. The conservative power in place, the restored Bourbon monarchy, thought that this bank would concentrate too much economic power and only accepted a more modest proposal for a bank with a capital of 35 million francs in 1837.[12] A number of similar institutions emerged in the same period, but they all disappeared during the crisis of 1847–1848.[13] The law of 23 May 1863 changed this state of affairs: it permitted the creation of joint stock banks with a capital of less than 20 million francs, without governmental authorization. Four years later, in 1867, all restrictions were lifted, and there were no more limitations on banks' capital.[14] These two laws ushered in a new era of banking in France. After these developments, many new banks were created, some of which continue to dominate French, European, and global finance to this day.

In Germany, the critical period for the development of joint stock banks was that which followed unification under Prussian domination, from the creation of the German Empire (1871) onward.[15] As small private banks could not meet the exponential increase in demand for capital, they first formed cooperative syndicates, a practice common in Britain and France. However, the "difficulties experienced in forming and holding such syndicates together motivated private bankers to search for an alternative institutional solution."[16] This new institutional solution was the joint stock bank.[17] Prussia and most other German states had hitherto not permitted the creation of such entities, aside from one exception in 1848.[18] The main reasons for their reticence was a fear of inflation, and the angst that this would disturb the fixed exchange rates on which the Zollverein was based. It was for this reason that new banks adopted legal structures that retained full liability, in the form of the Kommanditgesellschaft auf Aktien, so as to control monetary creation by making the shareholders fully liable.[19] This was the legal status of the Darmstädter Bank, as well as of the Berliner Handelsgesellschaft and the Disconto-Gesellschaft from 1856.[20] Because merchant bankers played a central role in their development, these were often referred to as "private banks of a higher order."[21] During the 1860s, everything changed: the Austro-Prussian War of 1866 led to the dissolution of the German Confederation and to the creation of a Prussian-dominated North German Confederation. The law of 1870 finally allowed joint stock companies with limited liability (including banks) to register freely.[22] The 1870s witnessed the creation of the likes of Deutsche Bank (1870) and the Dresdner Bank (1872). Increasingly, it was these new banks that financed trade and managed international capital movements.[23] Following the Franco-Prussian War and the creation of the German Empire in 1871, Berlin became the financial center of Germany.

For its part, the United States did not truly possess a national banking system before the 1860s.[24] Between 1780 and the 1860s, joint stock bank legislation developed in a rather piecemeal fashion, as "each of the states of the Union had developed its own joint stock banking laws."[25] To take an example, in the state of New York—which also happened to be the United States' financial capital—out-of-state and foreign banks were heavily restricted, in that these institutions could not engage in banking activities like receiving deposits, discount notes, or bills, and the issuance of debt. In April 1880, a bill was even passed to tax foreign bank capital.[26] In 1881, companies incorporated in New York were still limited to a capital of $2 million and in 1890 to $5 million when in England those limits had been abandoned for over thirty years. These changes were part of what legal scholar Morton J. Horwitz has termed "the transformation of American law," an abandonment of the conservative worldview of the role of the state due to the "rapid centralization of economic power" and "cartelization" of the American economy.[27] It was the National Bank Acts of 1863/64 that provided a legal framework for the incorporation of banks at the federal level. They created, as well as organized, a relatively coherent banking system for the United States.[28] Notwithstanding the permissive nature of these acts by contrast with a lot of state legislation, they continued to impose major limitations on joint stock banks.[29] For instance, though foreigners could be shareholders in joint stock banks, the directors had to be U.S. citizens and residents in the state where business was done. In addition, a national bank "could not grow as a firm beyond a specified and very limited locale,"[30] leading one scholar to claim that 'U.S. banks were confined to their home state, and most states restricted banks to a single office within that state."[31] The United States remained a debtor nation until World War I and was not a major lender to foreign sovereigns until the interwar period.[32] For this reason, the organization of its banking system does not carry much weight for my analysis of this period—less so, in any case, than the British, French, and German ones. In fact, it was European merchant bankers who possessed offices or correspondents in the United States that were key to channeling capital there.

The 1860s were truly pivotal for the development of joint stock banks. In the next two sections, I will examine how these new banks differed from merchant bankers in terms of their social composition and of their relation to sovereigns. I begin with the Anglo-American joint stock banks, before turning to the Franco-German case.

THE ANGLO-AMERICAN MODEL

British and American joint stock banks shared two key characteristics. First, joint stock banks differed profoundly from merchant banks in that they had a very distinct sociological profile. Ostensibly disdained by merchant bankers, joint stock banks were kept at a distance, a fact sometimes translated in their exclusion from key decision-making bodies. Second, joint stock banks were relatively poorly connected to sovereigns across the world. By contrast with merchant banks, they were very national institutions that did not possess the same type of international networks. As a result, they were mostly absent from international finance and, most crucially, from the business of sovereign lending.[33] In the few cases where they managed to partake in a sovereign debt issue, it was with the generous and somewhat reluctant assistance of merchant bankers, who were nonetheless happy to draw on their deep pockets.

The domestic banking system of England was well developed prior to the nineteenth century, albeit not very internationally oriented. By contrast with other European countries, English banking emerged to serve a domestically oriented trade starting in the late seventeenth century.[34] Indeed, as we saw in the section on the old sovereign lending, for international financial services Britain came to rely on continental bankers.[35] The domestic English banks were private deposit banks of six partners or less, as English law did not permit any more.[36] They were in this respect—their legal structure—similar to merchant bankers.[37] However, one important difference was that, until World War I, the merchant banks stood strong, "while the private bank disappeared almost completely" and was replaced by the joint stock bank.[38]

A number of joint stock banks, such as Midland Bank, London and Westminster Bank, and the National Provincial bank, were created in the 1830s, before the watershed of the previously mentioned Companies Act of 1862. But these banks did not have all the qualities of modern joint stock banks until this key piece of legislation. Other banks, like Lloyds, developed as joint stock banks in the 1860s, after the Companies Act. These developments culminated in 1880, when the number of joint stock banks in England and Wales reached an all-time high of 128.[39] Institutionally, they were only truly accepted in the world of deposit banking in 1854, when the leading London joint stock banks were admitted to the Clearing House, "an organisation hitherto reserved exclusively for private bankers."[40] Joint stock banks were in fact gaining so much ground that they would soon gobble up the private bankers.

Indeed, beginning in the 1880s, the new joint stock banks acquired the old London private banks, a development known as the "amalgamation movement."[41] Financial historian Youssef Cassis has characterized the disappearance of this type of bank as an "outstanding feature of the period."[42] In 1893, when this development was well underway, Lloyds amalgamated with Herries, Farquhar & Co.,[43] prompting the *Bankers' Magazine* to write that, "year by year, the private firms are growing fewer in number, and the large joint stock companies are becoming more powerful. . . . Who would have ever thought of Herries Bank ever amalgamating with Lloyds, or indeed with any bank from the City? . . . Herries! The name is familiar to most business men because there is about and around it an air of antiquity, and a history that commands respect."[44] The sense of surprise reveals that, in the 1890s, the contest between private banks and joint stock banks was not yet won. Indeed, to take an example, in 1891 a large private bank such as Coutts & Co. had similar capital, reserves, and deposits as the London and Provincial Bank, a large joint stock bank.[45] And yet, by 1909, there were only two private banks left in the City (see fig. 4.1).[46] The joint stock banks

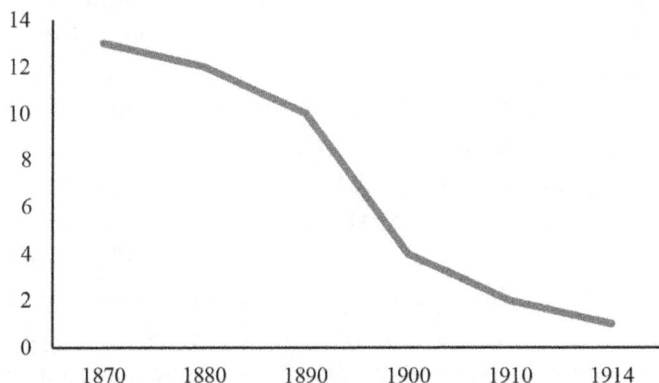

FIGURE 4.1. Private banks that were members of the Clearing House, 1870–1914. *Source*: Youssef Cassis, *City Bankers, 1890–1914* (Cambridge: Cambridge University Press, 1994), 18.

thus "rose to dominate the domestic banking system" during the last third of the nineteenth century and the first decade of the twentieth,[47] as "private banks were absorbed one by one."[48]

Some large private banks tried to grow their business to compete with joint stock banks. Barclays was the most notable of these. Even after incorporation in 1896, it attempted to maintain the structure of a private bank; it had only 110 shareholders, and each director was a "practitioner" who managed a bank branch.[49] But, as Barclays absorbed fourteen banks between 1897 and 1906, this structure became difficult to maintain. Private bankers such as Bertram Currie of Glyn, Mills, Currie & Co. came to the conclusion that groupings of select private banks could indeed only be run in the joint stock form.[50] Private bankers thus all eventually embraced the joint stock form or, alternatively, they were acquired by a joint stock bank.

It would, however, be inaccurate to say that private banking families disappeared entirely. Many, in fact, became joint stock bank directors. To put figures on this claim, in the period from 1890 to 1914, 96 percent of directors at Barclays were former private bankers, as compared with 64 percent at Lloyds, 50 percent at the Union of London and Smiths Bank, 45 percent at the Capital and Counties Bank, and 35 percent at Parr's Bank (see table 4.3). In the new joint stock banks, the social reproduction of banking families was, of course, not as easy as within a family-based private bank. And yet, some families, particularly those who belonged to old banking dynasties, managed to perpetuate themselves. To take an example, the chairman of the board at Barclays in 1982 was Timothy Bevan, while the first chairman in 1896 was Francis Augustus Bevan.[51] Barclays was admittedly a special case because it was quite literally a grouping of private banks. However, similar patterns can be observed in other banks (see table 4.3). This goes to show the extent of social reproduction in this sector of British society.

The private bankers that joint stock banks amalgamated stood rather high in terms of social status and bear some resemblance to the merchant bankers discussed in chapter 2. As Walter Bagehot, editor of the *Economist*, has put it, they represented "a certain union of pecuniary sagacity and educated refinement which was scarcely to be found in any other part of society."[52] This is in a clear sense totally unsurprising, as these bankers, particularly those in the West End of London, were for a long time providers of banking services to the aristocracy.[53] Private bankers were the most highly educated in the banking profession; 72 percent had a public school

TABLE 4.3
Proportion of Former Private Bankers and Merchants Among the Directors
of Joint Stock Banks, 1890-1914

Banks	Former private bankers (%)
Barclays & Co.	96
Lloyds Bank	64
Union of London and Smiths Bank	50
Capital and Counties Bank	45
Parr's Bank	35
London and Southwestern Bank	14
London City and Midland Bank	6
National Provincial Bank	0
London and Provincial Bank	0

Source: Youssef Cassis, City Bankers, 1890-1914 (Cambridge: Cambridge University Press, 1994), 55.

and/or an Oxbridge education, a higher number than for the merchant bankers.[54] This means, therefore, that a large number of joint stock bank directors who hailed from private banks had been well educated and qualified as gentlemen. What, then, made the British joint stock banks different from the merchant banks, if some of them had a large number of gentlemen at their head?

The answer is beguilingly simple. Though these were gentlemen, they lacked a key feature that merchant bankers possessed: an international network. They were, after all, domestic bankers. While they could obtain all the education they wanted, it was not going to make up for their lack of cousins in Frankfurt, Naples, and Paris, or the absence of family alliances across continents based on marriages. Because joint stock bankers who were formerly private bankers did not have networks, "they tended . . . to lack the detailed knowledge of foreign finances and connections with foreign governments needed to compete fully with the merchant banks."[55] In any case, most British joint stock banks were busy "digesting their successive absorptions,"[56] and so did not become seriously involved in foreign finance before the early twentieth century.[57]

When they eventually started engaging in foreign business, they had to get to know foreign sovereigns in a way that differed starkly from how merchant bankers went about this task. For instance, the joint stock bank that turned the most rapidly to foreign investments—and that also happened to be the largest—was Midland Bank (see table 4.1).[58] It was also one of the banks with the least well educated directors; only 17 percent had an Oxbridge or a public school education.[59] In order to proceed with this new endeavor, the bank's chairman, Edward Holden, opened a foreign exchange department early in 1905.[60] This was so unusual that the department "was criticized in the City as being outside the scope" of a joint stock bank's activities.[61] The next chapter will delve more thoroughly in the precise method and form of knowledge that these banks used to know sovereigns, but for now it is worth noting that those in charge of producing knowledge about foreign sovereigns in these new banks were not the directors, but a new class of professionals.

The differences between joint stock banks and merchant banks were sustained by the structure of British banking itself, which consecrated merchant banks as the core "Inner Sanctum" of the City.[62] The most striking institutional expression of this fact was the exclusion of joint stock banks (sometimes referred to as deposit banks) from the Court of Directors of the Bank of England until the 1950s, an issue I examined in my discussion of merchant bankers in chapter 2.[63] The result of this marginalization of joint stock banks meant that crises were managed without them, and that they were not informed of any measures regarding their resolution. Consider the case of the Argentine default of 1890, which nearly destroyed Barings, a merchant bank. During this crisis, the merchant banks relied only on themselves and on the governor of the Bank of England, Viscount Goschen—also a merchant banker at Goschen & Frühling. As Marcello De Cecco puts it, "All the outer layer of the financial system had to remain excluded . . . and even the existence of the crisis had to remain unknown to them as long as possible. . . . In the event of a panic, the joint-stock banks would inevitably act in a totally egotistic manner and engage in a *sauve qui peut* operation."[64] Joint stock banks were clearly not deemed to possess the ethos necessary to act in a sound manner. To save Barings, merchant banks therefore secretly pledged sums of money ranging from £200,000 to £500,000. The joint stock banks were only informed a day after this deal had been struck and were eventually asked to contribute to the financial package.[65] They were entirely excluded from important financial decisions. Merchant banks' perception of joint stock banks as second-class institutions is nicely captured in a letter from November 1890 written by Rodolphe Hottinguer, the head of Barings' sister house in Paris, after Barings had been forced to incorporate as a limited liability company. In this letter, Rodolphe Hottinguer conveys his hope that "it will quite soon be possible to do away with the word limited imposed by circumstances."[66] In 1914, over two decades after this crisis, joint stock bankers were still as marginalized. They went so far as to create a Secret Gold Reserve Committee, dominated by Edward Holden from Midland Bank, to "accumulate gold reserves to rival the official Bank of England reserves."[67] In addition to considering these reserves insufficient, they had no say in their use in times of crisis. All these examples go a long way to illustrate the position of joint stock banks in relation to merchant banks. They were true outsiders, excluded from the charmed circle of merchant bankers and deemed unfit to enjoy the privileges and assume the responsibilities of the far more gentlemanly merchant bankers.

Before I turn to the American case, which displays many similarities to the British one, I want to discuss one last British institution, which has received some attention in the literature but is not very well understood: the Corporation of Foreign Bondholders (CFB), created in 1868.[68] In this institution, it was joint stock banks that managed to exclude the merchant bankers. In addition to providing information about foreign states to bondholders, the CFB was meant to represent bondholders' interests in the negotiations that took place between creditors and sovereigns after defaults. The goal was to render access to the London market difficult prior to any satisfactory settlement of a sovereign's default. Bondholders had to be represented by a specific group of people; it was the Governing Council of the CFB that fulfilled this task. At the time, the inclusion in the council of "members of those eminent houses who have had experience in dealing with foreign governments" was a matter of course.[69] For this reason, until 1898 the CFB was criticized as an institution that pursued merchant banks' interests and did not push sufficiently strongly for settlements of sovereign defaults favourable to bondholders.[70] The rationale was that the issuing of sovereign debt was so lucrative a business for merchant banks that they had few incentives to punish defaulting states. After 1898 and the reorganization of the CFB with the Corporation of Foreign Bondholders Act, merchant bankers became ineligible for the Governing Council of the CFB, while the representatives of the Big Five joint stock banks all obtained representation.[71] It is in a sense unsurprising that joint stock banks and bondholders joined forces through the CFB, because, as we have seen, they were all outsiders in sovereign lending by comparison with merchant bankers.[72]

To a large extent, the American story follows the British model: merchant bankers were not involved in the creation of joint stock banks, and the same division of labor existed between the two types of banks. A prominent historian of banking therefore calls the United States the "mirror reflection" of Great Britain.[73] As the largest capital importer in the period between 1870 and 1914, the United States relied intensely on private bankers to channel the inflow of foreign capital.[74] As in Europe, these banks were truly private: they did not publish their financial statements and relied on the complete faith of the investing public, "based solely on reputation and word of mouth."[75] Their lending also followed similar precepts. During the 1912 Pujo Congressional Committee hearings, John Pierpont Morgan claimed that the banking system "was built on honor and character more than money," that banking "was a matter of trust," and that "in such matters social background was an important factor."[76] The persistence and strength of private bankers in the United States is so striking that one historian says of it that "it is a very astonishing phenomenon in the history of banking that in the United States a few big private bankers were able to uphold their position among the greatest financial powers in the country; what is more, well into our own century, the most influential money and credit institution in America was a private banker!"[77] Many of the American private houses engaged in international finance were European or linked through family to British and European bankers (e.g., the Morgans, Barings, Browns, Kleinworts, Lazards, Kuhns, Rothschilds, and Speyers).[78] The establishment of local agencies representing foreign banks was basically out of the question because of protectionist legislation, but copartnerships were possible if the bank had American citizens in it (e.g., Morgans).[79] An alternative was to act through agents—for instance, the Rothschilds, who relied on August Belmont Sr.[80]

Before 1919, American joint stock banks were rarely involved in international finance on their own, a rather different state of affairs than for French or German banks.[81] Some had opened foreign exchange departments to serve their multinational clients—for instance, the First National of Chicago as early as 1873, the Bank of New York in 1893, and National City Bank in 1897.[82] In fact, Edward Holden from Midland Bank (in Britain) had taken inspiration from the latter case to create his own foreign exchange service in 1905. But when the United States began exporting capital on a large scale, it was private banks, not joint stock banks, that played the leading role.[83] Only in 1914 did the Federal Reserve Act permit nationally chartered banks—those incorporated under the National Bank Act of 1863—with capital in excess of $1 million to establish branches overseas.[84] National City Bank (later Citibank), the largest American corporate bank, only opened an office abroad—in Buenos Aires—in 1914.[85] What happened was that the New York joint stock banks put their considerable financial resources in the hands of private bankers, as mentioned earlier.[86] Thus, National City Bank, the largest American joint stock bank, formed an alliance with private bank Kuhn, Loeb & Co.,[87] because it "had the ability to originate securities as well as European investment connections."[88] Despite its much larger size in terms of capital and deposits, National City Bank remained the junior partner.[89] The same point can be made with regard to J. P. Morgan's relation to First National Bank and National City Bank from the late nineteenth century to the interwar years.[90]

The dominance of private bankers in international finance continued throughout the interwar years. Soon, however, some of the regulatory hurdles to the participation of these large commercial banks in international finance were taken down. For instance, in 1927 commercial banks obtained the right to engage in equities underwriting.[91] Soon after, in 1933, the Glass-Steagall Act terminated the overlapping of commercial and investment banking, forcing banks to choose between the two activities. Most private banks chose to remain in the securities business, while J. P. Morgan, who had always accepted deposits from large commercial clients, split its business into two companies: J. P. Morgan & Co, which chose to focus on commercial banking, and the investment bank Morgan Stanley (created in 1935).[92] As one observer writes, by 1934 the New Deal had "delivered a severe blow to the independence and swagger of Wall Street."[93]

To sum up, in the American case as in the English case, there was little overlap between the individuals in merchant banks and those in the joint stock banks. The former were happy to invest the latter's capital, but that was the extent of their bonds.[94] On the whole, the picture painted here of American joint stock banks is that of a very domestically oriented class of actors, which, though it was much larger than private banks in terms of capital, remained subservient to the merchant banks in international finance, at least until the interwar period. Like their English counterparts, American joint stock banks were outsiders in the business of sovereign lending when compared with the merchant bankers. They would have to wait a few decades before becoming active in this business. On the European

continent, specifically in France and Germany, the picture was a little
more complicated.

THE FRANCO-GERMAN MODEL

In France and Germany, the separation between old and new banks was
not quite as clear cut as in Britain and the United States.[95] From the very
start, a number of merchant banks were involved in the creation of joint
stock banks.[96] And yet it is inaccurate to depict merchant bankers as having an entirely favorable attitude to these new banks. In this section, I make
two key points. The first is that it was often the most marginal merchant
banks that embraced joint stock status in France and Germany; in other
words, joint stock banks were a means for second-tier merchant banks
to realize their grand ambitions.[97] The second point pertains to the networks and connections that these new continental banks had to foreign sovereigns. Although many in France and Germany were created by merchant
bankers, these were second-tier institutions that were not very active in the
business of sovereign lending: they were not the Barings, Rothschilds,
Hottinguers, or Morgans of this world. To get involved in international
finance and sovereign lending more specifically, the new joint stock banks
either needed the help of merchant bankers, as in the American case, or to
build their own way of knowing foreign sovereigns (to be discussed in
chapter 5). The only exception to this rule was a specific subset of French
joint stock banks, the *banque d'affaires*.

After the passage of the law of 1863, French joint stock banks fell, practically speaking, in one of two broad categories: they were either deposit
banks (*banques de dépôt*) such as the Crédit Lyonnais and Société Générale,
or investment banks (*banques d'affaires*) such as the Banque de Paris et des
Pays-Bas—later Paribas—and the Banque de l'Union Parisienne. This distinction is central to understand how these banks differed in sociological
terms.[98] These bank types differed specifically in terms of their business
model and of the people who created them, though they sometimes worked
in tandem, with the deposit banks helping the investment banks to place
their securities.[99] The deposit banks were outsiders in international finance,
while the investment banks were to a large extent the continuation of the
haute banque.[100] In order to make these differences salient, I will briefly
explore an example from each end of the spectrum that runs from deposit

to investment banks: the Crédit Lyonnais and the Banque de Paris et des Pays-Bas.

Henri Germain founded the Crédit Lyonnais in 1863, with a capital of 20 million francs. Germain, it is important to note, was not part of a family like the Barings, Rothschilds, Morgans, or Hottinguers. Other individuals involved from the first board meeting included two bankers from Geneva, a money changer, three tradesmen, two minor Parisian bankers, one director of a public utilities company, a director of a railways company, and two administrators of ironworks.[101] While this group was certainly respectable by national standards, it was nothing like the banking aristocracy that gave rise to some of the investment banks, as we will see later. What one finds here is a very national, not to say regional, bank. Its business model was based on the large-scale collection of people's deposits. Germain had studied English banks closely, and it is thus no surprise that the Crédit Lyonnais decided to base its business on the collection of deposits.[102] Imitating English joint stock banks, it created a web of branches across France to collect laypersons' savings, so that by 1914 it was the leading French bank and had more than six hundred thousand account holders.[103] Because it was a deposit bank, the Crédit Lyonnais had to be extremely careful with the use of the capital it held. As soon as the bank decided to become involved in foreign lending in the 1870s—by 1879 it had offices in London, Geneva, Madrid, Alexandria, Constantinople, and St. Petersburg—it faced two problems. The first problem was the exceeding difficulty of entering the charmed circle of great merchant banks that dominated these types of transactions.[104] The second was that the Crédit Lyonnais simply had no knowledge of foreign states; it had to produce its knowledge from scratch.[105] In the next chapter, I will explore what this knowledge consisted of in more detail. For now, it is sufficient to say that the documentation and knowledge built up by the Crédit Lyonnais was so extensive that the work of the Versailles Peace Conference relied on it extensively.[106] This output was the result of the Crédit Lyonnais's position as an outsider in international finance, a characteristic reflective of the experience of deposit banks.

The Banque de Paris et des Pays-Bas (BPPB), later called Paribas, was created in 1872 and represents the alternative model, namely, the banque d'affaires. On the eve of World War I, it was the largest French banque d'affaires. These investment banks had a much larger starting capital than deposit banks, which they could use without fear of the rumors about mismanagement that sometimes led to runs on deposits.[107] In the case of the BPPB, the starting capital was 62.5 million francs and reached over 100 million francs by 1914.[108] The BPPB was the result of a bank merger. The first bank was the Banque de Paris, founded in 1869 by a group of Parisian bankers including A. Delahante, E. Joubert, and H. Cernuschi.[109] The second bank was the Banque de Crédit et de Dépôt des Pays-Bas, founded in 1863 in Amsterdam by the Bischoffsheims with branches in Paris, Brussels, Antwerp, and Geneva.[110] This bank, assembled around Louis-Raphaël Bischoffsheim, brought together French financiers such as Edouard Hentsch and Alphonse Pinard, as well as families originating from Germany and based in other European countries such as the Bischoffsheims, Goldschmidts, and Bambergers.[111] The Bischoffsheims (originally from Mainz) had started in Amsterdam, where two brothers married two Goldschmidt sisters, from a Frankfurt banking family. Out of this union later emerged Bischoffsheim, Goldschmidt & Cie. in Paris, and Bischoffsheim & Goldschmidt in London.[112] The Bambergers were the Bischoffsheims' cousins, and, interestingly, Ludwig Bamberger, who worked for the BPPB's predecessor in Paris, went on to be one of the two key founders of the Deutsche Bank.[113] The composition of the BPPB's leading group was, therefore, and quite obviously, more prestigious and international than the Crédit Lyonnais's. For this reason, the BPPB would not need to engage in thorough information-gathering activities. It might be able, so long as the founding merchant bankers were prominent in their structure, to rely on old networks.

It is clear, therefore, that in France the new joint stock banks were not all outsiders. The deposit banks surely were, but the investment banks (banques d'affaires) were in fact created by merchant bankers, not those of the same caliber as the Barings and the Morgans, but merchant bankers nonetheless. They could therefore rely to some degree on international networks.[114] What often happened was that deposit banks worked in tandem with investment banks. For instance, in the 43 million francs loan to Denmark in 1901, as in the 65 million francs loan to Sweden in 1914, the Crédit Lyonnais was present alongside the BPPB and obtained a similar share of the loan issue.[115] The question to ask here is, of course, until when could large investment banks count on their well-connected merchant banking founders to know foreign sovereigns? Before the interwar period, the old merchant banks had provided contacts (with their networks of connections), as well as contracts, to their newly created investment banks.[116] In return, the investment banks provided shares of their various transactions to the old banking houses.[117] And yet, even in the years running up to World War I, the chairman of the BPPB, Edouard Noetzlin, was trying to build his own links with English and American merchant bankers, who still reigned supreme in the business of sovereign lending.[118] In France, the decline of the influence of old banks within the new investment banks was a process that really gathered pace in the interwar period and was achieved with World War II.[119] In this period and thereafter, investment banks would need to develop new means of knowing sovereigns. Their structure made it difficult to maintain the same business model as the old merchant banks.

Despite the rise of these joint stock banks, what must be kept in mind, however, is the continued presence and importance of merchant bankers in French international finance. This fact was due to the still unshakable hold of merchant bankers on business in the world's financial center, London. Consider the following example. In 1907, a Japanese loan of £23 million was distributed equally between London and Paris. Rothschild Frères had the lion's share in the French issue, with 33.33 percent, whereas Paribas had 24.68 percent, and the Crédit Lyonnais a mere 13.33 percent. This distribution was intrinsically linked to the preeminence of merchant banks (by opposition to joint stock banks) in London and the fact that the London tranche of the loan was going to be underwritten by a syndicate led by N. M. Rothschild & Sons. If we consider the size of the Crédit Lyonnais in relation to the small Rothschild family partnership, this is truly astounding (see table 4.1).[120]

German joint stock banks were in many ways similar to French ones, falling somewhere in between the deposit bank and investment bank in terms of their "internationality." In short, both French and German joint stock banks operated in relatively similar ways when they lent to foreign sovereigns and companies, and in this they differed from their English counterparts, who were largely absent from this kind of business.[121] Contrary to the French case, however, there was no distinction between investment and deposit banks in Germany; most banks engaged in deposit collection, short-term lending, and long-term investment.[122] This was the beginning of German universal banks.[123] I do not want to dwell too long on the German case, as Berlin was much less important than London and New York (and even Paris) over the course of the long nineteenth century, and certainly in the interwar period.[124] I will simply outline the similarities of the German joint stock banks with the French ones.

Prior to the legal changes which permitted the free creation of joint stock banks in 1870, small private banking houses were Germany's most important financial institutions.[125] They dominated Germany's international banking scene until the 1870s, mainly by marketing securities for foreign governments and railways.[126] This was a world "governed by notables," where key characters were men such as Gerson Bleichröder, banker to Bismarck.[127] As an aside, it is worth noting that Bleichröder's importance seems to have been largely overblown, as his place was largely owed to his status as a Rothschild agent. For this reason, Paris-based James de Rothschild once said, "Bleichröder? What is Bleichröder? Bleichröder is the one per cent I let him have."[128]

German bankers were indeed dependent on foreign capital; they were unable to respond to the funding needs of German commerce and industry. For a long time, Germany in fact relied on the English—and, to a lesser extent, on the French—capital market to finance its trade.[129] As we saw in chapter 2, this was originally one of the key areas of business of German merchant bankers in London. As for industry, in the second half of the nineteenth century German demand for capital increased at a pace that far exceeded the savings available in the country—an experience that differed strongly from the British one.[130]

After 1870 and the legalization of modern joint stock banks, the most important institution for questions of international finance in Germany was the Deutsche Bank.[131] Consequently, it is interesting to examine its development to understand how the new joint stock banks engaged in international finance. This joint stock bank, as most German joint stock banks, was created by merchant bankers.[132] As in the French case, the top merchant banks tended to stay out of these new ventures, whereas the second-tier houses were very implicated in them. In Germany, the names of Rothschild, Bleichröder, and Bethmann are missing from joint stock bank rosters. In the case of the Deutsche Bank, whose founders were keen on teaming up with private bankers that would give their bank "the necessary *gravitas*," enlisting respectable banks such as Mendelssohn & Co turned out to be impossible.[133] The two founders of the Deutsche Bank were Adelbert Delbrück and Ludwig Bamberger. Adelbert Delbrück was part of the Berlin merchant bank Delbrück Leo & Co., which was not exactly in the front rank of Berlin banks but had a good reputation.[134] Ludwig Bamberger had worked in his cousins' banks in London, at Bischoffsheim & Goldschmidt, and, in Paris, at the Banque de Paris et des Pays-Bas (BPPB), where he specialized in foreign business.[135] Interestingly, and in a manner reminiscent of the usages of merchant banking families, he married Anna Belmont in 1852. She was a cousin of August Belmont's, the Rothschilds' agent in New York.[136] In addition to Delbrück and Bamberger, five other individuals sat on the administrative board, four of them German bankers.[137] In some sense, it looks as though the Deutsche Bank was trying to unify German banking by picking out bankers representing every part of the country, rather than trying to constitute an international network.

German banks generally, and the Deutsche Bank specifically, were involved in a number of foreign operations. The Baghdad Railway was, for example, one of the Deutsche Bank's most emblematic international projects of the pre–World War I period.[138] In sovereign lending, the old merchant banks such as the Rothschilds, Bleichröders, Behrens, and Warburgs were still crucial, and, in fact, joint stock banks often had to join them in syndicates to penetrate this area of business.[139] For instance, while the Disconto-Gesellschaft managed to make a foray in Austrian government finances in the 1860s, it nonetheless had to count on the support of the banking houses of Oppenheim, Mendelssohn, and Bleichröder.[140] This was equally true of the Russian loans of the late 1870s and 1880s, in which Mendelssohn and Bleichröder played leading parts.[141] The picture painted here is one in which the joint stock banks were still heavily reliant on merchant bankers that had *not* been involved in their creation. This reveals their nature as outsiders in relation to foreign sovereigns and their dependence on merchant bankers' networks and knowledge.

Here, as for the French banques d'affaires, the question must be posed as to how long merchant bankers' influence lasted *within* the new joint stock banks. The German case gives us an interesting answer, as, by 1884, a new Corporation Law was passed, establishing a strong distinction between management and supervisory boards in banks. It allocated great powers to the former and marked the "separation of capital ownership from company control."[142] In this way, the merchant bankers that were shareholders were distanced from the management of the bank. Though sons of merchant bankers continued to accede to the managing board in one way or another, they were "increasingly joined by the descendants of representatives of other professions" (e.g., civil servants, teachers, doctors, or priests).[143] These newcomers had a rather superficial knowledge of banking. For instance, one of the first two managing directors of the Deutsche Bank, a lawyer called Georg Siemens, wrote to his family, saying, "Though I understand little of American and Indian banking, I nevertheless try to look very erudite, give the occasional shrug, grin from ear to ear . . . and secretly refer, when I get home, to my encyclopaedia or dictionary . . . when I want to find a word I didn't understand. I've already just about grasped the difference between letter of credit and cash."[144]

Put simply, those at the head of joint stock banks had very little knowledge of banking. However, in an organization with 8,475 bank officials (Beamte) by 1914, knowledge of banking had become the affair of professional bureaucrats, not solely that of two or three managers (by contrast with merchant banks).[145] This was true not only for the Deutsche Bank but also for joint stock banks across the world. Even such a peculiar area of business as sovereign lending would not escape this transformation. In fact, from the brief sketch of joint stock banks drawn here, it is possible to hypothesize that the clearest outsiders in sovereign lending (i.e., those with the least means of knowing foreign sovereigns) would be the first to develop alternative methods, that is, methods that did not involve merchant bankers and their gentility, for knowing foreign sovereigns.

To sum up, in France and Germany, there undoubtedly existed some overlap between the individuals who populated merchant banks and those who created joint stock banks. The social composition of these banks was therefore different from their Anglo-American brethren's. My main observation, however, has been that it was primarily second-tier merchant bankers who partook in these new ventures. As a result, joint stock banks could rely to some degree on the networks of these founding members to engage in international business and, to a far lesser degree, in sovereign lending. Nonetheless, though continental joint stock banks engaged in international finance more thoroughly and precociously than their Anglo-American counterparts, their position remained precarious, particularly in the business of sovereign lending, for which they often relied on merchant bankers. In this sense, they remained outsiders in the business of sovereign lending.

Particularly important for the continued importance and dominance of old merchant banking houses against joint stock banks on the Continent was the fact that neither Paris nor Berlin was the center of nineteenth- and twentieth-century international finance.[146] Paris was a faithful second in the nineteenth century up until World War I and, after the war, moved further down the ranks once New York ascended. Berlin emerged as a second-tier financial center after 1870, precisely because of the rise of new German banks. The grip that merchant bankers kept on sovereign lending in London and, later, in New York, meant that their French and German counterparts, who were often family members or sister houses, were better placed to reap the benefits of sovereign debt issues that were regularly done across multiple financial centers simultaneously. In this sense, the specific structure of international banking in the world's two successive financial centers, first London and then New York, was absolutely crucial to containing the power of joint stock banks in continental Europe.

The rise of joint stock banks, a true financial revolution that eventually displaced the old world of family banks, has received no systematic attention in international political economy. The critical legal innovations that took place across Western countries in the 1860s and enabled this change deserve an entire study. By way of conclusion, I want to emphasize three points pertaining to joint stock banks. First, and somewhat counterintuitively, the rise of joint stock banks entailed a "nationalization" of international finance. Old merchant banks with connections across the world were replaced by financial institutions with a far less international structure. These joint stock banks would have to develop new strategies to become international, as family marriages and alliances were not tools suited to these commercial entities. This replacement of old banks meant that the movement of capital across the world was increasingly being managed by joint stock banks, which were nonetheless poorly integrated in the old structures of international financial cooperation. Though it is not the direct object of my study, I would suggest that this development made for an increasingly unstable international financial system.

The second point worthy of attention here is that it was continental joint stock banks that initially came to play a role in international finance, as they were more international in terms of their social composition and outlook than the Anglo-American banks. In other words, the corporatization of international finance cannot be attributed to "Anglo-Saxons" or to liberal countries. If anything, the dominance of corporate banks in international finance was a continental development anchored in polities that were in many ways illiberal: the Second French Empire and the German Empire. By contrast, the United Kingdom and the United States were characterized by the much clearer separation of joint stock banks from merchant banks, and the remarkable persistence and supremacy of the latter in international finance. In other words, a type of organization that could almost be characterized as premodern, namely, private family banks—retained a central place in the world's most economically advanced nation until the interwar period, while new corporate banks took the center ground in illiberal nations catching up with Britain.

Finally, joint stock banks were, for the most part, outsiders in the more specific area of sovereign lending; they had no connections with sovereigns across the world. It was thus relatively difficult for them to know sovereigns and to engage in the business of sovereign lending. This was particularly true for British and American joint stock banks, in which merchant bankers played no major role. Midland Bank in England and National City Bank in the United States are key examples. By 1913, they were the largest banks in terms of assets in their respective countries, and yet they were not the central actors in the business of sovereign lending. The continental situation was slightly different. In France and Germany, merchant bankers were sometimes involved in the creation of joint stock banks. These were in some sense the continuation of the "old" sovereign lending, insofar as a number of second-tier merchant bankers partook in their creation. It was, accordingly, easier for these banks to enter the business of sovereign lending than for the American and British joint stock banks, as they could at times count on their founding members' connections to foreign sovereigns. But, of course, as new shares were issued, partners died, and inheritances were scattered, merchant banks could not insure their eternal preponderance in these new banks.

As their influence waned, notably in the interwar period, the joint stock banks they created would have to develop new means of knowing sovereigns. The few banks in which merchant bankers were completely absent, such as the Crédit Lyonnais, experienced the problem of how to "know" foreign sovereigns far more quickly than the ones in which merchant bankers were involved. A temporary solution consisted in operating alongside merchant banks, but this could not last forever. How, then, did these new lenders get to know sovereigns? What form of knowledge did they use? This is the question to which I now turn.

STATISTICS AS A FORM OF KNOWLEDGE

The question with which we were left in the preceding chapter is what type of knowledge was used by the new actors of sovereign lending. In this chapter, I make the claim that the crucial form of knowledge on which they relied was statistics. A prevalent contemporary understanding of statistics equates the term with probability. In this sense, statistics have become omnipresent not only in the social sciences but also in medical research such as epidemiology, as well as in other natural sciences, and even in finance.[1] This view is so prevalent that the main English-language monographs about the history of statistics generally focus entirely on this aspect.[2] A second meaning of "statistics" refers to what many would call "descriptive statistics," the "systematic collection and arrangement of numerical facts or data of any kind."[3] In this second sense, statistics is even more widespread. Originally, however, the word "statistics" referred to something much more specific: the description and comparison of states with quantifiable data.[4] This is the meaning of statistics that underlies my argument.

How can such a practice ever have been novel? Nowadays, states are routinely compared on the basis of quantifiable data. The use of numbers to represent states has become ubiquitous, both in international organizations, ministries of foreign affairs, and scholarly research. But this was not always so. Some may want to argue that describing sovereigns through quantifiable facts is a practice that has always existed—for instance, in the form of the numbering of the people of Israel, Augustus's balance sheet of the Roman Empire, Charlemagne's inventory of his possessions, or the Doomsday book.[5] However, none of these cases were undertaken in the spirit of modern statistics, and to think so is to "fail to understand the basis of the statistical approach' and the 'nature of the statistical method."[6] In addition to being one-off events, these instances of "counting things" were not thought to be representations of sovereigns, which could be used as templates for other sovereigns. As I will explain, such a conception and practice only emerged in the late eighteenth century.

Therefore, my first task in this chapter will be to outline when, where, and why people started systematically describing, comparing, and ranking sovereigns with numbers. In other words, when did statistics emerge as a form of knowledge as I described it in chapter 1? The chapter's second task is to trace the transmission of statistics to the new sovereign lenders. To this end, the second section examines the dissemination of statistics in the public sphere, while the third focuses on the emergence of the real conveyor belt of statistical thinking for sovereign lenders, namely, business schools. The chapter concludes by briefly illustrating how the students trained in these new institutions brought statistics to the new joint stock banks, based on the case of the Crédit Lyonnais. In so doing, it shows that one of the outcomes of this process was the creation of systematic sovereign credit ratings.

THE DEVELOPMENT OF STATISTICS

In a passage of his *Italian Journey*, Goethe describes some of the features of the town of Bolzano, where he has just arrived. He then stops abruptly and states that "in our statistically minded times" all of what he observes must already be "printed in books."[7] Goethe's choice of words is interesting, as the term *Statistik* had only been coined in the 1740s by a German academic. And yet, as an administrator of the Duchy of Sachsen-Weimar since 1775, it is no surprise that Goethe came in contact with the emerging discipline of Statistik, developed precisely for rulers. But what was it?

Initially responsible for the rise of this discipline was a group of law and history professors engaged in the development of cameral science—the science of government—at the University of Göttingen.[8] One of them, Gottfried Achenwall (1719–1772), coined the term *Statistik* in 1749.[9] The main goal of this science, according to Achenwall and those who came after him, was to describe states' material and nonmaterial forces,[10] and to compare them on the basis of (mostly) quantifiable facts.[11] The adjective "statistical" (not the noun "statistics") had been used in earlier Italian writings such as those of Girolamo Ghilini, who relies on the adjective *statistica* in a monograph from 1647, mentioning an unpublished work of his on the "civile, politica, statistica, e militare scienza."[12] The main difference between the Italian tradition, which was concerned with collecting "information more or less systematically on foreign states," and the German tradition is in large part that the latter was far more numerically oriented.[13] Indeed, a comparative glance at the work of Italian writers such as Botero and Ghilini and late eighteenth-century German statisticians reveals this clear discrepancy.[14] Beginning with Achenwall's work, states are described and compared with quantitative data about, for example, population, debt, infantry, cavalry, and naval forces. The discipline of statistics as the practice of representing and comparing sovereigns on the basis of quantifiable facts cannot truly be said to have begun in earnest before the second half of the eighteenth century in Germany.

Though originally the matrices comparing states contained a great deal of "verbal descriptions," this changed for the use of figures, which in turn "favored topics which lent themselves to numerical presentation."[15] The standard presentation became two-dimensional schemata, which had a horizontal dimension, containing the countries to be compared, and a vertical one, presenting the categories for comparison.[16] Achenwall's student and successor, August Ludwig von Schlözer, called for the abandonment of discursive description, as he largely preferred quantitative data.[17] For him, statistics ought to become a "measuring discipline" and an "exact observational science" that did not describe but "contained general results as counts"—in other words, "the less adorned, the truer."[18] This movement took place in the second half of the eighteenth century and in the early nineteenth. Its spread, however, was not primarily caused by academic statisticians.

The increasing use of statistics by neighboring disciplines such as history and geography demonstrates how, in some sense, statistics was becoming a technique of investigation, a method of presentation of empirical facts, rather than a science in its own right.[19] Statisticians found themselves increasingly trying to defend the remit of their discipline, which has led to the slightly confusing claim that German statistics declined in the early nineteenth century.[20] This is a misrepresentation; though it was itself declining as a self-standing academic discipline, statistics was in fact becoming a widespread means of knowing and representing sovereigns in a variety of disciplines. Statistical descriptions of various European sovereigns started appearing in the most curious of places. It was possible, for example, to find them in the Almanac de Gotha, a German yearly almanac ranking European royalty and high nobility that enjoyed a broad audience from 1764 to the late nineteenth century. In the very late eighteenth century, statistical representations of sovereigns can be seen in a great deal of German academic scholarship, of which J. C. Gatterer and A. L. Crome's works are good examples.[21]

This quantitative turn to describe and know states was not to everyone's taste. Arnold Heeren, successor and erstwhile colleague of the famous statistician August Ludwig von Schlözer, once declared that statisticians who overrelied on numbers were "table hacks."[22] A later commentator in the pages of the widely read *Göttingische gelehrte Anzeigen* (which, incidentally, was founded by Schlözer) from as late as 1807 stated in a refreshingly blunt manner: "These poor fools are spreading the crazy idea that one can understand the power of a state simply by a superficial knowledge of its population, its national income, and the number of animals nibbling in its fields. . . . The machinations in which these criminal statistician-politicians indulge in their efforts to express everything through figures . . . are ridiculous and contemptible beyond all words."[23] Hardly a ringing endorsement of the practice, this statement illustrates the resistance with which the description of sovereigns through quantifiable facts was met, and the novelty it constituted, more than half a century after it had timidly appeared. And yet the transition from "statistics without counting" to table-statistics, oriented "largely on the methodological criteria of measurability," was already well underway.[24] This meant, for instance, that traditional topics such as the history of a state that were treated by the first statisticians, such as Achenwall, had to be "excluded from the sphere of interest" of Statistik.[25]

While the heavily quantitative aspect of late eighteenth-century German statistics differentiated it from previous Italian work, it was its interstate comparison that distinguished it from the early British discipline of political arithmetic.[26] The work of John Graunt (1620–1674), William Petty (1623–1687), and Charles Davenant (1656–1714)—central to this British tradition—was not primarily concerned with the comparison of states, but with taxes, births, deaths, and general questions of demography within specific regions or countries. Political arithmetic thus cannot be considered a form of knowledge in the sense of being an enduring way of knowing and representing sovereigns; only statistics fits this description. The Germans who picked up political arithmetic were not the international lawyers or academics developing cameral sciences at the universities of Halle, Jena, or Göttingen, but men like Johann Peter Süssmilch (1707–1767),[27] a pastor trained in medicine, just like William Petty.[28] This is why, when he introduced the word "statistics" to English in his *Statistical Account of Scotland* (1798), John Sinclair felt the need to explain that

> many people were at first surprised at my using the words, Statistics and Statistical. . . . In the course of a very extensive tour, through the northern parts of Europe, which I happened to take in 1786, I found that in Germany they were engaged in a species of political inquiry to which they had given the name of Statistics. By statistical is meant in Germany an inquiry for the purpose of ascertaining the political strength of a country or questions concerning matters of state.[29]

This was a rather different exercise than the one proposed by political arithmeticians. One of William Petty's treatises, *Political Arithmetic*, did compare England, Holland, Zealand, and France, based on a few criteria, as did Charles Davenant's various essays concerned with France and the Dutch.[30] However, the English development that approximates German statistics most closely was the work of a Scotsman named John Campbell. In *The Present State of Europe* (1752), a publication that enjoyed an international readership, Campbell presents statistical material in the form of numerical tables to assess, compare, and rank states' power.[31] This was part of a broader journalistic genre on the "present state of Europe," in which a discourse identifying states as "powers" developed.[32] Thus, the practice of describing and comparing states with numbers truly emerged across Europe in the late eighteenth century, distinctly in Germany, but in recognizably similar forms elsewhere, too.

In order to appreciate why this was the case, it is necessary to understand two developments in international relations and international political thought. First, there was the political context of the Holy Roman Empire and its constituent entities. Within this curious polity, the emperor's power was already largely diminished by the end of the Thirty Years' War, and even more so by the eighteenth century. While disputes between states themselves and between states and the emperor had previously been dealt with through the juridical framework of the empire, the emperor's declining power could hardly continue to impose this old method.[33] This became an even more acute issue in the eighteenth century with the rise of a powerful Prussia, which led to an intense rivalry with Austria.[34] Lawyers such as Achenwall did try to maintain the old legalistic framework of the empire by omitting Prussia and Austria from their statistical work. For them, Austria and Prussia still had to be dealt with and understood within the context of the empire, not as part of an international power game.[35]

The second important development linked to the emergence of statistics in the sense of a quantitative description and comparison of states was a new type of discourse that identified international actors as powers that were part of an "international system." The discourse on powers and on their gradation (i.e., great, middle, or small) developed rapidly, and by the mid-eighteenth century the use of this vocabulary was "commonplace."[36] It was only in the latter part of the eighteenth century that the discourse on powers merged with statistics, such that gradations of power were supported by statistical analysis—for instance, in the work of Bielfeld.[37] It is not a surprise, then, that statisticians made important contributions to debates about power and the balance of power in international relations. The idea that these European powers formed an international system, the basis of which was the freedom of each state, was most famously developed by a historian based at the University of Göttingen, Arnold Heeren, in his *Handbuch der Geschichte des europäischen Staatensystems und seiner Colonien* (1809).[38] Heeren developed his argument in reaction to the French wars and Napoleon's bid for supremacy in Europe, so as to assert that Europe had always been based on a system of free independent states. Thus, both the political context of the Holy Roman Empire and the intellectual environment in Europe were favorable to the development of statistical ideas. As an aside, it is interesting to mark the central role of the University of Göttingen in the emergence of a recognizably realist discourse on international relations organized around the notions of powers, balance of power, and international system. In the same way as we like to speak of a "Chicago school" in twentieth-century economics, or an "English school" in twentieth-century IR, there was a "Göttingen school" of international relations in the second half of the eighteenth century and the first half of the nineteenth.

Statistics was not just an obscure academic undertaking; it was eminently useful for practically oriented men, like civil servants. It was a "political discipline" meant to prepare "future practical statesmen for their duties" and impart to them the knowledge of states' constitution and the nature of their strengths and weaknesses.[39] The University of Göttingen, where Achenwall worked, was created in 1737 to answer the need for properly qualified statesmen.[40] This was part of a broader movement in the development of what has been termed "cameral sciences," or "sciences of the state," for which professional chairs were purposefully created in various protestant German universities.[41]

The Faculty of Law in which Achenwall worked was a key tool for dispensing education to future statesmen and administrators,[42] attracting such promising candidates as the young Prince von Metternich, who was taught by a colleague of Achenwall's, Johann Stephan Pütter.[43] More minor figures trained in statistics in the eighteenth century were responsible for the great expansion of the role this discipline played in politics in the following century. For instance, Baron von Stein, the founder of the Prussian statistical bureau, studied in Göttingen and then became state minister and head of the departments of excises, customs, manufactures, and commerce.[44] Johann Gottfried Hoffmann, head of the Prussian bureau from 1808 onward, came to play *the* central role in the statistical commission—the first of its kind—of the Congress of Vienna led by G. F. von Martens (another Göttingen alumnus), established after the defeat of imperial France.[45] The commission was created in part to appease the disagreements between Metternich and Hardenberg, respectively Austrian and Prussian Chancellors, about the characteristics (e.g., population) of the territories lost by Napoleon. The commission's work, unheard of in previous peace settlements, was key in the shift from a qualitative evaluation of state power to a quantitative one, and in the "unrestricted mathematical application of the balance principle."[46] Though lawyers, intellectuals, and journalists had been moving in this direction for some time, the Congress of Vienna really appears as a turning point in terms of statesmen's practice.

MAKING A MARKET: THE DISSEMINATION OF STATISTICS

Because they were so tied with the exercise of power, statistics remained rather secretive during the eighteenth century. Professors often "had to defend themselves from charges of presumptuousness and unauthorized diffusion of state secrets."[47] As Ian Hacking puts it, "If there is a contrast in point of official statistics between the eighteenth and nineteenth centuries, it is that the former feared to reveal while the latter loved to publish."[48] A good illustration of the reluctance to publicize data about the state is Austria, which only started publishing its annual accounts in 1860.[49] However, things were already changing in the early nineteenth century, not least because of the arguments of statisticians themselves.

Many thought that statistics should be a matter of state administration, because, as Schlözer claimed, "only the state, and not the private person can create the most important statistical data."[50] This view, which found many supporters, led to the rise of statistical bureaus across Europe. It was also conveniently suited to the enlightened-absolutist programs of modernization that many princes pursued. Though probably self-interested, Schlözer's stance was shared by statisticians who sought explicit participation as "advising experts in the business of politics."[51] There was, however, a more subversive dimension to this movement. First, it led to an increasing professionalization of the high civil service and, therefore, a move toward more bureaucratic forms of authority. Second, through their publications, many academics sought to make statistics public, that is, to bring them into the emerging bourgeois public sphere.[52] Hence, the dissemination of statistics is bound up with the emergence of a public sphere, not so much in salons and cafes, but, more importantly, in publications such as journals and manuals. The intention of this move to publicize, enabled by the University of Göttingen's freedom from censorship, was the emancipation of the citizenry, best expressed through Schlözer's belief that "despotisms became free polities through publicity."[53] A number of political-statistical journals were created in the late eighteenth century, the most famous in Germany being Schlözer's *Staatsanzeigen*, published in Hanover from 1782 to 1795, when it was eventually prohibited.[54] These private efforts went some way toward making statistics public, but things only really changed in the early nineteenth century, with the rise of statistical bureaux. These did not produce statistics in the sense of cross-country comparisons, as the initial German definition would have had it, but national statistics.

The years around 1830 were the real *Sattelzeit* in terms of the development of statistical bureaux and associations (see table 5.1).[55] A French statistical bureau, the Bureau de la Statistique Générale, opened in 1800, but it was closed in 1812 by Napoleon.[56] It reopened in 1833 as Statistique Générale de France, and, in the meantime, a number of private statistical writings had appeared, notably the famous *Recherches statistiques sur la ville de Paris et le department de la Seine* from 1821.[57] Prussia, following its defeat against Napoleon, reorganized the state and built a statistical service, which opened in 1805 and remained in place until 1934.[58] From 1805 to 1806, it was headed by Leopold Krug, who had been trained at the University of Halle in statistics, before Johann Gottfried Hoffmann took over in 1808. The foundation of the Zollverein at the initiation of Prussia in 1833 also required accurate official statistics, particularly about the population, so "triennial enumerations were prescribed for the whole territory of the union."[59] This was one of the developments that led to the establishment of statistical bureaus in minor German states, because "excise taxes for trade between states were apportioned according to the number of people in each state."[60] Saxony as well as Mecklenburg-Schwerin opened their statistical offices in 1851, Oldenburg in 1855, Hamburg in 1866, Bremen in 1867, and Lübeck in 1871.[61] The revolution of 1848 and German industrialization were additional triggers for this movement.[62] The creation of the German Empire after 1871 was followed up with the establishment of an imperial statistical bureau, the Kaiserliches Statistisches Amt, in 1872.[63] Austria only opened a statistical office in 1829,[64] conducted its first census in 1857, and established a central statistical commission in 1863.[65] England and Wales, by contrast, developed their statistical offices in the 1830s, opening the Board of Trade's bureau of statistics in 1832 and the General Register Office in 1836.[66] It should however be noted that the first British census had taken place in 1801.[67] Finally, the United States, while it had been conducting censuses for political reasons pertaining to the congressional weight of each state since 1800, only created a permanent census bureau in 1902.[68]

These developments in official statistics were emulated by nongovernmental actors. In France, the Société Statistique was created in 1803, but closed in 1804. In 1829, a statistical society called the Société Française de Statistique Universelle appeared, and, in 1860, the Société de Statistique de

Paris was created.[69] The latter of these two had been explicitly founded to assess the merits of free trade after the signature of the Cobden-Chevalier Treaty.[70] A journal of statistics, the *Annales de Statistique*, was published as early as 1802. In Britain, the famous statisticians Quételet (a Belgian) and Malthus created a statistical section of the British Association for the Advancement of Science, and in 1834 the Statistical Society of London (later Royal Statistical Society in 1887) was founded.[71] In Germany, it was the famous Verein für Sozialpolitik, created in 1872, that played a role similar to the London Statistical Society's.[72] Finally, the first International Statistical Congress was held in Brussels in 1853, followed by another eight in different locations over the next twenty-three years.[73]

Most of these institutions and associations were still engaging in a type of statistics that was "divorced from the developments in the mathematical theory of probability."[74] For this reason, in 1838 it was still possible for the London Statistical Society to claim that "the Science of Statistics differs from Political Economy, because, although it has the same end in view, it does not discuss causes nor reason upon probable effects; it seeks only to

TABLE 5.1
Summary of the Creation of Statistical Institutions

1800–1830	Bureau de la Statistique Générale *closed 1812*
	Prussian statistical service
	Société de Statistiques *closed 1806*
	Société Française de Statistique Universelle
	Austrian Statistical Bureau
1830–1860	Statistique Générale de France
	Board of Trade's bureau of statistics
	General Register Office
	Société Statistique de Paris
	Statistical Society of London
	First International Statistical Congress (Brussels)
	German Statistical Offices: Bayern, Saxony and Mecklenburg-Schwerin.
1860–1890	Verein für Sozialpolitik
	Kaiserliches Statistisches Amt
	German Statistical Offices: Oldenburg, Hamburg, Bremen, and Lübeck.
	Central Statistical Commission (Austria)

Sources: Alain Desrosières, *The Politics of Large Numbers: A History of Statistical Reasoning*, trans. Camille Naish (Cambridge, MA: Harvard University Press, 2002), 151, 167, 179, 196; Ian Hacking, *The Taming of Chance* (Cambridge: Cambridge University Press, 1990), 34; Harm Klueting, *Die Lehre von der Macht der Staaten: Das aussenpolitische Machtproblem in der "politischen Wissenschaft" und in der praktischen Politik im 18. Jahrhundert* (Berlin: Duncker & Humblot, 1986), 297; Theodore M. Porter, *The Rise of Statistical Thinking, 1820–1900* (Princeton, NJ: Princeton University Press, 1986), 38–39; Nico Randeraad, *States and Statistics in the Nineteenth Century: Europe by Numbers* (Manchester: Manchester University Press, 2010), 112; Harald Westergaard, *Contributions to the History of Statistics* (London: PSKing, 1932), 114–15, 119–20, 173.

correct, arrange and compare, the class of facts which alone can form the basis of correct conclusions with respect to social and political government."[75] The point here is that, even by this time, for statistical societies statistics did not mean probability; it still referred to what we would now call "descriptive statistics." However, it was not only official bureaus and learned societies that produced and published statistics. Soon, new periodicals started publishing a substantial amount of the data produced by these bureaus and private organizations. By comparison with statistical bureaus, they were very interested in cross-country comparisons. One of the most important ones was the *Statesman's Yearbook*, published from 1864, though there were also many more specialized outlets. In 1837 in London, Charles Fenn published a *Compendium of the English and Foreign Funds*, the endless title of which includes a reference to "debts and revenues of foreign states."[76] It underwent sixteen editions between 1837 and the end of the nineteenth century. From its ninth edition (1867) onward, the editor of *Fenn's Compendium* was Robert Lucas Nash, a man who had started a career at the *Economist* in 1864, a journal created by James Wilson in the 1840s.[77] Interestingly, during the latter part of Nash's career at the *Economist* and until a few months before his resignation, R. H. Inglis Palgrave had been the editor of the journal.[78] The 1850s witnessed the foundation of a Brussels-based francophone equivalent named *La Semaine Financière*, as well as the French *Manuel des Fonds Publics et des Sociétés par Action*, created by Alphonse Courtois.[79] *L'Economiste Français* was first published in 1862 by Paul Leroy-Beaulieu, and, a year later, the *Economist* started producing a monthly supplement called the *Investor's Monthly Manual*.[80] One financial historian speculates that Robert Lucas Nash (again) edited this supplement.[81] Modeled on the *Economist*, as was the *Statist* (1878), the *Commercial and Financial Chronicle* was published from 1865 by William Buck Dana in New York.[82] Later publications included Mulhall's *Dictionary of Statistics*, undergoing five editions between 1886 and World War I. This last publication, like Fenn's compendium, was not updated monthly or even yearly, but only every few years.

The period starting in the 1830s thus saw a huge increase in the publication of statistics, through official bureaus and scientific associations, but also in periodicals of all sorts. However, the quality of the numbers was still very much in doubt. By the end of the nineteenth century, there were estimates of national wealth for only ten countries, and, by 1929, for twenty.[83] For some countries, these estimates were intermittent. For instance, in the second half of the nineteenth century, Russia, Germany, and the Netherlands only had national wealth estimates from the late eighteenth and early nineteenth century.[84] In any case, the point here is that the "statistical gaze," a new way of thinking about sovereigns and of knowing them, would soon penetrate deeper into society by reaching higher education. It would be taught in universities, and, more importantly for sovereign lenders, in newly created business schools.

THE TRANSMISSION OF STATISTICS

Prior to the end of the nineteenth century, there was no advanced commercial education. Those who became merchant bankers in Britain, for instance, learned their trade in the family bank and abroad with their foreign partners. Some did attend Oxford or Cambridge, but this type of education "was not seen as appropriate preparation for a youth intended for business life, any more than it was seen as a useful preliminary to the army."[85] Though bankers like the Rothschilds did go to the ancient universities to study moral sciences (of which political economy was a component) it was, as we saw in chapter 3, certainly not for the specialized business training these universities offered.[86]

In the last decades of the nineteenth century, the first business schools were founded, and all of them taught courses about statistics. In France, the boom started in the 1870s. The École Supérieure de Commerce was created in 1830, but it only acquired importance from 1869 onward, when it was taken over by the Chamber of Commerce of Paris. At that point, about 100 to 150 students attended the school, and, in their third year, they could study banking and financial operations relating to interests, annuities, types of bonds, calculation of probability and its financial and commercial applications, life insurance, state borrowing, treasury bonds, and the links between the state and railway undertakings.[87] They also studied commerce and political economy, which comprised a section on statistics.

The École Libre de Sciences Politiques (later Sciences Po) was created in 1871, and the École des Hautes Etudes Commerciales (later HEC) in 1881.[88] Both of these schools dispensed commercial training. At the École Libre, one could study the financial history of Europe, specifically relating to state budgets, financial organization, debts, taxes, borrowing, and credit.[89] In the

1870s, the school introduced a course about statistics, along with a course on public accounts. In the 1880s, a whole section (out of two) was dedicated to economy and finance, the other one being the section *générale*.[90] By the end of the decade, there was an endowed chair in "Statistique et commerce extérieur" and one in "Finance," a novelty followed by two new courses, one about French and foreign finance and the other concerned with "Statistics, external commerce and economic geography." The former course dealt with issues of public credit, loans and debt, repayment, conversion, and floating debt, while the latter examined the objects and processes of statistics, demography, agricultural/industrial/commercial statistics of France compared to that of other states, populations and professions, mines, great industries, canals, railways, telegraph, and ports, and various colonial systems around the world.[91] All of this is rather unsurprising, as Paul-Leroy-Beaulieu, a famous economist whose main work was a book entitled *Traité sur la Science des Finances* (1877), directed the school for a number of years. By the end of the 1880s, the school had about four hundred students. The École des Hautes Etudes Commerciales (HEC) offered similar classes, and, because of this, "banking was the one activity in which HEC graduates had been able to assert themselves, thanks to the originality of their training."[92] In 1905, the school even dedicated one of its three sections to "Commerce et banque."[93]

In Britain, similar developments took place slightly later. The author of a manual on commercial education from the 1880s notes in a puzzled tone that there are "no proper commercial schools in England, Scotland, and Ireland," and that, "in sum, the most commercial nation on the globe possesses a poorly developed commercial education."[94] To my knowledge, the only form of financial education was the Gilbart Lectures on Banking dispensed by the internationally famous statistician Leone Levi at King's College starting in 1872.[95] His lectures were funded by the will of James Gilbart (erstwhile manager of the London & Westminster Bank—a joint stock bank) who had written a handbook on banking practice earlier in the century. Levi had, as it happens, also published estimates of the national incomes of four countries in 1860 (UK, France, Russia, and Austria), at a time when there were still no reliable sources.[96]

One response to the lack of commercial education was simply to recruit French and German men. A number of British banks, such as Midland, followed this strategy.[97] Midland Bank was by the early twentieth century the largest British bank along with Lloyds in terms of deposits. In the early 1900s, it decided to undertake foreign operations. Midland did not have competent staff among its five thousand employees to engage in this sort of business, but the supply of well-trained bankers, even from abroad, was insufficient. As a result, chairman Sir Edward Holden "urged British universities to offer courses in international finance, pointing out in 1905 that the American banks were recruiting from the American and German universities."[98] The words of Midland's chairman are indicative of the lack of proper training for banking in British higher education, specifically pertaining to foreign banking, and they illustrate his willingness to hire employees with advanced financial training. One of the institutional responses to the lack of education for businessmen was the Institute of Bankers, established in 1879, which offered training to people who were already bank employees.[99] As one might expect, the directing committee and council were mostly populated by men from joint stock banks, either based in Britain or in the empire, and a few small private banks that were quickly absorbed by joint stock banks at the close of the nineteenth century. No merchant banks seem to have taken part in this endeavor.[100] However, the institute's educational program was for clerks rather than for high-ranking managers. The most telling feature of the low level of training offered at this institution is the fact that, in the early 1900s, the institute replaced courses on commercial geography and algebra with a compulsory paper in English composition and banking correspondence.[101] In fact, future bank managers were to receive training at another institution, as Sir Felix Schuster, president of the Institute of Bankers and Governor of the Union of London and Smiths Bank, recognized: "The opportunities which [the London School of Economics] affords (probably unequalled in this country or any other) for training in the higher branches of business administration are certainly worth the attention of our students, especially those whose ambition it is to rise to the higher grades and to take command of large administrative work of any kind, and for whom scientific as well as business capacity is essential."[102]

The heads of British joint stock banks indeed perceived novel institutions such as the London School of Economics (LSE) as superior and more adequately suited to the training of bankers. The development of elite business schools took place slightly later than in France, and, in fact, one of them drew particular inspiration from there. Both public and private interests pushed for the creation of the London School of Economics and Political Science (LSE) in 1895.[103] Beatrice and Sydney Webb helped to found the LSE with a donation, admitting the influence that the French experience had had on them. Indeed, Sydney Webb claimed that "my wife and I resolved to . . . start a centre of economic teaching and research in London on the lines of Paris."[104] This school offered two commercial degrees, the B.Sc. (Econ) and the B.Com., which both required passing examinations in law, political science, economic history, statistics, and scientific method. The B.Com. offered additional training in questions of banking, currency, commerce, international transport, industry, and public institutions.[105] There were also schools of commerce operating in Manchester and Birmingham.[106] Interestingly, before the Faculty of Commerce of Birmingham opened in 1902, one of its professors, W. J. Ashley, "visited Germany to look at the recently created Handelshochschulen."[107]

Some in the past have pointed to the role of the Realschule in Germany, which dispensed practical training to students in their teenage years, but these schools had little in common with the French and British institutions mentioned previously. Indeed, the Realschule trained students from as early as 13 years old and did not even require an Abitur (A-level equivalent). In Germany, it was the Handelshochschulen created at the turn of the century that were intended for the "training of leaders of the economy."[108] The business schools of Leipzig, St Gallen, Aachen, and Vienna came first, in 1898; then came the ones of Cologne and Frankfurt am Main in 1901, Berlin in 1906, Mannheim in 1907, Munich in 1910, Königsberg in 1915, and Nuremberg in 1919.[109] Here, statistics were used and transmitted to future bankers. While languages were part of the curriculum, as the impressive pre-1914 list of classes at the Cologne business school demonstrates (language courses on offer included French, Russian, Japanese, Chinese, modern Arabic, modern Persian, modern Greek, Hindi, and Sanskrit), the central part of the curriculum was macroeconomics (Volkwirtschaftslehre), law, geography, science of trade, natural sciences, and technology.[110] Very rapidly, schools such as Cologne and Berlin developed courses on banking (Handelstechnik der Banken).[111] In Cologne, this course was taught by Ernst Walb, who had written about and been schooled in cameralism, the discipline that produced statistics.[112] This evidence makes it clear that German joint stock banks could not recruit any employees that were highly trained in financial and commercial sciences until the early twentieth century, as there were no business schools. It is therefore a misinterpretation to claim that the non-recruitment of such students was a conscious choice: there was simply no available source of well-trained employees.[113] The Deutsche Bank, for instance, mostly recruited people with GCSE-level qualifications, and only a few recruits seem to have had an Abitur.[114] The law students who did receive economic training generally became civil servants who would organize the German economy, rather than bankers.[115] One alternative for the Deutsche Bank was to recruit men with foreign experience—for instance, Georg Siemens and Herman Wallich, the former having worked for Siemens in Persia, and the latter setting up the Shanghai branch of the Comptoir d'Escompte.[116] These men, however, were the directors of the company, not the mid-level managers devising methods to assess sovereigns as rigorously as possible.

Developments in the United States, the world's financial center by the interwar years, followed a similar pattern. There, "the period of vigorous development in the teaching of commercial and economic subjects" began at "the end of first decade of the twentieth century."[117] W. J. Ashley, the same Englishman who had traveled to see German business schools before founding the Faculty of Commerce in Birmingham, spoke highly of American universities. He lauded that fact that, by comparison with the English universities, Harvard offered not only general courses on political economy, but also on subjects such as tariffs, money, and banking.[118] Because of this, he claimed, "business men there, for the last two or three decades, have sent their sons to the universities."[119] Accordingly, in the United States, it was also through universities that businesspeople acquired a commercial education, and not only in commercial schools, such as Wharton Business School. This stands in stark contrast to Britain, where the merchant bankers attended Oxbridge and public schools, while joint stock bankers received specialized training at the Institute of Bankers and, later, schools such as the LSE.

From around the 1880s to the 1910s, there was a boom in formal business education in France, Germany, Britain, and the United States. The students who studied in business schools, and, in the United States, in universities, took courses about statistics, states' finances, and banking. As the brief overview of courses reveals, they studied states in a comparative manner. There is, accordingly, little doubt that this statistical way of thinking about sovereigns was spreading throughout societies and reaching the graduates of these new institutions of higher education. In the same way as for other forms of knowledge—for instance, gentility—the spread of statistics was followed by two developments. First, with time, statistics was becoming more and more commonplace in society and, as a result, the importance of a specialized education to understand and use statistics declined. One need only realize that, nowadays, we start comparing states on the basis of quantifiable facts in primary school geography or history. The second development was that the meaning of statistics was also gradually shifting in the nineteenth century, such that it came to refer to the gathering and organization of data regarding objects other than the state (and, eventually, to probability as well). In order to understand how exactly statistics reached the new sovereign lenders, the final section examines the experience of the largest joint stock bank in terms of assets by 1913: the Crédit Lyonnais.

STATISTICS IN PRACTICE: THE CASE OF THE CRÉDIT LYONNAIS

Oddly enough, no sovereign lenders relied systematically on statistics before, at least, the very last decade of the nineteenth century. A large quantity of financial information was available in financial periodicals, but it is as if these statistics, which could be obtained at a relatively cheap price, were of little use to merchant bankers, who dominated the business of sovereign lending. By the interwar period, Guy de Rothschild's main way of keeping up with international financial developments was still to have his clerk read him the newspaper. The situation was different for the new lenders, joint stock banks, who were outsiders in the business of sovereign lending.

Staff was made up of young men from the rising bourgeoisie. As the nineteenth century drew to a close, these men were increasingly educated, and a number of the higher-ranking ones attended business schools. Naturally, their training shaped the way in which they thought about states and the assessment of their creditworthiness. With their statistical knowledge, business school graduates went on to work in banks and developed the first statistical ratings of sovereigns. They did this in order to guide their institutions in the risky business of sovereign lending—and in foreign lending more broadly—as well as to compete with merchant bankers.

This type of development can, for instance, be observed in the case of the Crédit Lyonnais, which was the first bank to produce sovereign rankings for financial purposes and that also happens to possess particularly well-preserved archives. On the eve of World War I, the Crédit Lyonnais was the largest French bank, comparable in size to the largest City banks.[120] Founded in 1863, it turned to foreign lending as early as the 1870s and, accordingly, needed to gather information about foreign states, companies, and public utilities. To this end, it created a specific division, the Service des Études Financières (SEF). While this service could tap into the statistical information available in various press outlets, it was not always clear how accurate this information was. Another issue was that there was no international agreement as to how national accounts should be kept; this made the systematic comparison of sources mandatory.[121]

The founder of the bank, Henri Germain, was allegedly inspired by positivism, a fact reflected in his "obsession of informing himself meticulously."[122] He was embedded in a social circle of French engineers from the École Polytechnique ,and he published widely on economics. One of his close friends was Emile Cheysson,[123] a statistician who propagated statistics through the *Journal de la Société Statistique de Paris*.[124] When he opened the SEF, he turned to Alphonse Courtois to lead the division. Courtois was an influential liberal who authored numerous books on finance, among which one finds a statistical series about the Paris Bourse mentioned earlier, the *Manuel des fonds publics et des sociétés par actions*.[125]

The biggest problem for the SEF was that of human capital. First, the bank was relatively young and therefore did not appeal to new graduates. Second, and more importantly, there were next to no "qualified" graduates. There were a few engineers from the Grandes Écoles who had basic training in political economy, but that discipline was "vague and theoretical," a complaint that echoes those concerning political economy in Oxford and Cambridge.[126] As a result, there was but a small team of twenty employees until November 1889. At this point the SEF grew in numbers from a budget of 200,000 francs to one of nearly 1 million francs in 1900, and from twenty people to one hundred after 1900.[127] The reason for this change was in great part the bank's turn to foreign investments and the Argentine debt crisis of 1890 (an almost deathly blow to the old merchant bank Barings).[128]

The key background condition for this development was that the problem of a lack of qualified candidates had been solved, as new higher education institutions dispensed training in statistics, public finances, and economics: the École Libre de Sciences Politiques, the Hautes Etudes Commerciales, and the École Superieure de Commerce.[129] It was the people who graduated from these new institutions of higher education who then went on to develop new methods for knowing sovereigns and assessing their credit-worthiness. The competence of the Crédit Lyonnais' employees was widely recognized by foreign banks. For this reason, foreign banks like Midland sometimes "recruited experienced dealers from the successful European banks" such as "David Miller and David Lorsignol from the Crédit Lyon-nais," though this practice was rare before World War I.[130] The outcome of the recruitment of such well-trained men at the Crédit Lyonnais was that, in 1898, the section dedicated to financial studies created the first sovereign credit ratings (see table 5.2). Sovereigns' credit was ranked according to revenue, expenses, difference between revenue and total spending, the ratio of the net product of assets to interests on the debt, and the ratio of debt interests to normal revenues. The output was a three-tiered table, containing three groups of states, separated according to their credit worthiness.

TABLE 5.2
Sovereign Credit Ratings Constructed by the Crédit
Lyonnais in 1898

States whose financial management is of first order

1. Germany	7. Denmark
2. Great Britain	8. Belgium
3. United States	9. Norway
4. Russia	10. Switzerland
5. Sweden	11–20. Swiss cantons
6. Finland	21. Transvaal

States whose financial management is of second order

Holland	British India
Egypt	Hungary
Japan	Romania
Austria	Italy
Dutch Indies	Chile

States whose financial management is of third order

Spain	Portugal
Bulgaria and Rumelia	Greece
Argentina	Serbia
Brazil	

Source: "Classification des Etats d'après les résultats de leur gestion financière," DEEF 72879/1, Archives Historiques du Crédit Lyonnais (AHCL). Only states in the first category were ranked.

These ratings were not public, as they were intended for the Crédit Lyonnais's exclusive use.[131] And yet, when the SEF was launched, the Crédit Lyonnais made sure to invite journalists, to get a simple message across: we are well informed.[132] The goal was for the public to know that they, too, had good information, and that it was possible to be well informed without being a part of the haute banque.[133] Statistics as a form of knowledge is what allowed these outsiders in the business of sovereign lending to achieve both goals. Although joint stock banks like the Crédit Lyonnais would not take the lead in the business of sovereign lending during the interwar period, it is with them that, in 1898, the now ubiquitous practice of ranking sovereigns on the basis of statistics for financial purposes emerged.[134] The next chapter provides further evidence of this development in financial practice over the course of the twentieth century.

In this chapter, I have historicized the development of statistics—in other words, the description of states through quantifiable facts—and shown how it eventually reached a specific group of sovereign lenders at the very end of the nineteenth century and in the early twentieth. Emerging in the mid-eighteenth century in Germany, statistics was initially concerned with measuring the power of states. A group of German international lawyers and historians (particularly those in Göttingen) were trying to make sense of the changing international context around them, not least of which the crumbling of the Holy Roman Empire and the rise of great power rivalries in a polity that had hitherto relied on law to regulate internal conflicts. There were some similar developments in other parts of Europe, particularly in England, as more and more journalists were developing a discourse that identified international actors as "powers." Gradually, it was thought that power ought to be measured, and this is exactly what Statistik did, by examining population and national wealth, among other increasingly quantifiable criteria. Some of the students exposed to this new discipline included the future Austrian statesman Prince von Metternich, and the famous nineteenth-century international lawyer Georg Friedrich von Martens, both key figures of the Congress of Vienna, which witnessed the creation of the first international statistical commission.

Statistics then gradually spread to the broader public and eventually to the new sovereign lenders. In this respect, the 1830s was the first real turning point with the significant multiplication of official statistical bureaux in Europe. One or two decades later, an increasing number of publications, including the *Economist*, were making statistics about different countries available to a broad public. One of the striking features of this process of dissemination of statistics is, to use Ian Hacking's words, that "economic need does not ... seem well correlated with growth of understanding; nor does growth of understanding seem well correlated with satisfaction of economic needs."[135] Indeed, until the interwar period, information about sovereigns' finances and other indicators was still in many ways limited and inaccurate. Furthermore, whatever was available was not being used in any systematic way by the old and dominant sovereign lenders, namely, the merchant bankers. For this to take place, one had to wait for the passage of a new generation of men through commercial schools and into key jobs in joint stock banks. Indeed, many graduates from the newly created business schools such as HEC, LSE, the German Handelshochschulen, or even from economics departments in American universities went on to work in the newly created joint stock banks.

This transmission resulted in the emergence of a new way of engaging with sovereigns among financiers. The case of the Crédit Lyonnais offers a vivid example—and the first known instantiation—of the systematic application of statistics to sovereign lending, resulting in the first sovereign credit rating. It was only at this time, on the cusp of the twentieth century, that what the prominent nineteenth-century statistician Schlözer called the "statistical gaze" reached sovereign lenders. This observation shows that the new sovereign lending was profoundly different from the old, both in terms of its core set of actors and the way in which they thought about states. A group of outsiders in sovereign lending began using a form of knowledge, statistics, that allowed them to engage in sovereign lending and compete with the merchant bankers.

Thus it was that the new world of sovereign lending came about and took root in the first half of the twentieth century. Notwithstanding this development, as we saw in chapter 2, the key protagonists of the old world of sovereign lending remained dominant in the interwar period. The last chapter, to which I now turn, examines when the new lenders and their statistical approach finally triumphed and became a defining feature of our world.

Chapter Six

THE NEW SOVEREIGN LENDING TRIUMPHS

Having shown that new lenders were indeed emerging and thinking about their sovereign borrowers in a new way, through systematic statistical assessment, I now wish to make three final points. First, I want to expose how this development continued into the interwar period. Beyond joint stock banks, which remain pivotal international financial actors in our time, a number of new institutions that are still crucial to sovereign lending today emerged: credit rating agencies and international institutions, in this case, the League of Nations.[1] My intention here is to demonstrate that these actors were part of the new sovereign lending, in the sense that they relied on a similar form of knowledge to the joint stock banks.

My second point is that the rise of the new sovereign lending was halted between the 1930s and the 1970s. By the interwar period, the old sovereign lenders and the new coexisted, using different forms of knowledge and pursuing, in some respects, different goals. While the new sovereign lenders were on the ascent, the old were still dominant (see table 2.1). This came to a halt with the suspension of most *private* international capital flows and, thus, private lending to foreign sovereigns for roughly four decades—excluding lending by public institutions such as the International Monetary Fund (IMF), the World Bank, export credit agencies, or governments. This financial setup, often associated with Bretton Woods, slowly unraveled during the 1960s, such that, by the mid-1970s, private international lending to sovereigns reemerged, except that this time it was of an entirely different type, dominated by the new lenders that had outflanked and dwarfed the old in the domestic context. By the early 1980s, the new sovereign lending fully triumphed, subjecting states across the world to continual statistical evaluations to determine where capital would travel.

The third point I want to make is that new forms of global regulation emerged in response to this epoch-making development, a fact most readily observable in the work of institutions such as the Basel Committee on Banking Supervision. After a few sovereign debt crises in the 1970s and early 1980s, this international body sought to deal with the new sovereign lenders head on, so as to avoid a proliferation of bank failures that might be triggered by sovereign default, and thereby maintain the integrity of the international financial system. The key point here is that the committee pursued this aim by regulating the new lenders' statistical assessments, opting in turn for two very different approaches in the last thirty years or so. This new type of regulation faces questions of an entirely novel kind.

BEYOND THE JOINT STOCK BANKS

During the interwar period, the old world of sovereign lending was creaking at the seams as new banks were making their way into sovereign lending, first in Paris and Berlin before World War I, and, slowly, in New York City in the interwar period. However, just as the old world was waning and new banks were rising, another group of actors became involved in sovereign lending. These were, on the one hand, credit rating agencies, and on the other, the League of Nations (specifically its Economic and Financial Organization). Neither sovereign lenders nor borrowers, they provided information and judgments for the former about the latter. Crucially, both relied on statistics to know states.

In the business of sovereign lending, rating agencies were the outsiders par excellence. Their story begins in the United States in the mid-nineteenth century.[2] From the mid-1850s until the early 1900s, Henry V. Poor and John Moody sold manuals compiling financial data from different railroads in the United States.[3] In 1880, Poor's *Manual of the Railroads of the United States* had over five thousand subscribers, and, in 1900, Moody first published his *Manual of Industrial Statistics*, already widening the scope of interest of his business.[4] These were not intended to offer a judgment regarding the creditworthiness of a business, but rather to allow investors to make informed judgments of their own. From the 1910s onward, these companies gradually changed their products by adding assessments of creditworthiness in the form of letter grades to their data compendia. By 1909, John Moody sold his manual business and created a new one assessing creditworthiness, Moody's Analyses Publishing Co., the first to ever rate securities.[5] Poor's followed suit in 1916.[6] In the meantime, John Knowles Fitch created his own financial statistics company in 1913, although he did not issue any ratings prior to 1924, two years after the Standard Statistics Company issued theirs.[7]

These early ratings were sold to investors instead of being issued for free to a broad public. Rating agencies' main clients were the commercial banks and investment funds, as well as individual investors. This was what is sometimes referred to as an "investor-pays" model. It is opposed to the "issuer-pays" model that came to dominate starting in the 1970s.[8] In this latter scheme, it is those who wish to be rated that pay for ratings, and the ratings are freely available to all investors.[9]

Rating agencies began producing ratings of sovereigns during the interwar period, twenty years after the Crédit Lyonnais. The obvious reason for this was that the United States had now become the world's banker.[10] In 1918, Moody's started ranking the credit of ten sovereigns—Argentina, Canada, Cuba, the Dominican Republic, France, Japan, Norway, Panama, Switzerland, and the United Kingdom—based on alphabetical "grades" (e.g., Aaa, Aa, B).[11] Poor's followed suit in 1922, while Standard Statistics and Fitch began sovereign ratings in 1924.[12] These companies followed the same modus operandi as the large commercial banks. They relied on a different form of knowledge than the kind used by merchant bankers. A clue as to what type of knowledge they used can be found in the name that was often used to designate rating agencies during the interwar: "statistical corporations."[13]

Because this was happening at a later time than when the Crédit Lyonnais started producing rankings based on statistics, two factors were altered. First, there was much more official information available, notably from the American departments and embassies and, crucially, from the newly created League of Nations.[14] Second, it was easier to find competent staff to produce ratings. From the meager available evidence concerning the profile of analysts in these companies, it appears that rating agencies prized individuals with PhDs in economics. By no means did all sovereign analysts hold this degree, but it was clearly valued, and ratings were assessed against the type of knowledge held by people with such qualifications. In addition, twenty years after the Crédit Lyonnais's experience, more and more people had become familiar with statistics without going through a specialized education.

Let me take two examples to illustrate my claims. Standard Statistics, later part of Standard & Poor's, frequently hired men with competences in statistics and economics. This is evident when one examines the profiles of contributing editors for their rating publications: Eugene E. Agger was an associate professor of economics at Columbia University, Lewis H. Haney was director of the New York University Bureau of Business Research, and Carl E. Parry was professor of economics at Tulane. Meanwhile, their consulting economists included Herbert J. Davenport, Professor of Economics at Cornell University, and T. E. Gregory, who held a B.Sc. from the London School of Economics. Although, as one scholar explains, it is "difficult to assess the role played by each staff member in the sovereign rating process" at Standard Statistics, there is a clear pattern in terms of the kinds of individuals that were hired and consulted.

Likewise, at Moody's, from 1922 until 1928, the head of the department tasked with sovereign ratings, Max Winkler, held a PhD in economics.[15] Winkler also published books on the question of sovereign lending such as the gloomily titled *Foreign Bonds, an Autopsy* (1933).[16] It was under Max Winkler's directorship—a man with a sociological and educational profile that was strikingly different from merchant bankers and much closer to joint stock bank analysts—that the sovereign ratings division at Moody's developed a comprehensive list of twenty-five criteria to judge the creditworthiness of sovereign bonds (see table 6.1).[17]

As in the case of the Crédit Lyonnais, these criteria were not part of an explicit formula, but constituted broad guidance to assess sovereign bonds.[18] The first striking point is that at least half of these criteria are quantifiable in a very clear sense. A second observation can be made regarding the presence of some puzzling criteria—for instance, "racial characteristics of population"— that differ greatly from those of the Crédit Lyonnais. The persistence of such criteria in 1924 should not be brushed aside, but considered as an indication that the rise of statistics as a form of knowledge used by sovereign lenders left plenty of room for what many today would deem to be highly objectionable criteria.

TABLE 6.1
Moody's Twenty-five Sovereign Rating Criteria in 1924

1. Legality and validity of issue	13. Ratio of growth in debt and wealth
2. Tax exemptions in the country of issue	14. Importance of state-owned industries
3. International alliances	15. Monetary system
4. Racial characteristics of population	16. Existence of sinking funds
5. Educational standards	17. Past record
6. Occupational statistics	18. Promptness of interest payments
7. Institutional and political stability	19. Bonds payable in gold or in bills
8. Risk of debt repudiation	20. Exchange rates
9. Natural resources	21. Government revenues, expenses and taxation
10. Per capita wealth	22. Visible foreign trade
11. Ratio of national debt to national wealth	23. Blind items of exchange
12. Ratio of annual debt charges to annual revenues	24. Currency system
	25. Degree of industrialization

Source: Norbert Gaillard, *A Century of Sovereign Ratings* (New York: Springer, 2012), 47–49.

As we will see later on, because of the increasing irrelevance of private international finance to sovereign borrowing in the Bretton Woods era, most rating agencies suspended their ratings of foreign sovereigns during the period.[19] For instance, Standard & Poor's suspended almost all sovereign ratings between 1968 and 1974, except for the United States and Canada.[20] During the same time frame, Fitch had put an end to their sovereign rating activity.[21] But before moving on to discuss this period, I want to briefly explain the role that the League of Nations came to play in sovereign lending and the form of knowledge on which it primarily relied.

The League of Nations had in common with rating agencies the characteristic of not being an actual sovereign lender and yet of being involved in sovereign lending. It was the first international organization to play an active role in the business, and in economics and finance more broadly.[22] The league had embraced these activities as a response to the postwar slump and hyperinflation of the early 1920s, activities that eventually "formed the basis of attempts to reinvent the organization and its role in international relations."[23] At the heart of this undertaking was the League of Nations' Economic and Financial Organization (EFO), created to deal with financial crises in Austria, Hungary, Bulgaria, and Greece, and eventually in other nations as well.[24] This body was crucial in the making of the so-called league loans.

The loans in which the league played a role were a series of nine long-term loans issued between 1923 and 1928, for five sovereigns—Austria,

Hungary, Greece, Bulgaria, and Estonia—and a partly sovereign entity, Danzig (see table 6.2).[25] They were intended to help the reconstruction and stabilization of new central and eastern European states' finances and currencies. Though it did not participate in the lending itself, the league's aim was to convince private creditors to invest in these newly created and/or war-torn countries. It was meant to act as a seal of approval, and, to achieve this, it needed to rely on a specific type of expertise. The league, like the joint stock banks and rating agencies, would experience its own statistical "moment" to pursue this goal. The EFO attempted to "collate global intelligence,"[26] seeking "to measure and consistently to compare constituent parts of the world."[27] As one historian puts it, tasks nowadays devolved to international financial institutions such as the International Monetary Fund were "already known by its League of Nations predecessors."[28]

With time, the fact that loans were endorsed with the assent of the League of Nations came to be seen as a badge of trustworthiness on financial markets. The mention "An International Loan Issued Under the Auspices of the League of Nations," absent from the original loan prospectuses, appeared clearly. Speyer—a leading New York merchant banker who issued many of these league loans—claimed in front of the Senate Committee on Finance that the "League of Nations' moral endorsement of course had a great deal of weight with many people."[29] The league was developing a reputation in the business of sovereign lending based on a type of knowledge that was different from merchant bankers'.[30]

TABLE 6.2
League of Nations Loans

Country	Total amount (millions £)	Year	Underwriter in New York
Austria*	33.78	1923	J. P. Morgan
Hungary	14.38	1924	Speyer
Greece	21.0	1924	Speyer
Danzig*	1.5	1925	(issued in London)
Bulgaria	3.3	1926	Speyer, Schröder, Blair
Estonia	1.5	1927	Hallgarten & Co.
Danzig*	1.9	1927	(issued in London)
Greece	7.56	1928	National City
Bulgaria	5.53	1928	Speyer

Source: Juan H. Flores Zendejas and Yann Decorzant, "Going Multilateral?," *Economic History Review* 69, no. 2 (2016): 661.
*This loan to Austria was guaranteed by other states. As for the free city of Danzig, it was not fully sovereign, and there is a body of literature that attempts to assess its legal status.

What was this reputation based on? The answer is that it was initially underpinned by an informal transnational network of financiers, economists, and statisticians, and eventually, after the financial crises in Austria, Hungary, Bulgaria and Greece, by its own staff of statisticians at the EFO.[31] They were the producers of the league's immensely consequential statistical information—an impact that was in part based on its efforts to standardize national statistics.[32] Many of the league's statisticians and other experts would continue their careers in the IMF and the World Bank, constituting a crucial dimension of continuity with the post–World War II period.[33] The league was indeed a critical professional experience for individuals like Jean Monnet, Paul-Henri Spaak, Pietro Stoppani, and Per Jacobsson, who would come to play a key role in contemporary European and international institutions. It further provided hands-on experience for economists the likes of James Meade, Tjalling Koopmans, Ragnar Nurkse, Gottfried Haberler, Jan Tinbergen, Jacob Viner, Oskar Morgenstern, and Kenneth Boulding, who would make their mark in the second half of the twentieth century.[34]

Hence, though it did not possess its own capital, the League of Nations' EFO acted as a "money doctor" by providing a seal of approval to those who sought its help, after a thorough examination of their financial situation.[35] This approval was based on extensive statistical information. The extent of data collection about these countries and all of the world's states can be observed through the extensive series of publications created by the Economic and Financial sections: for example, *Statistical Yearbook of the League of Nations, Monthly Bulletin of Statistics, Money and Banking, International Trade Statistics, World Economic Survey, Review of World Trade,* and *International Trade in Certain Raw Materials and Foodstuffs*.[36] Another indicator of the centrality of statistical data gathering to the certification of sovereign loans was the nature of the league's involvement in the elaboration and implementation of programs for economic and financial recovery.[37] In Austria, for instance, the league named a commissioner general of finances, who "collated and analysed intelligence as to Austria's budgetary and monetary performance."[38] This knowledge was the basis for the constitution of the League of Nations' "seal of approval" on financial markets.

One of the truly interesting aspects of the league loans is that they illustrate how the old world of sovereign lending coexisted with the new. The League of Nations, though it was producing its own kind of knowledge about sovereign borrowers—largely statistical—continued to rely on the old merchant banks, as it knew that these prestigious bankers inspired trust in investors. Indeed, only one of the New York league loans was issued by a joint stock bank, National City Bank (see table 6.2). Nonetheless, over the course of merely five years (1923–1928), the league became more independent and gained its own reputation on the market. Thus, National City Bank, a joint stock bank, relying on the League of Nations' support, was able to issue the Greek loan of 1928. It is, however, noteworthy that no other league loan issued in New York, the world's financial center, was the responsibility of a joint stock bank.

Thus, though it developed its own reputation through statistical expertise, the league nonetheless had to rely on the old sovereign lenders, such as J. P. Morgan or Speyer & Co., to issue its loans. Only their names would convince investors to buy these bonds.[39] After all, in a book published in 1919 entitled *The Masters of Capital*, John Moody, founder of the eponymous rating agency, was quite explicit about the individuals to whom the title of his book applied. Opposite the title page, one finds a portrait of John Pierpont Morgan, and, in the first few pages, Moody identifies some of the great financial houses of Wall Street, such as the Morgans, Kuhns, Loebs, and Seligmans.[40] The so-called masters of capital were adamantly not joint stock bankers, directors of rating agencies, or men of the League of Nations. During the interwar years, New York merchant bankers were the centerpieces of sovereign lending, the hinge on which the whole international system of long-term finance rested.

THE RESUMPTION OF PRIVATE SOVEREIGN LENDING

If by the interwar period the old lenders still had the upper hand, when, then, did the new sovereign lenders triumph? My claim is that this world was not fully developed at any point before the 1970s. Books on sovereign debt and sovereign lending tend to shun the period from the 1930s to the 1970s, preferring to focus on its immediate predecessor and aftermath.[41] The reason for this is that private lending to foreign sovereigns declined markedly during these years. After the Great Depression and its flurry of sovereign defaults, private international capital flows largely came to a halt. This remained the case throughout the 1940s until the late 1950s. As one scholar puts it, "The postwar consensus on regulating capital was opposite the nineteenth century's validation of capital mobility," an arrangement that constituted a key part of "embedded liberalism."[42]

In this context, capital to fund sovereign debt mostly came through two channels. One channel consisted of official creditors, chief among them international financial organizations such as the International Monetary Fund (IMF) and the International Bank for Reconstruction and Development (IBRD), to which one should add government-to-government loans, and quasi-governmental agencies (e.g., export credit agencies).[43] As one observer points out, it was only by 1980 that private international capital flows caught up with and overtook official aid.[44] Although such forms of public sovereign lending are excluded from the purview of this study, which is concerned with sovereign lending by private financiers, it is nonetheless worth noting, again, that the way in which the IMF and the World Bank operated and engaged in sovereign lending was inherited from the League of Nations.

The second crucial source of funding, which did not involve any cross-border lending and mostly concerned economically developed countries, was private capital from domestic sources. Indeed, under the arrangements of the Bretton Woods system, private capital was trapped within national boundaries, rendering it unable to move around the world in search of the most lucrative opportunities.[45] Capital controls allowed for what two economists have called the "liquidation of government debt."[46] Governments forced captive domestic financial institutions to hold low-interest-rate sovereign debt. It also limited the interest rates banks could charge on loans to individuals and companies, to give them an incentive to invest in sovereign debt. Put differently, this system was the equivalent of a tax on private creditors, which allowed governments to repay their debts without engaging in austerity measures, a set of arrangements sometimes referred to as "financial repression."[47]

The era of Bretton Woods did not, therefore, witness the triumph of the new world of sovereign lending, as joint stock banks and rating agencies were either made redundant by official creditors or forced to buy domestic sovereign debt, rendering their statistical methods pointless, as they had almost no choice to lend to their "home" sovereign. This is not only one of the reasons why credit rating agencies suspended their sovereign ratings until the 1970s but also why the rating activities of large joint stock banks "were downsized, and did not regain importance until the 1970s."[48] States' independence from private international creditors would only be short lived, however.

The new sovereign lenders came back to the business of sovereign lending with the reemergence of international finance that took place when Bretton Woods–era capital controls were gradually circumvented and stripped down, in the late 1960s and 1970s.[49] Ironically, however, the process through which this happened was initiated by the old merchant bankers. Having benefited greatly from the open international financial markets of the period before the 1930s, they sought ways to undermine the capital controls of the Bretton Woods system and to restore London's place as an international financial center.[50] In order to redevelop what had hitherto been a critical aspect of their business (i.e. international transactions), merchant bankers based in Britain—chief among them Siegmund Warburg—successfully lobbied for freer financial transactions, exempt from various taxes and also, in the case of foreign currency transactions, from most regulation.[51]

Conducted in a foreign currency, what became known as the Euromarkets were entirely unregulated.[52] Thus, a foreign bank could keep deposits denominated in a foreign currency—most often dollars—in London and lend money to foreign companies and sovereigns for whatever interest rate it wanted, with no specific reserve requirements. In regulatory terms, the Bank of England was happy to ignore this type of operation. Banks engaged in these Euromarkets could therefore lend greater sums relative to their capital than when conducting operations in the local currency.[53] The medium-to-long-term transactions conducted in this framework could take the form of bond issues (Eurobonds) or direct loans (Euroloans). Such operations were, in effect, subject to no regulation. This created an enormous loophole in the architecture of the Bretton Woods financial system, which European and American banks were only too happy to exploit to obtain higher returns for the capital they held. It was, therefore, the old merchant bankers who made the internationalization of European and American finance possible.

In the first decade of these Euromarkets, British merchant bankers did benefit from the developments they had helped to usher in. However, they were unable to compete with much larger joint stock banks as the Euromarkets grew (see fig. 6.1).[54] Yet it was not with British joint stock banks that they competed. These banks, which possessed "underdeveloped skills

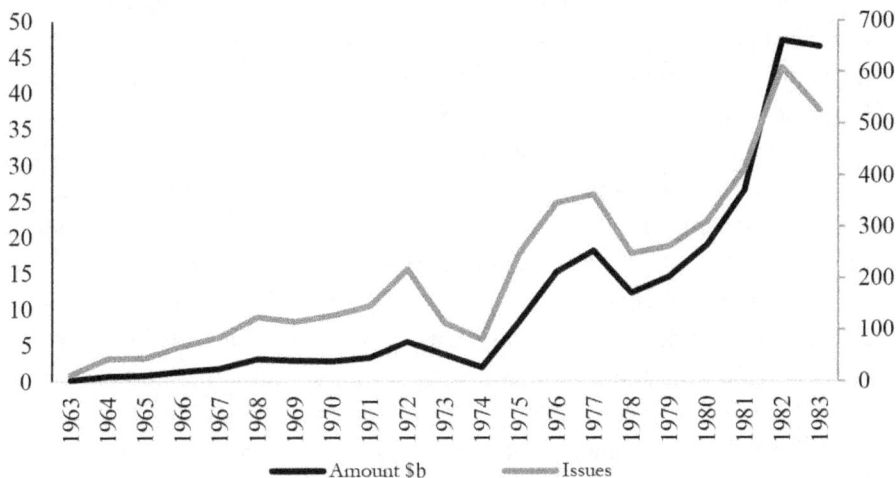

FIGURE 6.1. Number and volume (in $b) of Eurobond issues, 1963–1983. *Source:* Ian M. Kerr, *A History of the Eurobond Market: The First Twenty-One Years* (London: Euromoney, 1984).

outside retail banking," in fact avoided "a sustained entry" into the Euro-markets until the 1970s, continuing instead to focus on the financing of national industries.[55] In one sense, nothing was new here; the same division of labor as had been in operation until the interwar years remained, with merchant bankers leading the way in most international business, and joint stock banks focusing on domestic business. In Britain, the distinction between these different types of financial actors remained valid quite late, as many merchant banks were still operating under the legal framework of private partnership. N. M. Rothschild & Sons, for instance, only incorporated as a limited liability company in 1970.[56] By contrast, American merchant bankers such as J. P. Morgan & Co. had incorporated as early as 1940.[57]

The old division of labor between merchant banks and joint stock banks remained effective until the 1970s, save for one crucial fact, namely, the presence of Continental European and American joint stock banks in London, a shift that heralded what some have referred to as the "death of gentlemanly capitalism" in the United Kingdom.[58] And, indeed, to take an example, American banks came en masse to London in the 1960s, and, by the 1970s, they had fifty-eight branches in the City.[59] These competitors eventually led British joint stock banks to join the fray and engage in Euromarket operations, undermining the traditional division of labor in British banking.[60]

Following this momentous financial innovation, many developed countries began returning to conventional sovereign borrowing to finance public spending, as they no longer possessed a captive financial audience. Financiers could shirk financial repression. Groups of banks also began issuing loans (often called "syndicated loans") to developing countries such as Zaïre and Mexico, a practice that truly took off in the 1970s.[61] The need for oil exporting countries to recycle the growing dollar balances they accumulated, particularly after the oil shocks of 1973 and 1979, created a massive supply of capital for these loans.[62] Previously, such international financial imbalances would have been addressed by the IMF, but politicians and policymakers were warming up to the idea that commercial banks had a prominent role to play in the process of recycling petrodollars.[63] Thus, by 1982—the year in which Mexico would default—American banks had already lent large amounts of capital to foreign sovereigns and were owed $25.2 billion by Mexico, $20.5 billion by Brazil, and $10.7 billion by Venezuela, to name but a few.[64] The larger picture that emerges is one in which global levels of sovereign debt began rising very rapidly again from the late 1970s onward (see fig. 6.2).[65]

At about the same time, credit rating agencies resumed and expanded their sovereign rating activities, while formal country risk analysis made its return within most multinational banks after being sidelined for almost

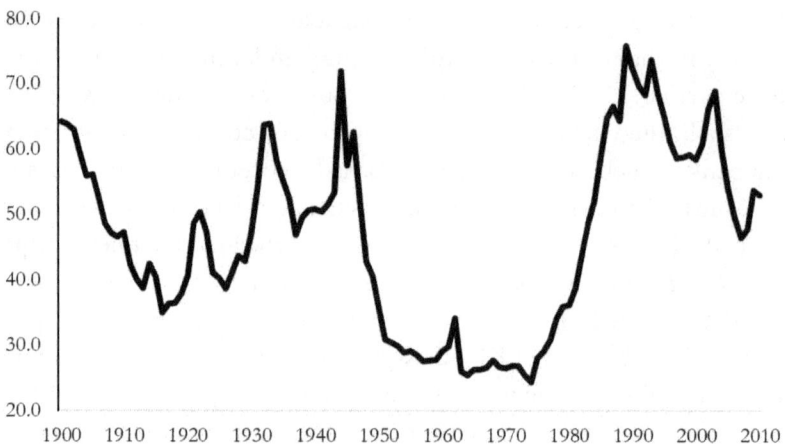

FIGURE 6.2. Average debt-to-GDP ratio (%), 1900–2010. *Source*: Calculated from Reinhart-Rogoff Series, http://www.carmenreinhart.com/data/browse-by-topic/topics/9/.

forty years.[66] It is generally agreed that Citibank led the way in 1973, under the chairmanship of Walter Wriston, when it recruited Irving Friedman, an economist previously employed by the World Bank and IMF—institutions that had been active in international lending.[67] Friedman then built the bank's country risk assessment method, the most sophisticated at the time, over the course of the 1970s.[68] But what were these methods based on?

In a survey of thirty-seven U.S. banks (including the twelve largest) conducted by the Export-Import Bank and published in 1977, four methods of evaluation are identified: 1) the fully qualitative system; 2) the structured qualitative system; 3) the checklist system, which was quantitative in character; and 4) more mathematically advanced techniques.[69] Most banks used a mix of two such systems. About 75 percent of the banks surveyed used a structured qualitative system, which was based on a list of criteria reproduced in table 6.3. Some, such as Chemical Bank and First National Bank of Chicago, converted these structured qualitative reports (overwhelmingly based on quantitative data) into actual country ratings to be compared, as the Crédit Lyonnais had done much earlier.[70] Only 13 percent of the banks surveyed used a weighted checklist system, the variables of which are also reproduced in table 6.3. The fully qualitative system was used by banks that were just beginning to do country reviews and represents 11 percent of the sample studied, while the advanced mathematical techniques were always paired with another method and are only found in 2 percent of the banks under review. Little to no information is provided on these two methods in the source I have found. For this reason, table 6.3 provides information on the two most important methods, which together account for 75 percent of the banks surveyed, holding 89 percent of the assets in the sample. Finally, it is worth noting that in about three-quarters of the banks under study, it was specialized staff, usually line personnel or staff economists, that conducted country risk analysis at the headquarters—a pattern typical of the new sovereign lenders.[71]

A comparison of the sovereign rating criteria used by American banks in the late 1970s with those of the new sovereign lenders of the first half of the twentieth century (see tables 5.2 and 6.1) reveals high degrees of similarity. And while the new sovereign lenders continued to face problems in terms of the quality or trustworthiness of the statistical information they could get their hands on—particularly with respect to developing and

TABLE 6.3
How U.S. Banks Evaluate Sovereign Risk in 1977

Structured qualitative (used by 73% of banks in survey)	Typical qualitative country evaluation report includes *Economics*: natural resources, demographics, GNP, inflation, budget, consumption, investment, trade account, current account, capital account and/or foreign debt analysis, managerial capability, investment in human capital, long-run projections *Politics*: type of government, orderliness of political successions, homogeneity of the populace, quality of relationships with major trading partners, quality of relationships with the United States, long run social and political trends Statistics frequently used *Internal economy*: GNP (per capita), inflation rate, money supply growth, net budget position *External economy*: balance of payments, external ratios, international reserves
Checklist system (used by 13% of banks in survey)	*Internal economy*: GNP, GNP per capita, growth in GNP per capita, inflation rate, money supply growth, investment-to-income ratio *External economy*: exports and export growth, imports and import growth, international reserves, reserves-to-import ratio, trade and current account balances, debt service ratio, IMF borrowing *Social and political*: political stability, past trend in unemployment

Eastern European countries—the key point here is that statistics was the main way in which they were seeking to evaluate sovereigns.[72]

By the 1980s, private sources of sovereign lending overtook public ones, and the new sovereign lending thus finally triumphed. New actors were at the helm of this world of sovereign lending, and they relied on their own, historically distinct, statistical way of knowing sovereigns. In this sense, the world in which private financiers continually evaluate states on the basis of a variety of statistical indicators in order to make their lending decisions is astonishingly new. This is a world we take completely for granted, and yet it is far more recent than we care to admit.

GRAPPLING WITH THE NEW SOVEREIGN LENDING

The triumph of the new sovereign lending did not go unnoticed in the financial world; indeed, its advent gave rise to major regulatory developments. Notable among these are the successive set of prudential rules issued by the Basel Committee on Banking Supervision (BCBS), a body until recently composed of the central banks and banking regulators of the G-10.[73] Located in the offices of the Bank for International Settlements (BIS), the BCBS has, over the last four decades, repeatedly debated how the new lenders' statistical models can be governed and, through them, the assets they hold on their balance sheets, not least of which is sovereign debt. Out of these efforts, one can observe two contrasting approaches to dealing with this issue, most clearly illustrated by comparing the first regulatory agreements produced by the BCBS, Basel I, with the second, Basel II.

In effect from roughly 1988 to 2007, the first Basel Accord was adopted by over 120 countries.[74] Its goal was to define minimum capital requirements for internationally active banks. To achieve this, it identified a minimum amount of capital (8 percent) that banks would need to hold in relation to the value of the assets on their balance sheets. But the committee did not think that all assets ought to call for the same amount of capital, as they differed markedly in terms of the risk they represented. A loan to a blue-chip company bore a different risk from a loan to a bank, a public sector entity, or a sovereign state. Bank assets would therefore need to be risk-weighted. The calculation of capital requirements in Basel I can be summed up with the following formula:

$$Asset\ value \times Minimum\ Capital\ Level\ (8\%) \times Risk\text{-}Weight$$

This formula, applied to the totality of a bank's assets, would produce a figure corresponding to the minimum capital requirement for that institution. One of the most crucial questions, therefore, concerned these risk-weights: How would the BCBS govern banks' risk assessment? While the committee faced multiple thorny questions, one recurring flash point was the issue of sovereign debt.[75] Indeed, fresh on the minds of BCBS members was the Latin American debt crisis of the 1980s, a stark reminder of the risks and implications of sovereign default. Who was going to determine the risk-weights of bank assets—of which sovereign debt—and what criteria would be used?

After much discussion, the striking choice made in Basel I was that the committee itself would design these risk-weights using criteria of its own choosing.[76] In the critical case of sovereign debt, the committee defined two broad risk categories. Whereas members of the Organisation for Economic Cooperation and Development (OECD) as well as signatories of the

International Monetary Fund's (IMF) General Arrangements to Borrow (GAB) would be considered riskless, receiving a zero percent risk-weight, all other states would be considered fully risky, receiving a one hundred percent risk-weight.[77] In turn, these risk-weights determined the risks associated with bank debt and public sector entity debt. The debt of a bank incorporated in an OECD or GAB country would be considered as a low-risk asset, receiving a twenty percent risk-weight, when that of a bank incorporated in a non-OECD or non-GAB state would be categorized as a fully risky asset, with a one hundred percent risk-weight (see table 6.4). This created considerable regulatory incentives to steer capital toward OECD and GAB members during a period of enormous growth for international finance.[78]

The fact that these risk-weights were essentially static, based on membership in existing international organizations, led to many complaints by those countries that were excluded from the privileges of riskless regulatory status.[79] As a result, the committee repeatedly debated, before and after the passage of the accord, whether it should instead draft a list of objective criteria that would determine if sovereign borrowers could enjoy riskless status. In practice, this choice meant that the BCBS would operate as a sort of world credit rating agency endowed with regulatory powers. But many other possibilities existed. Another alternative, which proved far more

TABLE 6.4
Selected Basel I Risk-Weights Using the OECD/Non-OECD Distinction

Risk-weight	Type of asset
0%	Claims on central governments and central banks denominated in national currency and funded in that currency Other claims on OECD central governments and central banks
20%	Claims on banks incorporated in the OECD and loans guaranteed by OECD incorporated banks Claims on banks incorporated in countries outside the OECD with a residual maturity of up to one year and loans with a residual maturity of up to one year guaranteed by banks incorporated in countries outside the OECD. Claims on non-domestic OECD public sector entities, excluding central government, and loans guaranteed by such entities.
100%	Claims on banks incorporated outside the OECD with a residual maturity of over one year. Claims on central governments outside the OECD (unless denominated in national currency and funded in that currency)

appealing in the long run, was to leave banks to evaluate the risk represented by their assets on their own.

Basel I was superseded by the Basel II framework, issued by the committee in 2004, but only implemented in 2006 in the European Union and 2007 in the United States.[80] Basel II was far more complex, as the sheer length of the document—by comparison with Basel I—indicates.[81] It profoundly altered the way in which the risk associated with different bank assets, notably sovereign debt, was to be calculated. Basel II empowered large banks to construct and rely on their own internal risk models to determine capital requirements, while smaller banks were made to depend on the ratings produced by rating agencies or export credit agencies.[82] This outcome was in no small part the result of heavy lobbying by large international banks, that is, the original group of new sovereign lenders.[83]

Thus, if Basel I represented an attempt by the Basel Committee to deal with the new sovereign lenders by actively steering their statistical assessments, Basel II and later agreements opted for an altogether different approach: a choice in favor of minimal interference in the statistical assessments of the new sovereign lenders. Joint stock banks, the "original" new sovereign lenders, were free to apply their statistical mode of evaluation to sovereign borrowers the world over so long as they were large enough, while the smallest would rely on another early actor of this new world of sovereign lending, namely, rating agencies. As the *Financial Times* tersely observed in 2008, now, banks were free to "use their own models for assessing risk."[84]

During the interwar period, as the world's financial center shifted from London to New York, new sovereign lenders emerged. They were credit rating agencies, which still play a prominent role in contemporary sovereign lending and international finance more broadly, as well as an international institution, the League of Nations, whose staff migrated to Bretton Woods financial institutions after World War II. These new lenders shared the joint stock banks' reliance on statistics as a form of knowledge. They had divisions dedicated to analyzing the creditworthiness of states based on a host of statistical indicators and staffed them with individuals trained to think in such a way. But, in spite of the presence of all these new actors, the old merchant bankers still dominated interwar sovereign lending.

From the 1930s to the 1970s, lending to foreign sovereigns was a relatively marginal activity, in large part because of the arrangements of the Bretton Woods system, which sought to drastically limit the role of private international finance. Merchant bankers based in London put great effort in undermining these arrangements. The key innovation that was used to circumvent existing capital controls was the Euromarkets. Under this ingenious scheme, banks could hold foreign currency in London and use it to make loans to foreign companies and sovereigns. These loans were not regulated by the Bank of England, as they were not made in sterling. Though British merchant banks initially benefited from these changes, it was American and continental European joint stock banks that most assiduously exploited the opportunity created by this loophole. Collectively, they issued loans to many developing countries, a business that really took off in the 1970s. By the 1980s, private lending to sovereigns had overtaken public sources of funding such as government-to-government loans, official aid, funding from international institutions, and the like. At that moment, the new sovereign lending triumphed. This world in which financiers continually evaluate states on the basis of a variety of statistical indicators in order to make their lending decisions is one we take entirely for granted, but it is astonishingly recent, barely forty years old, to be precise.

As a response to this momentous development, new forms of financial regulation aiming to grapple with the new sovereign lenders emerged. One such example is that of the BCBS, an international body that pursued this task by regulating the statistical evaluations used by banks to assess the risk of their assets and thus calculate their capital requirements. This type of regulation directly affects bank holdings of specific assets and, most importantly for my purposes, sovereign debt. In turn, the BCBS has adopted different approaches to regulate these new lenders. However, the key point is that this type of governance of balance sheets is only possible because of the unique properties of the new sovereign lending, that is, the use of statistical models by lenders that are structured as "public" companies. In this sense, the problems of the new world of sovereign lending along with the means developed to deal with them are fundamentally new.

CONCLUSION

The critical point with which I opened this book is that, like Alphonse Daudet's *arlésienne*, financiers are both pivotal to the stories that scholars of sovereign lending and sovereign debt tell and also glaringly absent from them. To the extent that they make an appearance, financiers are depicted as ahistorical profit-maximizing agents. The consequence of this analytical choice is that the only kinds of transformations this body of work can identify pertain exclusively to the world that surrounds financiers. The quality and quantity of information available to them may change, the structure of the market for sovereign debt might shift, and the political and legal framework governing sovereign lending could be altered. But financiers themselves never change. In all these accounts, financial markets are timeless beasts.

The bulk of my argument has been devoted to thinking historically about these financiers lending capital to sovereigns, by producing an account of how they have changed and how their thinking about states has shifted over the last two hundred years—my goal being to supplement, rather than replace, existing accounts of the transformation of sovereign lending. I began by explaining how one might go about recovering the thought of international practitioners—of which financiers are a subset—regarding the polities that constitute the international system. My first proposition was that we ought to locate this endeavor within a larger body of work on the history of international political thought, but that this came with two assorted issues. Financiers and other types of practically inclined individuals by and large produce no treatises clearly stating their ideas on this subject, in the way a famous jurist or philosopher would; exactly what one should be looking for and where one ought to look for it is thus an open question. As a response to these twin problems, I then argued that one could recover this dimension of their thought by analyzing the tools they use to know and represent polities in their everyday activities. These tools, which I called "forms of knowledge," are notably transmitted through education, a site that offered an excellent starting point to examine the ones financiers acquired and later came to rely on to carry out their business.

On this basis, I reconstructed two worlds of sovereign lending, the old and the new, populated by different kinds of financiers using different forms of knowledge. The old sovereign lending, dominant from the early nineteenth century to the interwar period, was led by merchant bankers such as the Rothschilds and the Barings. These banks were "naturally" international, as many were continental European families who had migrated and scattered across Europe. In other cases, marriage between banking houses served to create international bonds, a practice not unlike that of the dynasties of the early modern world. These financial institutions were mostly based on family ties—a feature whose significance has been largely underplayed—and the goals of families were almost entirely intertwined with those of the businesses, which were structured as private partnerships. When they engaged in sovereign lending, these families pursued both profit and status, seeking to enrich themselves and to rise socially. The fact that the acquisition of status was an end in itself has been unduly neglected, and it is important to understand merchant bankers' relation to sovereigns as one in which they also obtained this specific social asset. For this reason, relations between merchant bankers and states were not simply ones in which the former were continually evaluating the latter's creditworthiness, as they were extracting something other than profit.

In order to know sovereigns and to engage in sovereign lending, merchant bankers all used the same skill set, namely, gentility. This form of knowledge was rather common for such practitioners as early modern diplomats, who had no real alternative means of knowing sovereigns. They could only know them in person at the court. Merchant bankers were, in some respects, men of this ancien régime. They thought of states as sets of people to be known in person, rather than as series of statistical data points to be compared. The lack of any systematic use of the statistical information concerning states that became available toward the end of the nineteenth century is proof of merchant bankers' relative disinterest in this kind of information. They were not numerically illiterate; rather, statistics was quite obviously not the primary way in which they knew states.

The new world of sovereign lending, which overlapped with the old from the late nineteenth century onward, was different both in terms of the key actors that dominated it and the form of knowledge that underpinned it. The key actors of this world were and remain joint stock banks. Their rapid rise originated in a set of legal innovations in major European states in the period from 1850 to 1870, which enshrined principles of limited liability, unlimited shareholders and capital, and simple registration procedures not requiring political approval. By contrast with the merchant banks, the new joint stock banks were initially highly national, as they were created by individuals from one country, who possessed nothing resembling the strong transnational familial bonds of their venerable competitors. It is in this sense that we can speak of a process of nationalization of international finance in the period preceding World War I. The rise of joint stock banks in sovereign lending was faster and more pronounced in France and Germany than in the United Kingdom and the United States, but, by and large, these financiers were outsiders in the world of sovereign lending.

As they sought to invest in and, eventually, issue sovereign debt, joint stock banks found themselves at a loss to assess the creditworthiness of different states. Indeed, as national banks with few personal contacts with sovereigns across the world, they were in a disadvantaged position. Their solution was to hire employees who had been trained in new types of educational institutions: business schools. These had only just been founded in the late nineteenth and early twentieth century and had begun producing swathes of graduates. These men were trained to think of states through statistics, a relatively novel form of knowledge. As a result, they eventually produced the first systematic rankings of sovereign creditworthiness, as illustrated by the experience of the Crédit Lyonnais. The practice of using numbers to systematically represent and compare states, initially named *Statistik* in Germany, had slowly spread throughout the world, by means of publications and statistical bureaux, as well as, crucially, educational institutions. Thus, while merchant bankers were operating on the basis of their ad hoc knowledge of individual sovereigns, joint stock banks were developing systematic assessments and rankings of sovereigns, based on quantifiable data. Though these banks did not sell their ratings as credit rating agencies do, the form of knowledge on which these ratings were based was similar to that underlying those later produced by American rating agencies of the likes of Moody's and Standard & Poor's, beginning in the interwar period—a fact largely overlooked because of the emphasis put on the novelty of this latter type of company. The League of Nations' Economic and Financial Organisation (EFO), which gave its stamp of approval to a series of sovereign loans in the 1920s, also relied on statistical knowledge to do so.

The final step in my argument was to explain when the new sovereign lending had in fact triumphed and come to define our world. Old and new had overlapped into the 1930s, but the former was still dominant by the time private international capital flows broke down in the aftermath of the Great Depression. The pivotal development here was the resumption and rapid growth of those capital flows, especially in the form of private sovereign lending, from the 1970s onward. This was brought about by a number of old European merchant banks that sought to circumvent the heavy restrictions on international financial operations as early as the 1960s, eventually giving rise to the Euromarkets. On a side note, the persistent influence of these private partnerships in international finance is a striking indicator of the continued importance of family businesses at the highest levels of the world economy, deep into the twentieth century. But they were not the chief beneficiaries of the new opportunities created by this revival of private international capital flows. It was American and continental European joint stock banks that capitalized on this development, engaging in increasingly large sovereign lending operations in the 1970s. In this time frame they redeveloped their statistical models to evaluate sovereign borrowers, and rating agencies gradually began rating sovereigns across the world once more, providing assessments for a wide variety of joint stock companies investing in sovereign debt, like insurance companies and pension funds. For the first time, these actors and their form of knowledge were at the helm of sovereign lending, though for most developing countries, it would still take until the 1980s for private sovereign lending to overtake public sources of sovereign lending. It is at that point that the sovereign debt markets we know, dominated by large joint stock companies relying on statistical data to regularly evaluate sovereign borrowers, finally triumphed. This world is thus far more recent than we care to admit, only coming of age in the twenty-first century.

In my view, far too much scholarship, critical or otherwise, assumes that sovereign borrowers have always confronted the same old financial markets, pursuing the same goals, continually evaluating them with the same forms of knowledge. I think this point of view is completely wrong. Not only does it misconstrue the past but it also obscures one of the most distinctive features of contemporary sovereign lending. The condition in which states face purely profit-maximizing actors continually evaluating and comparing them with the help of reams of statistical data, ready to enforce market discipline on recalcitrant sovereign borrowers, is a fundamentally contemporary one. It is this world about which James Carville, a Clinton-era advisor, famously joked in 1994 when he explained that if reincarnation was possible, he would wish to "come back as the bond market" because it can "intimidate everybody."[1] This is also the world of "bond vigilantes," a term coined by brokerage house economist Edward Yardeni in 1983, denoting a world dominated by a constituency of financial investors constantly keeping tabs on sovereign borrowers, ready to suddenly demand higher interest rates from sovereigns whose policies they might consider unfavorable to them.[2]

Failure to pay attention to this transformation has not only hindered our understanding of the past and present of sovereign lending but also limited our grasp of the changing relationship between states and financial markets more generally. Traditionally, accounts of the evolution of this relationship begin with statespersons and policymakers' views about the place of financial markets in relation to society. Over a period of two hundred years, their views are thought to have oscillated between two poles, one being relatively accommodating of the freedom of global financiers, and the other—largely associated with the period from the 1930s to the late 1960s—deeply restrictive for global finance. On this account, the history of the relationship between states and financial markets is reduced to a pendulum swing between these extremes. By contrast, my account begins not with statespersons and policymakers, but with financial markets. Over the course of the past two centuries, financiers fundamentally reconceptualized what states were; from a set of individuals to be known in person, they became numbers on a page. Thus, what we have witnessed since the 1980s is not simply a reemergence of global finance or its disembedding, but the triumph of an entirely new kind of global finance, made up of financiers who think about states in a radically new way.

The characteristics of this new world of sovereign lending have raised new kinds of political questions. Should banks and other market actors be completely free to construct their evaluations of sovereigns as they wish and assess sovereign borrowers accordingly? Should national or international public institutions be entrusted with this task or, at the very least, be given an oversight role in the matter? Do some states deserve preferential treatment in these models, and, if so, which ones? Are some criteria for assessing creditworthiness illegitimate? A variety of regulatory bodies have confronted these questions, chief among them the Basel Committee on Banking Supervision, intervening directly in some of the new sovereign lenders' statistical assessments of states.[3] In its first major piece of regulation (Basel I), the Basel Committee did so rather heavy-handedly, assigning specific risk scores to different groups of states.[4] In its subsequent regulatory agreements, the Basel Committee adopted a very light-touch approach, allowing large banks to use their own "in house" statistical models to calculate sovereign risk, while smaller banks were made to rely on credit rating agencies. In the world of the old sovereign lending, no such regulatory possibilities arose as sovereign lending was conducted by private partnerships that used no systematic statistical assessments. Only in the world of the new sovereign lending does the possibility of governing lenders' behavior through their statistical assessments of sovereign borrowers even arise. We may think that this type of regulation is too weak, not used to good effect or insufficiently politicized, but it has arisen precisely on the back of the unique characteristics of the new sovereign lending, presenting opportunities to steer global capital that are historically distinct and raising its own specific set of political questions.

Every successive world of sovereign lending is characterized by specific sets of dominant lenders, with particular social positions and goals, as well as unique forms of knowledge. As a result, each inevitably raises its own historically distinct constraints, possibilities, and political questions. The dynamics set in motion after the crisis of 2007–2008 and accelerated during the COVID-19 crisis suggest at least two possibilities for the near future. One of these is a world in which the passively managed behemoths that are asset management companies of the likes of BlackRock and Vanguard become the dominant players in sovereign bond markets. While these are joint stock companies, their goal is to generate returns on investment without managing their capital actively. Their investments are based on index funds, which are designed by index providers, the most important of which are S&P, MSCI, and FTSE. The consequence of this approach is that passively managed asset management companies do not make decisions to invest in specific companies or, conversely, to withdraw their capital from them. As Larry Fink, CEO of BlackRock, explains it, the company's very mode of functioning means that it cannot decide to sell the securities of a specific company so long as "that company remains in the relevant index."[5] As a result, these kinds of companies provide what is perhaps the ultimate form of "patient capital."[6] In a world of sovereign lending dominated by these investors, the fate of sovereign bonds would largely be determined by their inclusion in various index funds, the composition of which would be determined by index providers. As in the case of equity, investment in sovereign bonds would therefore be geared toward the long term, in so far as asset management companies could not opt to sell the bonds of a specific country so long as it remained in the relevant sovereign bond index, to paraphrase Larry Fink. This would leave little scope for regular movements of capital in and out of specific countries' sovereign bonds, though the moments in which sovereign bond indexes change would create potentially large disruptions, much as when sovereign bonds are downgraded to "junk" status by credit rating agencies. The key political question would pertain to the inclusion or exclusion of specific sovereign borrowers from various index funds, which would itself depend on the form of knowledge these institutions use. Exactly what form of knowledge these actors would rely on to construct sovereign bond index funds operating with such a long-term view—by comparison with, say, rating agencies—is an open but critical question.

The other possibility that we have been able to glimpse in recent years is a world in which independent central banks become the dominant players in sovereign bond markets, as they have done during the recent COVID-19 crisis in many countries.[7] These actors are not primarily seeking profit, nor are they public institutions simply doing the government's bidding, as to some extent they did in the postwar years.[8] Pursuing ends of their own, independent central banks participate in sovereign bond markets for a variety of reasons. In moments of crisis, they may be interested in helping the central government access credit at an affordable price, but since 2007–2008, a crucial reason for massive interventions in these markets has been to support the booming but unstable shadow banking system. To support this system of credit intermediation in which sovereign bonds play a crucial role as collateral, central banks have bought and sold these assets in large quantities, becoming what some have called a "market-maker of last resort."[9] By contrast with merchant bankers or joint stock banks, central banks may not even be interested in becoming the dominant player in these markets; they have attained this position as a result of their attempts to maintain global financial stability. Were independent central banks to continue occupying this preponderant place in the market for sovereign bonds, it is unclear what form of knowledge they would rely on to determine the scope and conditions of their interventions. What is clear is that the political questions such a world would raise, if it were to prevail, would likely pertain to the democratic mandate and relative independence of central banks from governments.

My purpose here is not to predict whether these worlds will ever come to be in such ideal-typical forms, but rather to point out that the specific path I have taken to think about sovereign lending in this book can help us envision and conceptualize different potential futures of sovereign lending in a way that existing work on sovereign debt, because of the assumptions it makes about lenders, simply cannot.

To grasp the kind of relationship that exists between states and financial markets today, it is critical that we understand how it differs from what existed in the past, and we cannot do that if we simply assume, as many economists and political scientists do, that sovereign lenders are ahistorical actors with timeless motivations and patterns of thought, who have always adopted a similar outlook on states. The study I have presented here is an attempt to reframe two centuries of sovereign lending by historicizing the main protagonists, as well as to identify one of its unique contemporary features. Given its scope, I am convinced that it could be refined in all sorts of ways. At the very least, my hope is that it constitutes a useful starting point to better appreciate the distinctiveness of the contemporary relationship between states and financial markets.

NOTES

INTRODUCTION

1. For a sample of the voluminous literature on the determinants of sovereign states' ability to access capital, see, for example, Cameron Ballard-Rosa, Layna Mosley, and Rachel L. Wellhausen, "Contingent Advantage? Sovereign Borrowing, Democratic Institutions, and Global Capital Cycles," *British Journal of Political Science* 51, no. 1 (2021): 353–73; Emily Beaulieu, Gary W. Cox, and Sebastian Saiegh, "Sovereign Debt and Regime Type: Reconsidering the Democratic Advantage," *International Organization* 66, no. 4 (October 2012): 709–38; Michael D. Bordo and Hugh Rockoff, "The Gold Standard as a 'Good Housekeeping Seal of Approval,'" *Journal of Economic History* 56, no. 2 (1996): 389–428; Gary W. Cox and Sebastian M. Saiegh, "Executive Constraint and Sovereign Debt: Quasi-Experimental Evidence from Argentina During the Baring Crisis," *Comparative Political Studies* 51, no. 11 (2018): 1504–25; Niall Ferguson and Moritz Schularick, "The Empire Effect: The Determinants of Country Risk in the First Age of Globalization, 1880–1913," *Journal of Economic History* 66, no. 2 (2006): 283–312; Julia Gray, *The Company States Keep: International Economic Organizations and Investor Perceptions* (Cambridge: Cambridge University Press, 2013); Jana Grittersová, *Borrowing Credibility: Global Banks and Monetary Regimes* (Ann Arbor: University of Michigan Press, 2017); Jonathan Kirshner, *Appeasing Bankers: Financial Caution on the Road to War* (Princeton, NJ: Princeton University Press, 2007); Paolo Mauro, Nathan Sussman, and Yishay Yafeh, *Emerging Markets and Financial Globalization: Sovereign Bond Spreads in 1870–1913 and Today* (Oxford: Oxford University Press,

2006); Douglass C. North and Barry R. Weingast, "Constitutions and Commitment: The Evolution of Institutional Governing Public Choice in Seventeenth-Century England," *Journal of Economic History* 49, no. 4 (1989): 803–32; Maurice Obstfeld and Alan M. Taylor, "Sovereign Risk, Credibility, and the Gold Standard: 1870–1913 Versus 1925–31," *Economic Journal* 113, no. 487 (2003): 241–75; Sebastian M. Saiegh, "Do Countries Have a 'Democratic Advantage?' Political Institutions, Multilateral Agencies, and Sovereign Borrowing," *Comparative Political Studies* 38, no. 4 (2005): 366–87; Kenneth A. Schultz and Barry R. Weingast, "The Democratic Advantage: Institutional Foundations of Financial Power in International Competition," *International Organization* 57, no. 1 (2003): 3–42; David Stasavage, *States of Credit: Size, Power, and the Development of European Polities* (Princeton, NJ: Princeton University Press, 2011); David Stasavage, *Public Debt and the Birth of the Democratic State: France and Great Britain, 1688–1789* (Cambridge: Cambridge University Press, 2008); and Michael Tomz, *Reputation and International Cooperation: Sovereign Debt Across Three Centuries* (Princeton, NJ: Princeton University Press, 2007). This is true even of such excellent works as Layna Mosley's *Global Capital and National Governments* (Cambridge: Cambridge University Press, 2003); see especially 32. For a related critique, see Hassan Malik, *Bankers and Bolsheviks: International Finance and the Russian Revolution* (Princeton, NJ: Princeton University Press, 2020).

2. On sovereign lending and the structure of sovereign debt markets, see, in particular, Vinod K. Aggarwal, *Debt Games: Strategic Interaction in International Debt Rescheduling* (Cambridge: Cambridge University Press, 1996); and Jerome Roos, *Why Not Default? The Political Economy of Sovereign Debt* (Princeton, NJ: Princeton University Press, 2019). The best scholarship on the structure of sovereign debt markets (to which I will return later) is by Marc Flandreau and associates; see, for instance, Marc Flandreau and Juan H. Flores, "The Peaceful Conspiracy: Bond Markets and International Relations During the Pax Britannica," *International Organization* 66, no. 2 (2012): 211–41. I should nonetheless add that although this body of work certainly notes that financiers of different types were involved in sovereign lending at different points in time, its emphasis is entirely on *market structure*, rather than on the unique characteristics of actors doing the lending. On the political and legal framework governing sovereign debt and sovereign lending, see Jeremy I. Bulow and Kenneth Rogoff, "Sovereign Debt: Is to Forgive to Forget?," *American Economic Review* 79, no. 1 (1989): 43–50; Martha Finnemore, *The Purpose of Intervention: Changing Beliefs About the Use of Force* (Ithaca, NY: Cornell University Press, 2004), chap. 2; Stephen D. Krasner, *Sovereignty: Organized Hypocrisy* (Princeton, NJ: Princeton University Press, 1999), chap. 5; Odette Lienau, *Rethinking Sovereign Debt: Politics, Reputation, and Legitimacy in Modern Finance* (Cambridge, MA: Harvard University Press, 2014); and

Michael Waibel, *Sovereign Defaults Before International Courts and Tribunals* (Cambridge: Cambridge University Press, 2011). For an analysis of the difference between the global financial framework of Bretton Woods and that of the subsequent period, see Eric Helleiner, *States and the Reemergence of Global Finance: From Bretton Woods to the 1990s* (Ithaca, NY: Cornell University Press, 1994); and Rawi Abdelal, *Capital Rules: The Construction of Global Finance* (Cambridge, MA: Harvard University Press, 2007). On sovereign borrowing in this time frame, see Carmen M. Reinhart and M. Belen Sbrancia, "The Liquidation of Government Debt" (working paper, National Bureau of Economic Research, March 2011), http://www.nber.org/papers/w16893 (accessed 17 March 2022).

3. For a few works that deal with the history of this type of thought, see David Armitage, *Foundations of Modern International Thought* (Cambridge: Cambridge University Press, 2012); Hedley Bull, *The Anarchical Society: A Study of Order in World Politics*, 3rd ed. (New York: Columbia University Press, 2002); Adom Getachew, *Worldmaking After Empire: The Rise and Fall of Self-Determination* (Princeton, NJ: Princeton University Press, 2019); Edward Keene, *International Political Thought: A Historical Introduction* (Cambridge: Polity, 2005); James Muldoon, *Empire and Order: The Concept of Empire, 800–1800* (New York: Palgrave Macmillan, 1999); Daniel Philpott, *Revolutions in Sovereignty: How Ideas Shaped Modern International Relations* (Princeton, NJ: Princeton University Press, 2001); and Christian Reus-Smit, *The Moral Purpose of the State: Culture, Social Identity, and Institutional Rationality in International Relations* (Princeton, NJ: Princeton University Press, 1999).

4. Precisely for this reason, scholars who wish to tease out the financial assumptions of a given era frequently turn to academic books by prominent scholars. For a good example, see Marc Flandreau and Frédéric Zumer, *The Making of Global Finance, 1880–1913* (Paris: Organization for Economic Cooperation & Development, 2004).

5. I owe the phrase "form of knowledge" to Bernard S. Cohn, *Colonialism and Its Forms of Knowledge: The British in India* (Princeton, NJ: Princeton University Press, 1996).

6. On education and change in historical international relations, see Quentin Bruneau, "Converging Paths: Bounded Rationality, Practice Theory, and the Study of Change in Historical International Relations," *International Theory* 14, no. 1 (2022): 88–114.

7. The classic work here is Norbert Elias, *The Civilizing Process*, 2nd ed. (Oxford: Blackwell, 2000). But see also Jeroen F. J. Duindam, *Vienna and Versailles: The Courts of Europe's Major Dynastic Rivals, 1550–1780* (Cambridge: Cambridge University Press, 2003).

8. For this thesis, see P. J. Cain and A. G. Hopkins, *British Imperialism: 1688–2000* (London: Routledge, 2001).

9. See, for instance, Katharina Pistor, Yoram Keinan, Jan Kleinheisterkamp, and Mark D. West, "Evolution of Corporate Law: A Cross-Country Comparison," *University of Pennsylvania Journal of International Law* 23, no. 4 (2002): 791–871. As I will explain, these corporations are quite different from the ones that have recently attracted much attention in historical International Relations. On this latter theme, see Andrew Phillips and Jason Sharman, *Outsourcing Empire: How Company-States Made the Modern World* (Princeton, NJ: Princeton University Press, 2020).

10. On the origins of *Statistik*, see Harm Klueting, *Die Lehre von der Macht der Staaten: Das aussenpolitische Machtproblem in der "politischen Wissenschaft" und in der praktischen Politik im 18. Jahrhundert* (Berlin: Duncker & Humblot, 1986). For an overview of the history of sovereign debt statistics, see Eric Monnet and Blaise Truong-Loï, "The History and Politics of Public Debt Accounting," in *A World of Public Debts: A Political History*, ed. Nicolas Barreyre and Nicolas Delalande (Cham: Palgrave Macmillan, 2020), 481–511. On the history of statistics more generally, including what would typically have been known as probability, see William Deringer, *Calculated Values: Finance, Politics, and the Quantitative Age* (Cambridge, MA: Harvard University Press, 2018); Alain Desrosières, *The Politics of Large Numbers: A History of Statistical Reasoning*, trans. Camille Naish (Cambridge, MA: Harvard University Press, 2002); Ian Hacking, *The Taming of Chance* (Cambridge: Cambridge University Press, 1990); M. G. Kendall, "Where Shall the History of Statistics Begin?," in *Studies in the History of Statistics and Probability*, ed. E. S. Pearson and M. G. Kendall (London: Griffin, 1970), 45–46; Paul F. Lazarsfeld, "Notes on the History of Quantification in Sociology—Trends, Sources, and Problems," *Isis* 52, no. 2 (1961): 277–333; Donald A MacKenzie, *Statistics in Britain, 1865–1930: The Social Construction of Scientific Knowledge* (Edinburgh: Edinburgh University Press, 1981); Theodore M. Porter, *The Rise of Statistical Thinking, 1820–1900* (Princeton, NJ: Princeton University Press, 1986); Adam Tooze, *Statistics and the German State, 1900–1945: The Making of Modern Economic Knowledge* (Cambridge: Cambridge University Press, 2001); and Harald Westergaard, *Contributions to the History of Statistics* (London: PSKing, 1932).

11. See Patricia Clavin's excellent *Securing the World Economy: The Reinvention of the League of Nations, 1920–1946* (Oxford: Oxford University Press, 2013); and Yann Decorzant, *La Société des Nations et la naissance d'une conception de la régulation économique internationale* (Brussels: PIE-Peter Lang, 2011).

12. On the notion of "embedded liberalism," see John Gerard Ruggie, "International Regimes, Transactions, and Change: Embedded Liberalism in the Postwar Economic Order," *International Organization* 36, no. 2 (1982): 379–415.

13. This claim is different from Donald Mackenzie's regarding the development of models in financial economics in the 1960s and 1970s and their influence on derivatives markets. My contention, by contrast, is about the basic use of numbers to describe and compare states. See Donald MacKenzie, *An Engine, Not a Camera: How Financial Models Shape Markets* (Cambridge, MA: MIT Press, 2008).

14. On the rise of rankings for governance, see Alexander Cooley and Jack Snyder, eds., *Ranking the World: Grading States as a Tool of Global Governance* (Cambridge: Cambridge University Press, 2015); Kevin Davis, Angelina Fisher, Benedict Kingsbury and Sally Engle Merry, eds., *Governance by Indicators: Global Power Through Quantification and Rankings* (Oxford: Oxford University Press, 2012); Alain Desrosières and Emmanuel Didier, *Prouver et gouverner* (Paris: La Découverte, 2014); Sally Engle Merry, Kevin E. Davis, and Benedict Kingsbury, eds., *The Quiet Power of Indicators* (Cambridge: Cambridge University Press, 2015); and Richard Rottenburg, Sally E. Merry, Sung-Joon Park, and Johanna Mugler, eds., *The World of Indicators: The Making of Governmental Knowledge Through Quantification* (Cambridge: Cambridge University Press, 2015). See also the special issue "The Politics of Numbers," *Review of International Studies* 41, no. 5 (2015). For a recent exception focusing on the post–Bretton Woods era, see Quinn Slobodian, "World Maps for the Debt Paradigm: Risk Ranking the Poorer Nations in the 1970s," *Critical Historical Studies* 8, no. 1 (2021): 1–22.

15. On rating agencies, see Norbert Gaillard, *A Century of Sovereign Ratings* (New York: Springer, 2012); Bartholomew Paudyn, *Credit Ratings and Sovereign Debt: The Political Economy of Creditworthiness Through Risk and Uncertainty* (New York: Palgrave Macmillan, 2014); and Timothy J. Sinclair, *The New Masters of Capital: American Bond Rating Agencies and the Politics of Creditworthiness* (Ithaca, NY: Cornell University Press, 2005).

16. For examples, see Abdelal, *Capital Rules*; Jeremy Green, *The Political Economy of the Special Relationship: Anglo-American Development from the Gold Standard to the Financial Crisis* (Princeton, NJ: Princeton University Press, 2020); Helleiner, *States and the Reemergence of Global Finance*; and Louis W. Pauly, *Who Elected the Bankers? Surveillance and Control in the World Economy* (Ithaca, NY: Cornell University Press, 1997). This is particularly true of scholarship inspired by Karl Polanyi's *The Great Transformation: The Political and Economic Origins of Our Time*, 2nd ed. (Boston: Beacon, 2001). See, for instance, Nancy Fraser, "A Triple Movement? Parsing the Politics of Crisis After Polanyi," *New Left Review* 81 (2013): 119–32; Ronaldo Munck, "Globalization and Democracy: A New 'Great Transformation?,'" *Annals of the American Academy of Political and Social Science* 581, no. 1 (2002): 10–21; and Giovanna Zincone and John Agnew, "The Second Great Transformation: The Politics of Globalisation in the Global North," *Space and Polity* 4, no. 1 (2000): 5–21.

17. For a sense of these discussions, see Basel Committee on Banking Supervision, "The Regulatory Treatment of Sovereign Exposures" (Basel, December 2017); and European Systemic Risk Board, "ESRB Report on the Regulatory Treatment of Sovereign Exposures" (Brussels, March 2015). See also Quentin Bruneau, "In the Club: How and Why Central Bankers Created a Hierarchy of Sovereign Borrowers, c. 1988–2007," *Review of International Political Economy*, forthcoming.

18. The category of "semi-" or "demi-sovereignty" was commonplace among nineteenth-century lawyers and diplomats. To my mind, the best treatment is Arthur Learoyd, "Semi-Sovereignty and Relationships of Hierarchy" (PhD diss., University of Oxford, 2017). For a very condensed version, see Arthur Learoyd, "Configurations of Semi-Sovereignty in the Nineteenth Century," in *De-Centering State Making: Comparative and International Perspectives*, ed. Jens Bartelson, Martin Hall, and Jan Teorell (Cheltenham: Edward Elgar, 2018), 155–74; see also Peter Haldén, "A Non-Sovereign Modernity: Attempts to Engineer Stability in the Balkans, 1820–90," *Review of International Studies* 39, no. 2 (April 2013): 337–59. On the divisibility of sovereignty in modern international society, see Edward Keene, *Beyond the Anarchical Society: Grotius, Colonialism, and Order in World Politics* (Cambridge: Cambridge University Press, 2002). For a brief introduction to nineteenth-century international society that discusses these themes, see Quentin Bruneau, "The Long Nineteenth Century," in *The Oxford Handbook of History and International Relations*, ed. Mlada Bukovansky, Edward Keene, Christian Reus-Smit, and Maja Spanu (Oxford: Oxford University Press, forthcoming).

19. See Gerrit W. Gong, *The Standard of "Civilization" in International Society* (Oxford: Clarendon, 1984); and Turan Kayaoglu, *Legal Imperialism: Sovereignty and Extraterritoriality in Japan, the Ottoman Empire, and China* (Cambridge: Cambridge University Press, 2014).

20. On colonial borrowing, see Olivier Accominotti, Marc Flandreau, and Riad Rezzik, "The Spread of Empire: Clio and the Measurement of Colonial Borrowing Costs," *Economic History Review* 64, no. 2 (2011): 385–407; Lance Edwin Davis and Robert A. Huttenback, *Mammon and the Pursuit of Empire: The Political Economy of British Imperialism, 1860–1912* (Cambridge: Cambridge University Press, 1986); and Ferguson and Schularick, "Empire Effect." A small institution named the Crown Agents was in charge of borrowing on behalf of Crown colonies; it has received surprisingly little scholarly attention. The most recent study is David Sunderland, *Managing the British Empire: The Crown Agents, 1833–1914* (Woodgate: Boydell & Brewer, 2004). As for settler colonies, it was the Bank of England that was responsible for many of their debt issues until the late nineteenth century, when they had to turn to overseas banks.

21. In his study of the origins of the international legal regime for property rights, Charles Lipson adopts a similar line of argument to justify his focus on Latin America, rather than on Asia or Africa. See Charles Lipson, *Standing Guard:*

Protecting Foreign Capital in the Nineteenth and Twentieth Centuries (Berkeley: University of California Press, 1985), 16–18.

1. HOW INTERNATIONAL PRACTITIONERS
THINK ABOUT STATES

1. Marc Flandreau and Frédéric Zumer, *The Making of Global Finance, 1880–1913* (Paris: Organization for Economic Cooperation & Development, 2004), 14.
2. For a few examples, see Jens Bartelson, *A Genealogy of Sovereignty* (Cambridge: Cambridge University Press, 1995); Hedley Bull, *The Anarchical Society: A Study of Order in World Politics*, 3rd ed. (New York: Columbia University Press, 2002), 27–28, 31–35; Edward Keene, *Beyond the Anarchical Society: Grotius, Colonialism, and Order in World Politics* (Cambridge: Cambridge University Press, 2002); Daniel Philpott, *Revolutions in Sovereignty: How Ideas Shaped Modern International Relations* (Princeton, NJ: Princeton University Press, 2001); Andrew Phillips and J. C. Sharman, *International Order in Diversity: War, Trade, and Rule in the Indian Ocean* (Cambridge: Cambridge University Press, 2015); and Christian Reus-Smit, *The Moral Purpose of the State: Culture, Social Identity, and Institutional Rationality in International Relations* (Princeton, NJ: Princeton University Press, 1999).
3. Robert Gilpin, *War and Change in World Politics* (Cambridge: Cambridge University Press, 1981), 39–40; John Gerard Ruggie, "Territoriality and Beyond: Problematizing Modernity in International Relations," *International Organization* 47, no. 1 (1993): 143–44; Daniel H. Nexon, *The Struggle for Power in Early Modern Europe: Religious Conflict, Dynastic Empires, and International Change* (Princeton, NJ: Princeton University Press, 2009), 11.
4. Bull, *Anarchical Society*, 245, 254–55, 266, 275; Edward Keene, *International Political Thought: An Historical Introduction* (Cambridge: Polity, 2005), chap. 4; Ruggie, "Territoriality and Beyond"; Martin Wight, *Power Politics* (London: Leicester University Press, 1995), 23–26. The seminal statement remains Quentin Skinner, *Visions of Politics*, vol. 2: *Renaissance Virtues* (Cambridge: Cambridge University Press, 2002), chap. 14. The empirical accuracy of this story is coming under increasing strain. See, for instance, Nexon, *Struggle for Power*; Andreas Osiander, "Sovereignty, International Relations, and the Westphalian Myth," *International Organization* 55, no. 2 (2001): 251–87; Andreas Osiander, *Before the State: Systemic Political Change in the West from the Greeks to the French Revolution* (Oxford: Oxford University Press, 2007); and Benno Teschke, *The Myth of 1648: Class, Geopolitics, and the Making of Modern International Relations*, 2nd ed. (London: Verso, 2009).
5. David Armitage, *Foundations of Modern International Thought* (Cambridge: Cambridge University Press, 2012); Jens Bartelson, *Visions of World Community* (Cambridge: Cambridge University Press, 2009); Duncan Bell, ed., *Victorian*

Visions of Global Order: Empire and International Relations in Nineteenth-Century Political Thought (Cambridge: Cambridge University Press, 2012); Annabel S. Brett, *Changes of State: Nature and the Limits of the City in Early Modern Natural Law* (Princeton, NJ: Princeton University Press, 2014); Keene, *International Political Thought*; Jennifer Pitts, *A Turn to Empire: The Rise of Imperial Liberalism in Britain and France* (Princeton, NJ: Princeton University Press, 2006); Jennifer Pitts, *Boundaries of the International: Law and Empire* (Cambridge, MA: Harvard University Press, 2018).

6. For two recent examples, see Adom Getachew, *Worldmaking After Empire: The Rise and Fall of Self-Determination* (Princeton, NJ: Princeton University Press, 2019); and Patricia Owens and Katharina Rietzler, eds., *Women's International Thought: A New History* (Cambridge: Cambridge University Press, 2021).

7. This disinterest in financiers, by contrast with the emphasis placed on how great political and legal figures think about states, is somewhat puzzling, as markets and access to capital occupy a prominent place in many accounts of international relations, even in those concerned with the transition to a system of states. See, in particular, Hendrik Spruyt, *The Sovereign State and Its Competitors: An Analysis of Systems Change* (Princeton, NJ: Princeton University Press, 1996); and Charles Tilly, *Coercion, Capital, and European States, A.D. 990–1992* (Cambridge, MA: Basil Blackwell, 1990).

8. For related critiques, see Edward Keene, "International Intellectual History and International Relations: Contexts, Canons, and Mediocrities," *International Relations* 31, no. 3 (2017): 341–56; Claire Vergerio, "Context, Reception, and the Study of Great Thinkers in International Relations," *International Theory* 11, no. 1 (2019): 110–37; and Tomas Wallenius, "The Case for a History of Global Legal Practices," *European Journal of International Relations* 25, no. 1 (2019): 108–30.

9. For methodological discussions of this issue, see Kimberly Hutchings, Jens Bartelson, Edward Keene, Lea Ypi, Helen Kinsella, and David Armitage, "Foundations of Modern International Theory," *Contemporary Political Theory* 13, no. 4 (2014): 398–401. For an interesting treatment of Locke (related to this issue), see Armitage, *Foundations of Modern International Thought*, chaps. 5–7.

10. This obstacle is precisely why some financial historians interested in the question of how financiers evaluate states give such weight to academic writings in the fields of economics and finance, as well as to journalistic writings such as those found in the *Economist*, *Fenn on the Funds*, or *Mulhall's Dictionary*. Flandreau and Zumer, *Making of Global Finance*, 14, 30–35.

11. Two excellent references on this more general problem are Vergerio, "Context, Reception"; and Wallenius, "Case for a History."

12. For broad overviews of this literature, see Mai'a K. Davis Cross, "Rethinking Epistemic Communities Twenty Years Later," *Review of International Studies*

39, no. 1 (2013): 137–60; Peter M. Haas, "Introduction: Epistemic Communities and International Policy Coordination," *International Organization* 46, no. 1 (1992): 1–35; and Bentley B. Allan, "From Subjects to Objects: Knowledge in International Relations Theory," *European Journal of International Relations* 24, no. 4 (2017): 841–64.

13. Bentley B. Allan, "Producing the Climate: States, Scientists, and the Constitution of Global Governance Objects," *International Organization* 71, no. 1 (2017): 131–62.

14. Bartelson, *Genealogy*, 71. Following Ian Hacking, I do not find it necessary to attribute priority to either epistemology or ontology or methodology. See his notion of "styles of reasoning" in Ian Hacking, *Historical Ontology* (Cambridge, MA: Harvard University Press, 2002).

15. Vincent Pouliot, "'Sobjectivism': Toward a Constructivist Methodology," *International Studies Quarterly* 51, no. 2 (2007): 360.

16. J. Samuel Barkin and Laura Sjoberg, "Calculating Critique: Thinking Outside the Methods Matching Game," *Millennium—Journal of International Studies* 43, no. 3 (2015): 854.

17. Gary King, Robert O. Keohane, and Sidney Verba, *Designing Social Inquiry: Scientific Inference in Qualitative Research* (Princeton, NJ: Princeton University Press, 1994), 7–9.

18. Patricia Clavin, *Securing the World Economy: The Reinvention of the League of Nations, 1920–1946* (Oxford: Oxford University Press, 2013); Alain Desrosières, *The Politics of Large Numbers: A History of Statistical Reasoning*, trans. Camille Naish (Cambridge, MA: Harvard University Press, 2002); Timothy Mitchell, *Rule of Experts: Egypt, Techno-Politics, Modernity* (Berkeley: University of California Press, 2002); Tooze, *Statistics and the German State*, introduction.

19. Vincent Pouliot, "The Logic of Practicality: A Theory of Practice of Security Communities," *International Organization* 62, no. 2 (2008): 258.

20. Emanuel Adler and Vincent Pouliot, "International Practices: Introduction and Framework," in *International Practices*, ed. Emanuel Adler and Vincent Pouliot (Cambridge: Cambridge University Press, 2011), 8.

21. Pouliot, "Logic of Practicality," 259n14.

22. James Scott, *Seeing Like a State: How Certain Schemes to Improve the Human Condition Have Failed* (New Haven, CT: Yale University Press, 1999), 311–33.

23. Pierre Bourdieu, *Le sens pratique* (Paris: Editions de Minuit, 1980), 87, 101; Pierre Bourdieu, *Esquisse d'une theorie de la pratique: précédé de trois études d'ethnologie kabyle* (Paris: Seuil, 2000), 256, 261.

24. Pierre Bourdieu, *Langage et pouvoir symbolique* (Paris: Seuil, 2001).

25. Though the term "form of knowledge" is taken from the work of Bernard Cohn, others such as Michel Foucault and Ian Hacking have used it as well. See Bernard S. Cohn, *Colonialism and Its Forms of Knowledge: The British in*

India (Princeton, NJ: Princeton University Press, 1996); Hacking, *Historical Ontology*, 74; and Michel Foucault, *Sécurité, territoire, population: cours au Collège de France, 1977–1978* (Paris: Seuil, 2004), 104. The complete definition that Cohn offers explains that forms of knowledge might take the form of "published reports, statistical returns, histories, gazetteers, legal codes, and encyclopedias" (5), sources that are in large part related to his focus on forms of knowledge as colonial tools deployed by states.

26. In this sense, they are much more specific than John Ruggie's "social epistemes," which are sets "of spatial, metaphysical, and doctrinal constructs" that shape "the visualization of collective existence on the planet." See Ruggie, "Territoriality and Beyond," 173. Precisely for this reason, Ruggie and Branch direct our attention to different times, tools, and people when identifying the causes and advent of a system of territorially defined sovereign states. Whereas Ruggie points to single point perspective, the Renaissance, and Filippo Brunelleschi, Branch directs us to modern cartography, diplomats, and the early nineteenth century.

27. Jordan Branch, *The Cartographic State: Maps, Territory, and the Origins of Sovereignty* (Cambridge: Cambridge University Press, 2014).

28. Branch, *Cartographic State*, chap. 6.

29. Branch, 135.

30. Josef Konvitz, *Cartography in France, 1660–1848: Science, Engineering, and Statecraft* (Chicago: University of Chicago Press, 1987), 33, cited in Branch, 133.

31. Branch, 74–76; David Buisseret, "The Cartographic Definition of France's Eastern Boundary in the Early Seventeenth Century," *Imago Mundi* 36, no. 1 (1984): 72–80.

32. Branch, 5.

33. Edward Keene, "The Naming of Powers," *Cooperation and Conflict* 48, no. 2 (2013): 278; Edward Keene, "International Hierarchy and the Origins of the Modern Practice of Intervention," *Review of International Studies* 39, no. 5 (2013): 1082.

34. William J. Roosen, "Early Modern Diplomatic Ceremonial: A Systems Approach," *Journal of Modern History* 52, no. 3 (1980): 452–76; Peter R. Coss and Maurice H. Keen, *Heraldry, Pageantry, and Social Display in Medieval England* (London: Boydell, 2002).

35. Maurice Keen, *Chivalry* (New Haven, CT: Yale University Press, 1984), 148.

36. Maurice Keen, *Origins of the English Gentleman: Heraldry, Chivalry and Gentility in Medieval England, c.1300–c.1500.* (Stroud: Tempus, 2002), 97.

37. This section draws in part on Bruneau, "Converging Paths."

38. Keene, "International Intellectual History."

39. In IPE, however, see Jeffrey M. Chwieroth, *Capital Ideas: The IMF and the Rise of Financial Liberalization* (Princeton, NJ: Princeton University Press, 2010); and Donald MacKenzie, *An Engine, Not a Camera: How Financial Models Shape Markets* (Cambridge, MA: MIT Press, 2008).

40. Emanuel Adler and Vincent Pouliot, eds., *International Practices* (Cambridge: Cambridge University Press, 2011); Christian Bueger and Frank Gadinger, *International Practice Theory: New Perspectives* (New York: Palgrave Macmillan, 2014); Silviya Lechner and Mervyn Frost, *Practice Theory and International Relations* (Cambridge: Cambridge University Press, 2018). One might object, as Erik Ringmar does, that "practices of one kind or another are what scholars of international relations always have studied," diplomacy and the balance of power being two notable examples. But this criticism misses the mark. While the study of practices such as diplomacy or balancing has indeed long constituted a key object of research in international relations, the little attention previously paid to practitioners is perplexing. The quote is from Erik Ringmar, "The Search for Dialogue as a Hindrance to Understanding: Practices as Inter-Paradigmatic Research Program," *International Theory* 6, no. 1 (2014): 2. For a similar point about the lack of attention paid to practitioners in the case of diplomacy, see Iver B. Neumann, "The English School on Diplomacy: Scholarly Promise Unfulfilled," *International Relations* 17, no. 3 (2003): 341–69. For a recent exception, see Mai'a K Davis Cross, *The European Diplomatic Corps: Diplomats and International Cooperation from Westphalia to Maastricht* (Basingstoke: Palgrave Macmillan, 2008).

41. Adler and Pouliot, *International Practices*; Bueger and Gadinger, *International Practice Theory*; Peter Jackson, "Pierre Bourdieu, the 'Cultural Turn,' and the Practice of International History," *Review of International Studies* 34, no. 1 (2008): 155–81; Ted Hopf, "The Logic of Habit in International Relations," *European Journal of International Relations* 16, no. 4 (2010): 539–61; Lechner and Frost, *Practice Theory and International Relations*; Iver B. Neumann, "Returning Practice to the Linguistic Turn: The Case of Diplomacy," *Millennium—Journal of International Studies* 31, no. 3 (2002): 627–51; Pouliot, "Logic of Practicality"; Vincent Pouliot, *International Security in Practice: The Politics of NATO-Russia Diplomacy* (Cambridge: Cambridge University Press, 2010).

42. See Martti Koskenniemi, *The Gentle Civilizer of Nations: The Rise and Fall of International Law, 1870–1960* (Cambridge: Cambridge University Press, 2004); and Markus Mösslang and Torsten Riotte, eds., *The Diplomats' World: The Cultural History of Diplomacy, 1815–1914* (Oxford: Oxford University Press, 2008).

43. Edward Keene, "The English School and British Historians," *Millennium—Journal of International Studies* 37, no. 2 (2008): 391. See also William J. Bouwsma, "Lawyers and Early Modern Culture," *American Historical Review* 78, no. 2 (1973): 303–27.

44. Nathalie Bulle, "Pierre Bourdieu (1930–2002)," *L'année sociologique* 52, no. 2 (2008): 231.

45. See Pierre Bourdieu, *Homo academicus* (Paris: Éditions de Minuit, 1984); and Pierre Bourdieu, *La noblesse d'Etat: grandes écoles et esprit de corps* (Paris: Editions de Minuit, 1989).

46. See Pierre Bourdieu and Jean-Claude Passeron, *Les héritiers: les étudiants et la culture* (Paris: Editions de Minuit, 1964); and Pierre Bourdieu and Jean-Claude Passeron, *La reproduction: eléments pour une théorie du système d'enseignement* (Paris: Editions de Minuit, 1970). For a view that endows education with a diminished role in the making of the habitus, see Bernard Lahire, *L'homme pluriel* (Paris: Hachette, 2006). For an interesting comment on the role of education in Bourdieu's work, see Michel de Certeau, *L'invention du quotidien, tome 1: arts de faire* (Paris: Gallimard, 1990).

47. See, in particular, Yves Dezalay and Bryant G. Garth, *The Internationalization of Palace Wars: Lawyers, Economists, and the Contest to Transform Latin American States* (Chicago: University Of Chicago Press, 2002); and Yves Dezalay and Bryant G. Garth, *Dealing in Virtue: International Commercial Arbitration and the Construction of a Transnational Legal Order* (Chicago: University of Chicago Press, 1998). Beyond Bourdieu and Bourdieusians, one could turn to the equally towering figure of Michel Foucault, no less interested in the role of disciplines in structuring social practices, such as punishment and the treatment of madness, across entire historical epochs. Nearly all of Foucault's work is concerned with such questions, which means one could potentially cite his entire oeuvre to demonstrate this assertion. For excellent examples, see Michel Foucault, *Histoire de la folie à l'âge classique* (Paris: Gallimard, 1999); Michel Foucault, *Surveiller et punir: naissance de la prison* (Paris: Gallimard, 1993); and Michel Foucault, *Les mots et les choses: une archéologie des sciences humaines* (Paris: Gallimard, 1966).

48. Etienne Wenger, *Communities of Practice: Learning, Meaning, and Identity* (Cambridge: Cambridge University Press, 1999), chap. 12.

49. Donald Cameron Watt, *What About the People? Abstraction and Reality in History and the Social Sciences: An Inaugural Lecture* (London: London School of Economics and Political Science, 1983), 2.

50. Watt, *What About the People?*, 2–3; Donald Cameron Watt, *Succeeding John Bull: America in Britain's Place, 1900–1975* (Cambridge: Cambridge University Press, 1984), 3–4.

51. See, especially, Norbert Elias, *The Civilizing Process*, 2nd ed. (Oxford: Blackwell, 2000), 363–447.

52. C. Stephen Jaeger, *The Origins of Courtliness: Civilizing Trends and the Formation of Courtly Ideals, 939–1210* (Philadelphia: University of Pennsylvania Press, 1985), 7–9; Aldo Scaglione, *Knights at Court: Courtliness, Chivalry, and Courtesy from Ottonian Germany to the Italian Renaissance* (Berkeley: University of California Press, 1992). In his study, Jaeger explains that the educational changes he identifies precede "by a century that train of social changes in which Elias locates the birth of the civilizing process in the Middle Ages," an observation that allows him to turn Elias's argument on its head (8–9).

53. See, especially, Koskenniemi, *Gentle Civilizer.*

54. I should add that it constitutes an obvious site to study "dead" practitioners, who cannot be observed. In this sense, it complements ethnographic methods by giving us access to a world of deceased practitioners. See the comments in Bruneau, "Converging Paths"; Wallenius, "Case for a History," 111; and Peter Wilson, "The English School Meets the Chicago School: The Case for a Grounded Theory of International Institutions," *International Studies Review* 14, no. 4 (2012): 587.

55. John Lawson and Harold Silver, *A Social History of Education in England* (London: Routledge, 2013), 2.

56. Lawson and Silver, *Social History of Education*, 1.

57. Thomas S. Kuhn, *The Structure of Scientific Revolutions* (Chicago: University of Chicago Press, 1996), 19.

58. Matthew S. Anderson, *The Rise of Modern Diplomacy, 1450–1919* (London: Routledge, 1993), chap. 2; H. M. A. Keens-Soper, "The French Political Academy, 1712: A School for Ambassadors," *European History Quarterly* 2, no. 4 (1972): 329–55; Heidrun Kugeler, "Le Parfait Ambassadeur: The Theory and Practice of Diplomacy in the Century Following the Peace of Westphalia" (PhD diss., University of Oxford, 2006).

59. On this question, see Edward Keene, "The Age of Grotius," in *Routledge Handbook of International Law*, ed. David Armstrong (London: Routledge, 2009), 126–40.

2. THE INSIDERS—MERCHANT BANKERS

1. Heinrich Heine, *Heine's Wit, Wisdom and Pathos*, trans. J. Snodgrass, 2nd ed. (London: Alexander Gardner, 1888), 192.

2. Lord Byron, *Don Juan* (London: Penguin, 2004), Canto 12, 136.

3. Benjamin Disraeli, *Coningsby or, The New Generation* (Leipzig: Berhn. Tauchnitz, 1844), 198–99.

4. Honoré de Balzac, *La Maison Nucingen* (Paris: Gallimard, 1989).

5. A few recent studies overlook this key historical feature. See Jonathan Kirshner, *Appeasing Bankers: Financial Caution on the Road to War* (Princeton, NJ: Princeton University Press, 2007); and Michael Tomz, *Reputation and International Cooperation: Sovereign Debt Across Three Centuries* (Princeton, NJ: Princeton University Press, 2007. For a similar critique, see Marc Flandreau and Juan H. Flores, "The Peaceful Conspiracy: Bond Markets and International Relations During the Pax Britannica," *International Organization* 66, no. 2 (2012): 211–41.

6. See Layna Mosley, *Global Capital and National Governments* (Cambridge: Cambridge University Press, 2003), chap. 7.

7. Stanley D. Chapman, *The Rise of Merchant Banking* (London: Allen & Unwin, 1984), 173.

8. Vinod Aggarwal, *Debt Games: Strategic Interaction in International Debt Rescheduling* (Cambridge: Cambridge University Press, 1996), 19–25. For Aggarwal's full periodization, see 19–41. He identifies the end of the first epoch of sovereign debt with the 1860s and the creation of bondholder corporations. On this issue, see Rui Pedro Esteves, "The Bondholder, the Sovereign, and the Banker: Sovereign Debt and Bondholders' Protection Before 1914," *European Review of Economic History* 17, no. 4 (2013): 389–407. The identification of the 1860s as a pivotal time for the decline of an international bourgeoisie is an argument put forward by Charles Jones—though, tellingly, he has very little to say about merchant bankers. See Charles A. Jones, *International Business in the Nineteenth Century: The Rise and Fall of a Cosmopolitan Bourgeoisie* (New York: New York University Press, 1987).

9. Aggarwal, *Debt Games*, 25–29.

10. Marc Flandreau, Juan H. Flores, Norbert Gaillard, and Sebastián Nieto-Parra, "The End of Gatekeeping: Underwriters and the Quality of Sovereign Bond Markets, 1815–2007" (working paper, National Bureau of Economic Research, Chicago, 2010), http://www.nber.org/papers/w15128 (accessed 21 March 2022).

11. One might expect a German financial center to be part of this group, but "German foreign trade was wholly dependent on English intermediaries as far as finance was concerned," at least until the creation of Deutsche Bank in 1870. See Marcello De Cecco, *Money and Empire: The International Gold Standard, 1890–1914* (Oxford: Blackwell, 1974), 108.

12. Some even argue that it lasted until the 1960s. See, for example, Michael Lisle-Williams, "Beyond the Market: The Survival of Family Capitalism in the English Merchant Banks," *British Journal of Sociology* 35, no. 2 (1984): 245; and Herbert Feis, *Europe, The World's Banker, 1870–1914* (London: Cass, 1961), 8.

13. R. H. Tawney, cited in Andrew Walter, *World Power and World Money: The Role of Hegemony and International Monetary Order* (New York: Harvester Wheatsheaf, 1993), 30.

14. Chapman, *Rise of Merchant Banking*, 3–4; Hubert Bonin, *La banque et les banquiers en France: du Moyen Age à nos jours* (Paris: Larousse, 1992), 49.

15. Sovereign lending on the Amsterdam market was in the hands of very few merchant banks among which one finds Hope & Co. (the most preeminent one), Goll & Co., George Clifford & Co., Andries Pels & Zoonen, Jacob Dull, and R. & Th. De Smeth. Interestingly, a number of these firms came from Scotland and northern England—for instance, Hope & Co. and Clifford & Co, respectively. These firms had an oligopolistic control of loans to foreign powers. This position was reinforced by the fact that wealthy investors had virtually no information about sovereigns' financial state, so as to make informed decisions about lending. The best they could do was to trust merchant bankers' judgments, despite the fact that these bankers also had very little information. On these matters, see James Riley, *International Government Finance and the*

Amsterdam Capital Market, 1740–1815 (Cambridge: Cambridge University Press, 2009), 38–44, and chaps. 7–8 more broadly.

16. Chapman, *Rise of Merchant Banking*, 2–5.
17. One of the reasons put forth by Ellen Wood to explain the absence of such bankers in England and their presence on the continent is that, contrary to many continental states, England had a highly developed *domestic* market and was less dependent on long distance trade with the rest of Europe. See Ellen Meiksins Wood, *The Pristine Culture of Capitalism: A Historical Essay on Old Regimes and Modern States* (London: Verso, 1991), 98.
18. Goethe, cited in Niall Ferguson, *The House of Rothschild: Money's Prophets, 1798–1848* (London: Penguin, 1998), 35.
19. Ferguson, *House of Rothschild: Money's Prophets*, 48–49.
20. Lisle-Williams, "Beyond the Market," 268n25; Toshio Suzuki, *Japanese Government Loan Issues on the London Capital Market, 1870–1913* (London: Athlone, 1994), 8.
21. As we will see later, leading American private banks were often made up of families that had reimmigrated to England and established their main branch there or who were deeply connected to the Continent (e.g., Jacob Schiff from Kuhn, Loeb & Co.). On American private banking in the interwar, an excellent reference is Susie J. Pak, *Gentlemen Bankers: The World of J. P. Morgan* (Cambridge, MA: Harvard University Press, 2013).
22. Suzuki, *Japanese Government Loan Issues*, 7.
23. Louis Bergeron, "Banquiers, négocants et manufacturiers Parisiens du Directoire à L'Empire—Tome I" (PhD diss., Paris, Paris IV-Sorbonne, 1975), 90, 149–210.
24. See Nicolas Stoskopf, "Qu'est-ce que la haute banque Parisienne au XIXe siècle?," in *Journée d'études sur l'histoire de la haute banque* (2000): 3.
25. Lecouteulx de Canteleu was a prominent figure, as he held a post as regent of the Banque de France from 1800 to 1804. See Romuald Szramkiewicz, *Les régents et censeurs de la Banque de France nommés sous le Consulat et l'Empire* (Paris: Droz, 1974), LVI.
26. See Bonin, *La banque et les banquiers*, 50.
27. Eighteenth-century Dutch banking families did not stand in this tradition, but they were also not the ones to migrate to London and Paris, and they declined in importance in the nineteenth century.
28. Jerold Siegel, *Modernity and Bourgeois Life* (Cambridge: Cambridge University Press, 2012), 286.
29. This is the year in which the North German Confederation was founded. On this issue, see Hans A. Schmitt, "From Sovereign States to Prussian Provinces: Hanover and Hesse-Nassau, 1866–1871," *Journal of Modern History* 57, no. 1 (1985): 24–56. Of course, the final key step in the destruction of minor German states was 1871, which marks the foundation of the German Empire.

30. Ferguson, *House of Rothschild: Money's Prophets*, 126.
31. Bertrand Gille, *Histoire de la maison Rothschild*, 2 vols. (Geneva: Droz, 1965), 430–32.
32. Chapman, *Rise of Merchant Banking*, 25.
33. Chapman, 34–37. Chapman identifies two models of merchant banking, one represented by the House of Rothschild, which focused on "pure finance," and one epitomized by the House of Baring, which was more broadly based on general merchanting. Chapman however stresses that these differences should not be overemphasized.
34. Chapman, 36.
35. Chapman, 36.
36. Kathleen Burk, *Morgan Grenfell, 1838–1988: The Biography of a Merchant Bank* (Oxford: Oxford University Press, 1989), 32–33.
37. Chapman, *Rise of Merchant Banking*, 37.
38. For some exceptions, see Kristine Bruland and Patrick O'Brien, *From Family Firms to Corporate Capitalism: Essays in Business and Industrial History in Honour of Peter Mathias* (Oxford: Clarendon, 1998); and Harold James, *Family Capitalism: Wendels, Haniels, Falcks, and the Continental European Model* (London: Belknap Press of Harvard University Press, 2006). For a brief discussion regarding the Rothschilds, see Niall Ferguson, "The Rise of the Rothschilds: The Family Firm as Multinational," in *The World of Private Banking*, ed. Youssef Cassis and Philip Cottrell (Farnham: Ashgate, 2009), 1–30.
39. Walter Bagehot cited in Jehanne Wake, *Kleinwort, Benson: The History of Two Families in Banking* (Oxford: Oxford University Press, 1997), 107.
40. Burk, *Morgan Grenfell*, 28.
41. Colin Arthur Cooke, *Corporation, Trust, and Company: An Essay in Legal History* (Manchester: Manchester University Press, 1950), 122.
42. For an interesting take on the role of status in social stratification, see Frank Parkin, *Marxism and Class Theory: A Bourgeois Critique* (Taylor & Francis, 1979).
43. Mark Häberlein, *The Fuggers of Augsburg: Pursuing Wealth and Honor in Renaissance Germany* (Charlottesville: University of Virginia Press, 2012), 6. On the broader question of the social acceptability of pursuing one's interests, see Albert O. Hirschman's classic *The Passions and the Interests: Political Arguments for Capitalism Before Its Triumph* (Princeton, NJ: Princeton University Press, 2013).
44. Häberlein, *Fuggers of Augsburg*, 208–10, 222.
45. Häberlein, 222.
46. Marten G. Buist, *At Spes Non Fracta: Hope & Co., 1770–1815* (The Hague: Nijhoff, 1974), 279.
47. Fritz Stern, *Gold and Iron* (New York: Vintage, 1979), xvii. This status-seeking was also broadly shared by the rising European bourgeoisie, the "nouveaux riches"—a term imported from French in the Napoleonic period. See J.

Mordaunt Crook, *The Rise of the Nouveaux Riches: Style and Status in Victorian and Edwardian Architecture* (London: John Murray, 1999), 7.

48. Youssef Cassis, *City Bankers, 1890–1914* (Cambridge: Cambridge University Press, 1994), 269.

49. Niall Ferguson, *The House of Rothschild: The World's Banker, 1849–1999* (London: Penguin, 2000), 20–21.

50. Philip Ziegler, *The Sixth Great Power: Barings, 1765–1929* (London: Collins, 1988), 33–34.

51. Peter J. Cain and Antony G. Hopkins, *British Imperialism, 1688–2000*, 2nd ed. (London: Routledge, 2001), 38.

52. See, for instance, the remarks in Wake, *Kleinwort, Benson*, 134.

53. Ferguson, *House of Rothschild: Money's Prophets*, 184.

54. Ferguson, 184. On the importance of dynasties for international relations until the nineteenth century, see Jeroen F. J. Duindam, *Dynasties: A Global History of Power, 1300–1800* (Cambridge: Cambridge University Press, 2015).

55. Ziegler, *Sixth Great Power*, 31.

56. Ziegler, 54.

57. Ziegler, 55.

58. It is worth noting that, though Protestants from Switzerland were numerous in French banking, a number of German banking families arrived just after the fall of the first French Empire—for instance, the Gontards or Bethmans of Frankfurt and the Mendelssohns from Berlin. Bertrand Gille, *Histoire de la maison Rothschild, Vol. 1* (Geneva: Droz, 1965), 59. These families, however, never opened a branch in Paris, but simply had representatives there. This was in all likelihood because they had moved with the German troops stationed in France after the fall of the empire.

59. Besides differences in name, these banks were in fact rather similar. See David S. Landes, "Vieille banque et banque nouvelle: la révolution financière du dix-neuvième siècle," *Revue d'histoire moderne et contemporaine* 3, no. 3 (1956): 207–8n5. For a different view, see Joseph Wechsberg, *The Merchant Bankers* (London: Weidenfeld & Nicolson, 1967), 10–11. For a useful overview of different terms, see Richard Roberts, "What's in a Name? Merchants, Merchant Bankers, Accepting Houses, Issuing Houses, Industrial Bankers, and Investment Bankers," *Business History* 35, no. 3 (1993): 22–38.

60. Elizabeth Hennessy, "The Governors, Directors, and Management of the Bank of England," in *The Bank of England: Money, Power, and Influence, 1694–1994*, ed. David Kynaston and Richard Roberts (Oxford: Oxford University Press, 1995), 186.

61. Lisle-Williams, "Beyond the Market," 254.

62. Cassis, *City Bankers*, 88.

63. Lisle-Williams, "Beyond the Market," 254; Cassis, *City Bankers*, 86.

64. Wechsberg, *Merchant Bankers*, 13.

65. Hennessy, "Governors," 194–95.

66. Lisle-Williams, "Beyond the Market," 254.

67. Szramkiewicz, *Les régents et censeurs*, LVII.

68. Bonin, *La banque et les banquiers*, 50.

69. Alain Plessis, *Régents et gouverneurs de la Banque de France sous le Second Empire* (Paris: Droz, 1985), 18.

70. Ferguson, *House of Rothschild: Money's Prophets*, 82; Plessis, *Régents et gouverneurs*, 421.

71. Ferguson, *House of Rothschild: The World's Banker*, 82–84.

72. Ferguson, 342. On the role of Rothschilds as arbitrageurs between the British-based gold standard and French-dominated bimetallic zone, see Marc Flandreau's excellent *The Glitter of Gold: France, Bimetallism, and the Emergence of the International Gold Standard, 1848–1873* (Oxford: Oxford University Press, 2004).

73. Siegel, *Modernity and Bourgeois Life*, 286.

74. Andrew Richard Dilley, "Gentlemanly Capitalism and the Dominions: London Finance, Australia and Canada, 1900–14" (PhD diss., University of Oxford, 2006), 39, 41.

75. Lisle-Williams, "Beyond the Market," 245.

76. Ziegler, *Sixth Great Power*, 58. Though Barings had helped financed the American wars, the sums involved were much smaller than in the French wars.

77. Charles P. Kindleberger, *A Financial History of Western Europe* (London: Routledge, 2006), 220.

78. A few French merchant banking houses were entrusted with tranches of the loan, among which one finds Hottinguer, Lafitte, and Delessert.

79. Jean Bouvier, *Les Rothschild: Histoire d'un capitalisme familial* (Paris: Editions Complexe, 1992), 71; Chapman, *Rise of Merchant Banking*, 83; Ferguson, *House of Rothschild: The World's Banker*, xxiv; Youssef Cassis and Philip Cottrell, eds., *The World of Private Banking* (Farnham: Ashgate, 2009), 8.

80. See Ferguson, xxiv; and R. C. Michie, *The Global Securities Market: A History* (Oxford: Oxford University Press, 2006).

81. Alain Plessis, "The Parisian 'Haute Banque' and the International Economy in the Nineteenth and Early Twentieth Centuries," in *The World of Private Banking*, ed. Youssef Cassis and Philip Cottrell (Farnham: Ashgate, 2009), 135–40. See also the remarks in Philip Cottrell, "London's First 'Big Bang?' Institutional Change in the City, 1858–1883," in *The World of Private Banking*, ed. Youssef Cassis and Philip Cottrell (London: Ashgate, 2009), 98.

82. Chapman, *Rise of Merchant Banking*, 4.

83. Bonin, *La banque et les banquiers*, 49.

84. Burk, *Morgan Grenfell*, 5. See also the comments in Landes, "Vieille banque et banque nouvelle," 208.

85. Ziegler, *Sixth Great Power*, 20.

86. Ziegler, 20.

87. Ziegler, 30; Wechsberg, *Merchant Bankers*, 11–12.

88. Ziegler, 30.
89. John Orbell, "Private Banks and International Finance in the Light of the Archives of Baring Brothers," in *The World of Private Banking*, ed. Youssef Cassis and Philip Cottrell (London: Ashgate, 2009), 141–58; Landes, "Vieille banque et banque nouvelle," 208.
90. Ziegler, *Sixth Great Power*, 30.
91. Paul Ferris cited in Wechsberg, *Merchant Bankers*, 41.
92. Jack Morgan cited in Pak, *Gentlemen Bankers*, 2.
93. Marc Flandreau, "Anatomy of Regime Change: Underwriters' Reputation, New Deal Financial Acts, and the Collapse of International Capital Markets (1920–1935)" (draft, Graduate Institute of International Studies and Development, Geneva, August 18, 2011), 2, http://econ.as.nyu.edu/docs/IO/21858/Flandreau_10142011.pdf; Marc Flandreau, Juan Flores, and Sebastiàn Nieto-Parra, "The Changing Role of Global Financial Brands in the Underwriting of Foreign Government Debt (1815–2010)" (IHEID Working Paper, Economics Section, Graduate Institute of International Studies, 2011), http://ideas.repec.org/p/gii/giihei/heidwp15-2011.html (accessed 21 March 2022), 4.
94. Flandreau, "Anatomy of a Regime Change," 2–3. By contrast, research shows that there is no such relation nowadays. See Flandreau, Flores, and Nieto-Parra, "Changing Role of Global Financial Brand."
95. Burk, *Morgan Grenfell*, 6.
96. Flandreau and Flores, "Peaceful Conspiracy," 221–23; Mosley, *Global Capital and National Governments*, 260–61; Aggarwal, *Debt Games*, 20.
97. Flandreau and Flores, 223.
98. Chapman, *Rise of Merchant Banking*, chap. 9.
99. See, for instance, the comments in Rui Pedro Esteves, "Quis Custodiet Quem? Sovereign Debt and Bondholders' Protection Before 1914" (Discussion Paper 323, University of Oxford, April 2007), https://ideas.repec.org/p/oxf/wpaper/323.html (accessed 22 April 2022), 4.
100. Ferguson, *House of Rothschild: Money's Prophets*, 132.
101. On underwriting, see Flandreau, Flores, and Nieto-Parra, "Changing Role of Global Financial Brands"; Flandreau et al., "End of Gatekeeping"; Anders L. Mikkelsen, "Dealing with Risk: Underwriting Sovereign Bond Issues in London 1870–1914," (Paper No. 14-06, European Association for Banking and Financial History, June 2014), http://www.eabh.info/fileadmin/user_upload/documents/eabhpapers14_06.pdf (accessed 29 April 2022).
102. Kirshner, *Appeasing Bankers*; Tomz, *Reputation and International Cooperation*.
103. For an analysis of the situation in the preceding period (sixteenth and seventeenth century), see Laurence Fontaine, *The Moral Economy: Poverty, Credit, and Trust in Early Modern Europe* (Cambridge: Cambridge University Press, 2014); Häberlein, *Fuggers of Augsburg*; and Richard Ehrenberg, *Capital and Finance in the Age of the Renaissance: A Study of the Fuggers and Their Connections* (New York: Augustus M. Kelley, 1963).

104. As for the broader group of investors, they mostly relied on their trust in the banking houses themselves. Regarding the eighteenth-century capital market in Amsterdam, Riley claims that "borrowers appear generally to have understood that there were only a few houses that could handle issues competently" and goes on to describe the importance of these houses to the sovereign bond market; see Riley, *International Government Finance*, 42–44. This pattern is reminiscent of the observations of Flandreau and Flores regarding the nineteenth-century London market. See, in particular, Marc Flandreau and Juan H. Flores, "The Peaceful Conspiracy: Bond Markets and International Relations During the Pax Britannica," *International Organization* 66, no. 2 (2012): 211–41; and Marc Flandreau, Juan Flores, and Sebastiàn Nieto-Parra, "The Changing Role of Global Financial Brands in the Underwriting of Foreign Government Debt (1815–2010)" (Working Paper 15/2011, Graduate Institute of International Studies, Geneva, 2011), http://ideas.repec.org/p/gii/giihei /heidwp15-2011.html (accessed 5 April 2022).

105. Ehrenberg, *Capital and Finance*, 319–20.

106. Riley, *International Government Finance*, 38.

107. Riley, 39.

108. Riley, 38–40.

109. Riley, 39–40. Regarding accounting, Riley mentions that even the Netherlands, generally considered to be financially more advanced at the time, did not have the same accounting clarity. However, according to recent literature on national accounting, it appears that Riley overstates British advances in national accounting. See André Vanoli, *A History of National Accounting* (Oxford: IOS, 2005), 3–11.

110. Tomz, *Reputation and International Cooperation*, 44.

111. Marc Flandreau and Juan H. Flores, "Bonds and Brands: Foundations of Sovereign Debt Markets, 1820–1830," *Journal of Economic History* 69, no. 3 (2009): 660.

112. George G. Carey, *A New Guide to the Public Funds: Or, Every Man His Own Stock-Broker* (London: D. B. Woodward, 1825), 118, 120, 125. According to Mosley, even later in the century (1880–1914), the few prospectuses that were issued for loans—this was not the norm—contained the same basic information. See Mosley, *Global Capital and National Governments*, 290.

113. Thomas Fortune, *Fortune's Epitome of the Stocks and Public Funds, Containing Every Necessary Information for Perfectly Understanding the Nature of Those Securities and the Mode of Doing Business Therein: With a Full Acount of All the Foreign Funds and Loans*, 13th ed. (London: J. J. Secretan, 1833), 121. This excellent passage was brought to my attention in an early working paper version of Flandreau and Flores, "Bonds and Brands," https://www.princeton.edu /~pcglobal/conferences/globdem/papers/Bonds_and_Brands14.pdf (accessed 21 March 2022).

114. See Landes, "Vieille banque et banque nouvelle," 211.

115. Flandreau and Flores, "Bonds and Brands," 660.

116. David Sinclair, *The Land That Never Was: Sir Gregor MacGregor and the Most Audacious Fraud in History* (London: Headline, 2003).

117. See, for example, Mosley, *Global Capital and National Governments*, 262–63.

3. GENTILITY AS A FORM OF KNOWLEDGE

1. Peter J. Cain and Antony G. Hopkins, *British Imperialism: 1688–2000* (London: Routledge, 2001).

2. I should like to add that, since the 1980s, prominent scholars in the social sciences and history have gradually returned to the study of manners and tastes. To take two examples, the 1980s witnessed the delayed publication of the English translation of Norbert Elias's *The Civilizing Process*, which analyzed the critical role of manners in the development of court societies and the formation of modern states, as well as the English translation of Pierre Bourdieu's *Distinction*, which still constitutes one of the most highly regarded theoretical statements on the importance of tastes and manners in social stratification. See Pierre Bourdieu, *Distinction: A Social Critique of the Judgement of Taste* (Routledge, 2010); and Norbert Elias, *The Civilizing Process* (Oxford: Blackwell, 1994).

3. Marc Flandreau, *Anthropologists in the Stock Exchange: A Financial History of Victorian Science* (Chicago: University of Chicago Press, 2016). Edward Beasley's review of the book—though I do not agree with it in its entirety—provides a useful critique of Flandreau's account of gentlemanliness and gentlemanly capitalism. See Edward Beasley, "Marc Flandreau, *Anthropologists in the Stock Exchange*: A Financial History of Victorian Science," *American Historical Review* 123, no. 1 (2018): 306–7.

4. Though claims to this effect do exist in Cain and Hopkins, *British Imperialism*.

5. Jeroen F. J. Duindam, *Vienna and Versailles: The Courts of Europe's Major Dynastic Rivals, 1550–1780* (Cambridge: Cambridge University Press, 2003); Nobert Elias, *The Civilizing Process*, 2nd ed. (Oxford: Blackwell, 2000); and William J. Roosen, "Early Modern Diplomatic Ceremonial: A Systems Approach," *Journal of Modern History* 52, no. 3 (1980): 452–76; Miloš Vec, *Zeremonialwissenschaft im Fürstenstaat: Studien zur juristischen und politischen Theorie absolutistischer Herrschaftsrepräsentation* (Frankfurt am Main: Klostermann, 1998). This development stood in opposition to the earlier, but declining, peripatetic courts. See C. Stephen Jaeger, *The Origins of Courtliness: Civilizing Trends and the Formation of Courtly Ideals, 939–1210* (Philadelphia: University of Pennsylvania Press, 1985), 19–20.

6. In the early modern period, courts were defined in Furetière's and Zedler's famous dictionaries as "the residence of a king or sovereign prince." It was also sometimes defined as "the officers and the suite of a prince." See Duindam, *Vienna and Versailles*, 3.

7. Elias, *Civilizing Process*, 1994, 50.

8. Duindam, *Vienna and Versailles*; Elias, 1994.

9. Kugeler, "Le parfait ambassadeur," 35.

10. Kugeler, 40.

11. Kugeler, 64–65, 81–85.

12. Baldassare Castiglione, *Il Cortegiano* (Venetia: Nelle case d'Aldo Romano & d'Andra d'Asola suo suocero, 1528); Nicholas Terpstra, *Religious Refugees in the Early Modern World* (Cambridge: Cambridge University Press, 2015), 319. This popularity was related to the decline of Italian republics (and their *palazzo publico*) and the rise in their stead of duchies and princely states centered on private courts. I thank Claire Vergerio for this point. See Quentin Skinner, *Visions of Politics, Vol. 2: Renaissance Virtues* (Cambridge: Cambridge University Press, 2002), 135–36. In his seminal work Norbert Elias puts overwhelming emphasis on Erasmus's *De civilitate morum puerilium* published in 1530 for enshrining a new standard of manners. This book underwent 130 editions in a century. Castiglione's manual, published in 1528, went through an almost equally astounding number of editions in less than a century (108). It was, however, much more clearly directed at courtiers and ambassadors, a group to which he belonged, than to the education of the nobility more broadly. I think that this book, rather than being subsumed to the general style of civility manuals of the kind represented by Erasmus's treatise, constitutes a different strand of literature, directed at professionals of a sort—courtiers—and not at noble offspring in general. See Peter Burke, *The Fortunes of the Courtier: The European Reception of Castiglione's Cortegiano* (Cambridge: Polity, 1995), 124–26; and Elias, *Civilizing Process*, 1994, 43.

13. Burke, *Fortunes of the Courtier*, 124.

14. See Baldassare Castiglione, *The Courtyer of Count Baldessar Castilio: Diuided into Foure Bookes. Very Necessary and Profitable for Yonge Gentilmen and Gentilwomen Abiding in Court, Palaice, or Place, Done into English by Thomas Hoby*, trans. Sir Thomas Hoby (London: By Wyllyam Seres at the Signe of the Hedghogge, 1561).

15. François de Callières, *De la manière de négocier avec les souverains: de l'utilité des negociations, du choix des ambassadeurs & des envoyez, & des qualitez nécessaires pour réussir dans ces emplois* (Amsterdam: La Compagnie, 1715); Abraham de Wicquefort, *L'ambassadeur et ses fonctions* (La Haye: Chez Jean & Daniel Steucker, 1681). Famous ambassadors wrote treatises entirely dedicated to courtesy with no reference to diplomacy; see François de Callières, *De la science du monde, et des connoissances utiles a la conduite de la vie* (Bruxelles: Chez Jean Leonard, 1717).

16. Wicquefort cited in Burke, *Fortunes of the Courtier*, 129–30.

17. Roosen, "Early Modern Diplomatic Ceremonial," 456–57.

18. The same is true of Callières's manual; see Callières, *De la manière de négocier*, chaps. 3–5, 10, 14–15.

19. Callières, chaps. 3–5, 10, 14–17, 22.
20. Kugeler, "Le parfait ambassadeur," 70, 91–92. Early eighteenth-century Russian diplomats like Postnikov introduced Wicquefort's treatise to Russia in 1701 and wrote a translation published in 1712. In the same vein, Matveev and Shafirov purchased for themselves and the czar copies of Wicquefort's treatise, but also of Vera's and Callières's. Similarly, American diplomat and later president John Adams taught himself with diplomatic and legal treatises, notably with Wicquefort's and Mably's.
21. Duindam, *Vienna and Versailles*. Outside Europe, see Charles H. Alexandrowicz, *An Introduction to the History of the Law of Nations in the East Indies (16th, 17th, and 18th Centuries)* (Oxford: Clarendon, 1967); Andrew Phillips and Jason Sharman, *International Order in Diversity: War, Trade, and Rule in the Indian Ocean* (Cambridge: Cambridge University Press, 2015), 87–89, 150–51; and Sanjay Subrahmanyam, *Courtly Encounters: Translating Courtliness and Violence in Early Modern Eurasia* (Cambridge, MA: Harvard University Press, 2012), chap. 3.
22. Matthew S. Anderson, *The Rise of Modern Diplomacy, 1450–1919* (London: Routledge, 1993), 10.
23. Alexandrowicz, *Law of Nations*, 15.
24. Duindam, *Vienna and Versailles*, 199–200.
25. Alexandrowicz, *Law of Nations*, 185; Johann Christian Lünig, *Theatrum Ceremoniale Historico-Politicum, Oder Historisch- Und Politischer Schau-Platz Aller Ceremonien.*, 2 vols. (Leipzig: Moritz Georg Weidmann, 1720).
26. Simon de La Loubère, *Du royaume de Siam* (Amsterdam: Chez Abraham Wolfgang près de la Bourse, 1691), ii; Maurice Keens-Soper, "The French Political Academy, 1712: A School for Ambassadors," *European History Quarterly* 2, no. 4 (1972): 329–55.
27. See the interesting examples of the Portuguese in China, and Warren Hastings with regard to the Raja of Benares in Alexandrowicz, *Law of Nations*, 17, 20.
28. The works of Mably, Bielfeld, and Nourar provide good illustrations of the decline of courtesy in diplomatic manuals. See Kugeler, "Le parfait ambassadeur," 39. To be perfectly clear, courtesy never disappeared completely, but it was marginalized by an array of alternative forms of knowledge.
29. Duindam, *Vienna and Versailles*, 6; Kugeler, 46.
30. Quentin Skinner, *The Foundations of Modern Political Thought: Vol. 2, The Age of Reformation* (Cambridge: Cambridge University Press, 1978), 349.
31. Osiander, *Before the State*, 485.
32. Edwin Green, *Debtors to Their Profession: A History of the Institute of Bankers 1879–1979* (London: Methuen, 1979), 5.
33. Green, *Debtors to Their Profession*, 5. Incidentally, John Dalton also founded the *Bankers' Magazine* in 1844. Even the *Bankers' Magazine* was basically "reserved for the world of deposit banking." See Youssef Cassis, *City Bankers, 1890–1914* (Cambridge: Cambridge University Press, 1994), 28–29.
34. Cassis, *City Bankers*, 28.

35. Jacques Peuchet, *Manuel du banquier, de l'agent de change et du courtier: con-tenant les lois et réglemens qui s'y rapportent, les diverses opérations de change, courtage et négociations des effets à la Bourse* (Paris: Roret, 1829). Peuchet also happened to be one of the key characters who introduced German *Statistik* in France (to be discussed in chapter 5). In France, from the seventeenth century onward, a number of works about bookkeeping appeared. These manuals were a source of teaching added to in-house training. Over the course of the eigh-teenth century, these manuals became more theoretical and attempted to dis-cern general laws. See Yann Lemarchand, "'A la conquête de la science des comptes': variations autour de quelques manuels de comptabilité des XVIIe et XVIIIe siècles," in *Ecrire, compter, mesurer /2 : vers une histoire des ratio-nalités pratiques*, ed. Natacha Coquery, François Menant, and Florence Weber (Paris: Editions Rue d'Ulm, 2013), 34–65.

36. Wake, *Kleinwort, Benson*, 107.

37. Monika Pohle Fraser, "Personal and Impersonal Exchange—The Role of Rep-utation in Banking: Some Evidence from Nineteenth- and Early Twentieth-Century Banks' Archives," in *Centres and Peripheries in Banking: The Historical Development of Financial Markets*, ed. Philip Cottrell, Even Lange, and Ulf Olsson (Aldershot: Ashgate, 2007), 177.

38. David S. Landes, *Bankers and Pashas: International Finance and Economic Imperialism in Egypt* (London: Heinemann, 1958), 14–15.

39. Cassis, *City Bankers*, 98–106; Niall Ferguson, *The House of Rothschild: The World's Banker, 1849–1999* (London: Penguin, 2000), 43–45, 223–25.

40. Cassis, 102. In his study, Cassis examines partners from the following mer-chant banks: Arbuthnot, Latham & Co.; Baring Brothers & Co. Ltd.; R. Benson & Co.; Brown, Shipley & Co.; Erlanger & Co.; R. Fleming & Co.; Fruehling & Goschen; Antony Gibbs & Sons; C. J. Hambro & Son; Frederick Huth & Co.; Kleinwort, Sons & Co.; H. S. Lefevre & Co.; Matheson & Co.; Morgan, Gren-fell & Co.; Samuel Montagu & Co.; N. M. Rothschild & Sons; M. Samuel & Co.; D. Sassoon & Co.; J. Henry Schröder & Co.; and Stern Brothers (10).

41. Cassis, 99.

42. Cassis, 102n19.

43. Cassis, 104.

44. Cassis, 103.

45. Cassis, 106.

46. Ferguson, *House of Rothschild: The World's Banker*, 43.

47. E. S. Leedham-Green, *A Concise History of the University of Cambridge* (Cam-bridge: Cambridge University Press, 1996), 153.

48. Sir Norman Chester, *Economics, Politics, and Social Studies in Oxford, 1900–85* (London: Globe Education, 1986), 2.

49. Alon Kadish and Keith Tribe, "Introduction: The Supply of and Demand for Economics in Late Victorian Britain," in *The Market for Political Economy: The Advent of Economics in British University Culture* (London: Routledge, 1993), 2.

50. Chester, *Economics, Politics, and Social Studies*, 2, 6–8.

51. Leedham-Green, *Concise History*, 162.

52. I discuss these institutions of higher education and their importance for a specific group of financiers in chapter 5.

53. Chester, *Economics, Politics, and Social Studies*, 54.

54. Ferguson, *House of Rothschild: The World's Banker*, 43–45.

55. Ferguson, 20.

56. Ferguson, 43–44.

57. Todd M. Endelman, *The Jews of Britain, 1656 to 2000* (Berkeley: University of California Press, 2002), 98–103.

58. Ferguson, *House of Rothschild: The World's Banker*, 44.

59. Ferguson, 224–25.

60. Ferguson, 249.

61. Ferguson, 249.

62. Ferguson, 225.

63. See Cain and Hopkins, *British Imperialism*, chap. 1; Landes, *Bankers and Pashas*, chap. 1; and Cassis, *City Bankers*, chap. 7. I should note that Niall Ferguson does not think that the Rothschilds' outlook is properly captured by the term "gentlemanly capitalist." Instead, he argues that they were unalloyed capitalists, dating back to their time in the Frankfurt Judengasse. See Niall Ferguson, *The House of Rothschild: Money's Prophets, 1798–1848* (London: Penguin, 1998), 10.

64. The authoritative reference is Cain and Hopkins, *British Imperialism*. For a discussion of the return of the ideal of gentlemanliness in nineteenth-century Britain, see Mark Girouard, *The Return to Camelot: Chivalry and the English Gentleman* (New Haven, CT: Yale University Press, 1985); and Maurice Keen, *Origins of the English Gentleman: Heraldry, Chivalry, and Gentility in Medieval England, c.1300–c.1500* (Stroud: Tempus, 2002). For a discussion of this theme with regard to France, see David Todd, "Republican Capitalism: The Political Economy of French Capital Exports in the Nineteenth Century" (working paper, King's College, London, 2015).

65. Cain and Hopkins, *British Imperialism*, 40.

66. Cain and Hopkins, 44.

67. Other important service sector jobs included the upper reaches of the law, upper echelons of the established church, and the officer class of the armed services. See Cain and Hopkins, 40.

68. Cain and Hopkins, 38.

69. Cain and Hopkins, 39.

70. Cain and Hopkins, 39. The opposition between entrepreneurial wealth and propertied wealth is a famous theme in classical sociology, particularly in the works of Max Weber and Thorstein Veblen. See Max Weber, *Economy and Society: An Outline of Interpretive Sociology*, ed. Guenther Roth and Claus Wittich (Berkeley: University of California Press, 1978), chap. 4; and Thorstein Veblen, *The Theory of the Leisure Class* (New York: Penguin, 1994).

71. Cain and Hopkins, *British Imperialism*, 49.
72. Cain and Hopkins, 39.
73. Cain and Hopkins, 41–42.
74. Cain and Hopkins, 45–46.
75. Cassis, *City Bankers*, 205.
76. Cassis, 205.
77. Cassis, 207–8.
78. Cassis, 205. This figure includes small private bankers, but it is nonetheless telling regarding the overlap between these two social characteristics.
79. See J. Mordaunt Crook, *The Rise of the Nouveaux Riches: Style and Status in Victorian and Edwardian Architecture* (London: John Murray, 1999), 62–63.
80. Ferguson, *House of Rothschild: The World's Banker*, 46.
81. Ferguson, 20.
82. Wake, *Kleinwort, Benson*, 134.
83. See Cassis, *City Bankers*, 202–8, 257–61.
84. Guillaume de Bertier de Sauvigny, *The Bourbon Restoration*, trans. Lynn M. Case (Philadelphia: University of Pennsylvania Press, 1966), 247–49.
85. Youssef Cassis, "Businessmen and the Bourgeoisie in Western Europe," in *Bourgeois Society in Nineteenth-Century Europe*, ed. Jürgen Kocka and Allen Mitchell (Oxford: Berg, 1993), 119–20.
86. Ferguson, *House of Rothschild: The World's Banker*, 54.
87. The German case was also characterized by a deep penetration of elites by merchant bankers that had ties either to Britain or the United States—for instance, the Warburgs. Thus, it was perfectly normal for Max Warburg to dine with the kaiser in Hamburg "to discuss the general situation." Eduard Rosenbaum and A. J Sherman, *M. M. Warburg & Co., 1798–1938: Merchant Bankers of Hamburg* (London: C. Hurst, 1979), 111.
88. Bertrand Gille, *Histoire de la maison Rothschild*, 2 vols. (Geneva: Droz, 1965), 1:487.
89. Ferguson, *House of Rothschild: Money's Prophets*, 389.
90. Layna Mosley, *Global Capital and National Governments* (Cambridge: Cambridge University Press, 2003), 290.
91. For a different though related argument, see Pohle Fraser, "Personal and Impersonal Exchange."
92. Ferguson, *House of Rothschild: The World's Banker*, 458.
93. Mira Wilkins, *The History of Foreign Investment in the United States to 1914* (Cambridge, MA: Harvard University Press, 1989), 463, 467.
94. Wilkins, *History of Foreign Investment*, 476–77.
95. Richard Roberts, "What's in a Name? Merchants, Merchant Bankers, Accepting Houses, Issuing Houses, Industrial Bankers, and Investment Bankers," *Business History* 35, no. 3 (1993): 34.
96. Leslie Hannah, "What Did Morgan's Men Really Do?" (paper presented at the Business History Conference, Cleveland, OH, 2007), https://www.researchgate

.net/profile/Leslie_Hannah2/publication/24135378_What_did_Morgan's_Men
_really_do/links/0a85e537b748780abb000000.pdf (accessed 23 March 2022), 7.

97. *Money Trust Investigation: Investigation of Financial and Monetary Conditions in the United States Under House Resolutions 429 and 504 Before a Subcommittee of the Committee on Banking and Currency, Parts 1–29* (Washington, DC: Government Printing Office, 1913), 1056.

98. Susie J. Pak, *Gentlemen Bankers: The World of J. P. Morgan* (Cambridge, MA: Harvard University Press, 2013), 8.

99. Kathleen Burk, *Morgan Grenfell, 1838–1988: The Biography of a Merchant Bank* (Oxford: Oxford University Press, 1989), 62–63.

100. Burk, 65.

101. Burk, 66–67.

102. *Money Trust Investigation*, 1083–84.

103. *Money Trust Investigation*, 1084.

104. *Money Trust Investigation*, 1084.

105. Vincent Carosso, *The Morgans: Private International Bankers, 1854–1913* (Cambridge, MA: Harvard University Press, 1987), 202.

106. The whole notion of "character" has indeed been shown to be a cultural trait specific to the Victorian era. See Stefan Collini, "The Idea of 'Character' in Victorian Political Thought," *Transactions of the Royal Historical Society* 35 (1985): 29–50.

107. It should come as no surprise, then, that the author of a recent monograph on the Morgans took as her title *Gentlemen Bankers*. See Pak, *Gentlemen Bankers*. There is (rather oddly, I must admit) no discussion of the Cain and Hopkins thesis in this book.

108. Even actors such as the Dutch Republic, not structured around a court and a sovereign, found themselves relying on courtesy, lest they fell into a precarious position. See Burke, *Fortunes of the Courtier*, 129. Unlike the Venetian Republic headed by a doge (duke), the Republic could not be treated as a duchy or monarchy, though it certainly did seek such recognition. The office of *stadtholder* and the reliance on the House of Orange-Nassau was in part an attempt to remedy this problem, so the Republic might fit in the international society of which it was part.

4. THE OUTSIDERS—JOINT STOCK BANKS

1. The first "financial revolution" was the establishment of a permanent public debt. See Peter George Muir Dickson's classic *The Financial Revolution in England: A Study in the Development of Public Credit, 1688–1756* (London: Macmillan, 1967).

2. John Micklethwait and Adrian Wooldridge, *The Company: A Short History of a Revolutionary Idea* (London: Weidenfeld & Nicolson, 2003).

3. The Bank of England falls in this category. See David Kynaston, *Till Time's Last Sand: A History of the Bank of England, 1694–2013* (London: Bloomsbury, 2020), 1–8, 11–31.

4. Arthur Sullivan and William S. Gilbert, *Utopia Limited, Or, The Flowers of Progress: An Original Comic Opera in Two Acts* (London: Chappell, 1893).

5. For a good starting point, see Katharina Pistor, Yoram Keinan, Jan Kleinheisterkamp, and Mark D. West, "Evolution of Corporate Law: A Cross-Country Comparison," *University of Pennsylvania Journal of International Law* 23, no. 4 (2002): 791–871.

6. On this question, see Charles W. Munn, "The Emergence of Joint-Stock Banking in the British Isles: A Comparative Approach," *Business History* 30, no. 1 (1988): 69–83. There was, of course, the exception of the Bank of England.

7. Colin Arthur Cooke, *Corporation, Trust, and Company: An Essay in Legal History* (Manchester: Manchester University Press 1950), 121–23; Margaret Ackrill and Leslie Hannah, *Barclays: The Business of Banking, 1690–1996* (Cambridge: Cambridge University Press, 2001), 49.

8. Cooke, *Corporation, Trust, and Company*, 124–25.

9. Cooke, 166.

10. Cooke, 167; David Foucaud, "The Impact of the Companies Act of 1862," *Revue Économique* 62, no. 5 (2011): 873.

11. Foucaud, "Impact of the Companies Act," 873.

12. Youssef Cassis, *Capitals of Capital: The Rise and Fall of International Financial Centres, 1780–2009* (Cambridge: Cambridge University Press, 2010), 47; Charles P. Kindleberger, *A Financial History of Western Europe* (London Routledge, 2006), 104. On the details of Lafitte's experience, see Fritz Redlich, "Jacques Lafitte and the Beginnings of Investment Banking in France," *Bulletin of the Business Historical Society* 22, nos. 4–6 (1948): 137–61.

13. Kindleberger, *Financial History of Western Europe*, 104; Alain Plessis, "The History of Banks in France," in *Handbook on the History of European Banks*, ed. Manfred Pohl and Sabine Freitag (Aldershot: Edward Elgar, 1994), 188–89. This was the crisis that led to the creation of the Comptoir d'Escompte de Paris, by statesmen of the Second Republic (1848–1852), the second French experience with joint stock banks. See Nicolas Stoskopf, "La fondation du comptoir national d'escompte de Paris, banque révolutionnaire (1848)," *Histoire, économie et société* 21, no. 3 (2002): 395–411.

14. Jean Bouvier, *Un siècle de banque française* (Paris: Hachette, 1973), 91–94.

15. For a good overview of the history of German corporate law, see Peter Muchlinski, "The Development of German Corporate Law to 1990: An Historical Reappraisal," *German Law Journal* 14, no. 2 (2013): 339–79.

16. Richard Tilly, "Germany," in *Handbook on the History of European Banks*, ed. Manfred Pohl and Sabine Freitag (Aldershot: Edward Elgar, 1994), 302.

17. This is one of the points made in Alexander Gerschenkron, *Economic Backwardness in Historical Perspective: A Book of Essays* (Cambridge, MA: Belknap

Press of Harvard University Press, 1962). For a different view, see Caroline Foh-lin, "The History of Corporate Ownership and Control in Germany," in *A History of Corporate Governance Around the World: Family Business Groups to Professional Managers*, ed. Randall K. Morck (Chicago: University of Chicago Press, 2005), 223–82.

18. Tilly, "Germany," 303. The exception was the A. Schaffhausen'scher Bankver-ein from Cologne, which obtained joint stock status during the crisis of 1848 as an emergency measure.

19. Richard Tilly, "International Aspects of the Development of German Bank-ing," in *International Banking, 1870–1914*, ed. Rondo Cameron and Valerii I. Bovykin (Oxford: Oxford University Press, 1991), 303.

20. P. Barrett Whale, *Joint Stock Banking in Germany: A Study of the German Cred-itbanks Before and After the War* (London: Cass, 1968), 9.

21. Tilly, "Germany," 302.

22. Lothar Gall, Gerald D. Feldman, Harold James, Carl-Ludwig Holtfrerich, and Hans E. Büschgen, *The Deutsche Bank, 1870–1995* (London: Weidenfeld & Nicolson, 1995), 3. Banking laws and policy were largely decentralized in the German Confederation and, later, the North German Confederation. Some, such as Hanseatic cities, had a rather free incorporation policy for limited lia-bility companies (based on the Allgemeines Deutsches Handelsgesetzbuch of 1861). Others, such as Prussia and other large German states, did not, until 1870. See Timothy W. Guinnane, "Delegated Monitors, Large and Small: Ger-many's Banking System, 1800–1914," *Journal of Economic Literature* 40, no. 1 (2002): 79–80.

23. Tilly, "Germany," 304.

24. Mira Wilkins, *The History of Foreign Investment in the United States to 1914* (Cambridge, MA: Harvard University Press, 1989), 455.

25. Vincent P. Carosso and Richard Sylla, "U.S. Banks in International Finance," in *International Banking, 1870–1914*, ed. Rondo Cameron and Valerii I. Bovykin (Oxford: Oxford University Press, 1991), 51.

26. Wilkins, *History of Foreign Investment*, 467.

27. Morton J. Horwitz, *The Transformation of American Law, 1870–1960: The Cri-sis of Legal Orthodoxy* (Oxford: Oxford University Press, 1992), 4.

28. The regulations imposed by these two acts created three classes of banks: non-reserve ("country") banks, reserve city banks, and central reserve city banks. The country banks had to have a reserve of 15 percent against their liability deposits, and 9 percent could take the form of deposits in reserve city banks. In turn the reserve city banks had to amass reserves of 25 percent against their liability deposits, of which 12.5 percent could take the form of deposits in cen-tral reserve city banks. The latter category were essentially "national banks of New York City" and were in some sense the nation's central bank, acting as lenders of last resort until 1914. Carosso and Sylla, "U.S. Banks in International Finance," 54.

29. Wilkins, *History of Foreign Investment*, 455.

30. Wilkins, 455.

31. Thomas F. Huertas, "U.S. Multinational Banking: History and Prospects," in *Banks as Multinationals*, ed. Geoffrey Jones (London: Routledge, 1990), 249.

32. Mira Wilkins, "Foreign Investment in the U.S. Economy Before 1914," *Annals of the American Academy of Political and Social Science* 516, no. 1 (1991): 9–21; on America's rise as the world's banker from about 1916 onward, see Adam Tooze, *The Deluge: The Great War, America, and the Remaking of the Global Order, 1916–1931* (New York: Penguin, 2015), chap. 1.

33. To restate a point made earlier: there were of course joint stock banks that were active within empires. In the British Empire, these were referred to as "overseas banks." Similar institutions existed in France, Germany, and even the United States, where the International Banking Corporation (IBC) was perhaps the most famous such institution. On the last example, see Peter James Hudson, *Bankers and Empire: How Wall Street Colonized the Caribbean* (Chicago: University of Chicago Press, 2017). See also note 61.

34. Ellen Meiksins Wood, *The Pristine Culture of Capitalism: A Historical Essay on Old Regimes and Modern States* (London: Verso, 1991), 97–98.

35. On this question, see Stanley D. Chapman's interesting "The International Houses: The Continental Contribution to British Commerce, 1800–1860," *Journal of European Economic History* 6, no. 1 (1977): 5–48.

36. Cooke, *Corporation, Trust, and Company*, 122. There were thus four types of banks in England: 1) the small private deposit banks; 2) the merchant banks, both of which have in common the unlimited liability of their six (or fewer) partners; 3) the joint stock banks; and 4) the overseas banks, which were essentially joint stock banks based in the Empire.

37. Youssef Cassis, *City Bankers, 1890–1914* (Cambridge: Cambridge University Press, 1994), 14. The confusion between private bankers and merchant bankers, which can be observed in some of the literature, leads to confusing claims, such as the one made by David Landes that "the founders of British finance companies were established bankers . . . of the same stripe as those who had created the Crédit Mobiliers on the continent." See David S. Landes, *Bankers and Pashas: International Finance and Economic Imperialism in Egypt* (London: Heinemann, 1958), 58.

38. Cassis, *City Bankers*, 14–15.

39. Philip L. Cottrell, "United Kingdom," in *Handbook on the History of European Banks*, ed. Manfred Pohl and Sabine Freitag (Aldershot: Edward Elgar, 1994), 1144.

40. Cassis, *City Bankers*, 16.

41. Outside London, the shift took place from the mid-1860s onward, and by 1880 joint stock banks had "totally gained the upper hand." Philip Cottrell, "London's First 'Big Bang?' Institutional Change in the City, 1858–1883," in *The*

World of Private Banking, ed. Youssef Cassis and Philip Cottrell (London: Ashgate, 2009), 97.

42. Cassis, *City Bankers*, 18.
43. Cottrell, "London's First 'Big Bang?,' " 97–98.
44. *Bankers' Magazine*, 60 (1893): 745–46, cited in Cassis, *City Bankers*, 21.
45. Cassis, 20.
46. Cassis, 15.
47. Andrew Richard Dilley, "Gentlemanly Capitalism and the Dominions: London Finance, Australia, and Canada, 1900–14" (PhD diss., University of Oxford, 2006), 32.
48. Cassis, *City Bankers*, 27.
49. Cassis, 24.
50. Cassis, 25.
51. Cassis, 27.
52. Walter Bagehot cited in Ackrill and Hannah, *Barclays*, 49.
53. Cassis, *City Bankers*, 17.
54. Cassis, 102. The common features of private bankers and merchant bankers' educational profiles and lifestyle sometimes lead to confusion between the two groups. See Cottrell, "United Kingdom," 1143.
55. Dilley, "Gentlemanly Capitalism and the Dominions," 32. See also John Atkin, *The Foreign Exchange Market of London: Development Since 1900* (New York: Routledge, 2005), 5–22.
56. Cassis, *City Bankers*, 43.
57. There are two exceptions to note here. The first concerns Parr's, a bank involved in loan issues to Japan in the late 1890s and early 1900s. The main reason for this development was rather idiosyncratic: Parr's hired Allan Shand, who had worked for the Yokohama branch of the Chartered Mercantile Bank, a British imperial bank. While in Japan, Shand had taught a course on public finance organized by the Ministry of Finance and attended by Japan's first generation of modern bankers as well as government officials. He thus had extensive contacts with Japan's government and banking community. Philip L. Cottrell, "Great Britain," in *International Banking 1870–1914*, ed. Rondo Cameron and Valerii I. Bovykin (Oxford: Oxford University Press, 1991), 37; A. R. Holmes and Edwin Green, *Midland: 150 Years of Banking Business* (London: Batsford, 1986), 135. On the broader question of Japanese relations to the London capital market, see the interesting Toshio Suzuki, *Japanese Government Loan Issues on the London Capital Market, 1870–1913* (London: Athlone, 1994). In addition to Parr's curious case, there was the London Joint Stock Bank case, also noted as an exception by a number of scholars. In 1870, the German Disconto-Gesellschaft asked N. M. Rothschild & Sons to issue a loan to finance the Franco-Prussian War, but the London-based Rothschilds refused in part because of their strong connection to Rothschild Frères, based in France. At

this point, David Hansemann, chairman of the Disconto-Gesellschaft, approached the London Joint Stock Bank, which issued the Treasury bonds. The key point here is that the shift toward joint stock bank involvement in sovereign lending was taking place in Germany, not in England. It crept up in Britain, but remained extremely marginal. On this issue, see John Martin Kleeberg, "The Disconto-Gesellschaft and German Industrialization: A Critical Examination of the Career of a German Universal Bank, 1851–1914" (PhD diss., University of Oxford, 1988), 190; and Thomas Balogh, *Studies in Financial Organization* (Cambridge: Cambridge University Press, 1950), 112.

58. Holmes and Green, *Midland*, 134.

59. Cassis, *City Bankers*, 104.

60. Holmes and Green, *Midland*, 134.

61. Holmes and Green, 134–35. Of course, there was another type of joint stock bank involved in foreign operations, and that was the overseas bank of which the Hongkong and Shanghai Bank (later HSBC) is the prime example. A fascinating introduction to this area of international finance is Roberta A. Dayer, *Finance and Empire: Sir Charles Addis, 1861–1945* (Basingstoke: Macmillan, 1988). For an institutional history, see also Frank H. H. King, *History of the Hongkong and Shanghai Banking Corporation*, 4 vols. (Cambridge: Cambridge University Press, 1987). However, I will not deal with this type of bank in the present chapter, or in the rest of the book. In the introduction, I set out to explore how bankers knew sovereigns specifically in order to engage in the practice of sovereign lending. The overseas banks did not lend to sovereigns; they dealt with colonies where credit risk was mitigated by a unified jurisdictional system, and with countries whose finances were in part managed by Western powers—for instance, the Ottoman Empire and China. See Peter J. Cain and Antony G. Hopkins, *British Imperialism, 1688–2000* (London: Routledge, 2001), 360; and Olivier Accominotti, Marc Flandreau, and Riad Rezzik, "The Spread of Empire: Clio and the Measurement of Colonial Borrowing Costs," *Economic History Review* 64, no. 2 (2011): 385–407. The Bank of England and the London & Westminster Bank were both also involved in bond issues for self-governing colonies and their constituent states. See David Sunderland, *Managing the British Empire: The Crown Agents, 1833–1914* (Woodgate: Boydell & Brewer, 2004) 152–53.

62. Marcello De Cecco, *Money and Empire: The International Gold Standard, 1890–1914* (Oxford: Blackwell, 1974), 95.

63. Michael Lisle-Williams, "Beyond the Market: The Survival of Family Capitalism in the English Merchant Banks," *British Journal of Sociology* 35, no. 2 (1984): 246.

64. De Cecco, *Money and Empire*, 95.

65. De Cecco, 92–95.

66. Cassis, *City Bankers*, 25.

67. De Cecco, *Money and Empire*, 132–33.

68. Esteves, "Bondholder," 393.

69. Edwin Borchard, "Foreign Bondholders' Protective Organisations" (Faculty Scholarship Series Paper No. 3444, Yale University, 1933), http://digitalcommons .law.yale.edu/fss_papers/3444 (accessed 24 March 2022), 285.

70. Herbert Feis, *Europe: The World's Banker, 1870–1914* (London: Cass, 1961), 113.

71. Borchard, "Foreign Bondholders' Protective Organisations," 288–89.

72. Because the opposition between merchant banks and joint stock banks was less pronounced in France and Germany, we do not see similar fighting over their CFB equivalents. In France, the association created in 1898 was said to be too subservient to political power; in Germany, most banks were opposed to the creation of such an institution, apart from the Deutsche Bank (it appears to have been its chairman's—Georg Siemens—personal project). Such an association only saw the light of day in 1927. See Rui Pedro Esteves, "Quis Custodiet Quem? Sovereign Debt and Bondholders' Protection Before 1914," (Discussion Paper 323, University of Oxford, April 2007), 5–7, appendix 1.

73. Rondo Cameron, "Introduction," in *International Banking, 1870–1914*, ed. Rondo Cameron and Valerii I. Bovykin (Oxford: Oxford University Press, 1991), 14–15.

74. Wilkins, *History of Foreign Investment*, 463, 467.

75. Charles R. Geisst, *Wall Street: A History* (Oxford: Oxford University Press, 2012), 120.

76. Geisst, *Wall Street*, 124.

77. Karl Erich Born, cited in Carosso and Sylla, "U.S. Banks in International Finance," 50–51.

78. Wilkins, *History of Foreign Investment*, 476–77.

79. Wilkins, 456.

80. Wilkins, 474.

81. Hannah, "What Did Morgan's Men Really Do?," 7.

82. Carosso and Sylla, "U.S. Banks in International Finance," 68.

83. Cameron, "Introduction," 15.

84. Huertas, "U.S. Multinational Banking," 250; Carosso and Sylla, "U.S. Banks in International Finance," 52–53.

85. Huertas, 250; on the International Banking Corporation (ICB), see note 33.

86. Carosso and Sylla, "U.S. Banks in International Finance," 54–55; Hannah, "What Did Morgan's Men Really Do?," 7.

87. Partners in this bank included Jacob Schiff and Paul Warburg.

88. Carosso and Sylla, "U.S. Banks in International Finance," 68.

89. Carosso and Sylla, 69.

90. Susie Pak, *Gentlemen Bankers: The World of J. P. Morgan* (Cambridge, MA: Harvard University Press, 2013), 20–26.

91. Geisst, *Wall Street*, 178.

92. Interestingly, after this splitting of the banks, companies continued to use the same underwriters they had used in the past to issue their securities. As a

top-tier house inheriting J. P. Morgan & Co.'s prestige, Morgan Stanley remained the most reputable securities issuer. See Geisst, 256–59.

93. Geisst, 241. A key element of the blow dealt to Wall Street and particularly the main investment banks was the Securities and Exchange Commission's (SEC) Rule U-50. This rule required public utility companies to obtain competitive bids from underwriters. In other words, the SEC was forcing investment banks to compete, allowing public utilities to move beyond the more opaque relationship banking. See Geisst, 263–64.

94. Merchant bankers sometimes had shares in these joint stock banks. In England, some of them even had seats on the boards of London joint stock banks, but "there were not very many," and they were "not necessarily the most important." Cassis, *City Bankers*, 58–59.

95. Cameron, "Introduction," 9. On France in particular, see Rondo Cameron, *France and the Economic Development of Europe, 1800–1914: Conquests of Peace and Seeds of War* (Princeton, NJ: Princeton University Press, 1961). These commonalities may be indicative of Germany's—and, to a lesser extent, France's—economic "backwardness" in relation to England, and in this respect might be explained by the theory of uneven and combined development. On the relation between economic backwardness and the theory of "uneven and combined development," see Ben Selwyn, "Trotsky, Gerschenkron, and the Political Economy of Late Capitalist Development," *Economy and Society* 40, no. 3 (2011): 421–50. The classic statement on economic backwardness is Alexander Gerschenkron, *Economic Backwardness in Historical Perspective* (Cambridge, MA: Belknap Press of Harvard University Press, 1962).

96. David S. Landes makes this point in his classic article "Vieille banque et banque nouvelle: la révolution financière du dix-neuvième siècle," *Revue d'histoire moderne et contemporaine* 3, no. 3 (1956): 217.

97. Landes, "Vieille banque et banque nouvelle," 218. On these French banks, see Hubert Bonin, "The Case of the French Banks," in *International Banking, 1870–1914*, ed. Rondo Cameron and Valerii I. Bovykin (Oxford: Oxford University Press, 1991), 78.

98. The distinction is central to two key works on French finance; see Robert Bigo, *Les banques françaises au cours du XIXe siècle* (Paris: Recueil Sirey, 1947); and Hubert Bonin, *Le monde des banquiers français au XXe siècle* (Paris: Editions Complexe, 2000). Of course, there were also imperial banks, equivalent to the British overseas banks—for instance, the Banque de l'Indochine, which lasted far into the twentieth century. In fact, 40 percent of the Banque de l'Indochine's business was related to Chinese affairs: the HSBC's home market. See Plessis, "History of Banks in France," 210–12.

99. Bonin, *Le monde des banquiers français*, 41–42.

100. Prior to 1863, there was a vigorous contest between Rothschild Frères and the Crédit Mobilier, a powerful joint stock bank whose creation by the Péreire brothers had been supported by Napoleon III. For a history of their

confrontation across European markets, see the brief accounts in Bigo, *Les banques françaises*, 189; Bonin, "Case of the French Banks," 73; Cameron, "Introduction," 8–11; Landes, "Vieille banque et banque nouvelle," 205–6; and Plessis, "History of Banks in France," 189.

101. Bigo, *Les banques françaises*, 169.
102. Plessis, "History of Banks in France," 189.
103. Plessis, 189.
104. Bertrand Gille, *La banque en France au XIXe siècle: recherches historiques* (Paris: Droz, 1970), 243.
105. Marc Flandreau, "Le service des etudes financières sous Henri Germain (1871–1905): une macro-économie d'acteurs," in *Le Crédit Lyonnais, 1863–1986: études historiques* (Paris: Droz, 2003), 273.
106. Bernard Desjardins and Alain Plessis, "L'entreprise, ses hommes, ses métiers," in *Le Crédit Lyonnais, 1863–1986: études historiques*, ed. Bernard Desjardins, Michel Lescure, Roger Nougaret, Alain Plessis, and André Straus (Paris: Droz, 2003), 31–32.
107. Bonin, *Le monde des banquiers français*, 43.
108. Plessis, "History of Banks in France," 246.
109. Plessis, 246.
110. Plessis, 246.
111. This episode is recounted in more detail in Bernard van Marken and Piet A. Geljon, "La banque de crédit et de dépôt des Pays-Bas (Nederlandsche Credit en Deposito Bank): aux origines de la Banque de Paris et des Pays-Bas, 1863–1872," *Histoire, économie et société* 32, no. 1 (2013): 19–43.
112. Van Marken and Geljon, "La banque de crédit," 25. Bischoffsheim & Goldschmidt in London was the first employer of the famous financier Ernest Cassel.
113. Gall et al., *Deutsche Bank*, 3.
114. One cannot escape the observation that France seems to have evolved so differently from its neighbor across the Channel. Why did merchant bankers in France regroup in these new banks, while in England (and in the United States as well) they continued as independent houses? I have not come across a good explanation for these diverging paths, but see Bonin, "Case of the French Banks," 78; and Bonin, *Le monde des banquiers français*, 41.
115. Samir Saul, "Banking Alliances and International Issues on the Paris Capital Market, 1890–1914," in *London and Paris as International Financial Centres in the Twentieth Century*, ed. Eric Bussière and Youssef Cassis (Oxford: Oxford University Press, 2005), 136.
116. Bonin, *Le monde des banquiers français*, 44–45.
117. Bonin, 44–45.
118. Bonin, "Case of the French Banks," 78.
119. Bonin, *Le monde des banquiers français*, 46.
120. Saul, "Banking Alliances and International Issues," 132.

121. For a related point, see Youssef Cassis, "Le Crédit Lyonnais et Ses Concurrents Européens," in *Le Crédit Lyonnais, 1863–1986: études historiques,* ed. Bernard Desjardins, Michel Lescure, Roger Nougaret, Alain Plessis, and André Straus (Paris: Droz, 2003), 720. An obvious institution that linked the development of French and German joint stock banking was the Crédit Mobilier. For many European countries, and particularly Germany, the Crédit Mobilier provided an early example of a functioning joint stock bank engaged in many different financial operations. It had participated as early as 1853 in the creation of the first German joint stock bank, the Bank für Handel und Industrie in Darmstadt (Darmstädter). Some of the founders or first subscribers to the shares of the Crédit Mobilier, specifically the Cologne banking firm Sal. Oppenheim Jr. & Cie, were key players in the development of the Darmstädter. Tilly, "Germany," 303; Cameron, *France and the Economic Development,* 137, 148–49; Michael Stürmer, Gabriele Teichmann, and Wilhelm Treue, *Striking the Balance: Sal. Oppenheim Jr. & Cie—A Family and a Bank,* trans. Ewald Osers (London: Weidenfeld & Nicolson, 1994), 135–40. One German bank, the Cologne-based A. Schaffhausen'scher Bankverein, in fact preceded the Darmstädter as a joint stock bank, receiving a joint stock charter from the Prussian government in 1848 as an emergency measure to prevent its default.
122. Tilly, "International Aspects," 92.
123. On this issue, see Manfred Pohl, *Entstehung und Entwicklung des Universalbankensystems: Konzentration und Krise als wichtige Faktoren* (Frankfurt am Main: F. Knapp, 1986). To an extent, over time, the barrier between investment and deposit banks also broke down in France.
124. Cassis, *Capitals of Capital,* 108–9.
125. Tilly, "Germany," 301.
126. Tilly, "International Aspects," 91–93.
127. Fritz Stern, *Gold and Iron: Bismack, Blecihröder, and the Building of the German Empire* (New York: Vintage, 1979), xvii.
128. Niall Ferguson, *The House of Rothschild: Money's Prophets, 1798–1848* (London: Penguin, 1998), 285.
129. Gall et al., *Deutsche Bank,* 2.
130. Tilly, "Germany," 300.
131. Tilly, "International Aspects," 93.
132. Gall et al., *Deutsche Bank,* 6–7.
133. Gall et al., 6.
134. Gall et al., 3.
135. Gall et al., 5.
136. Stanley Zucker, *Ludwig Bamberger: German Liberal Political and Social Critic, 1823–1899* (Pittsburgh: University of Pittsburgh Press, 1975), 35.
137. Gall et al., *Deutsche Bank,* 6. The individuals in question were Baron Victor von Magnus, Hermann Zwicker, Adolph vom Rath, Gustav Kutter, and Gustav Müller.

138. Gall et al., 67–77.

139. Tilly, "International Aspects," 100.

140. Karl Erich Born, *Geld und Banken im 19. und 20. Jahrhundert* (Stuttgart: Kröner, 1977), 257.

141. Tilly, "International Aspects," 104.

142. Gall et al., *Deutsche Bank*, 118.

143. Gall et al., 119.

144. Gall et al., 14. The other managing director was Hermann Wallich.

145. Gall et al., 109.

146. On this broad issue, see Youssef Cassis and Eric Bussière, *London and Paris as International Finance Centres in the Twentieth Century* (Oxford: Oxford University Press, 2005); and Cassis, *Capitals of Capital*.

5. STATISTICS AS A FORM OF KNOWLEDGE

1. On the role of statistical models in finance, see particularly Donald MacKenzie, *An Engine, Not a Camera: How Financial Models Shape Markets* (Cambridge, MA: MIT Press, 2008).

2. For two examples, see Ian Hacking, *The Taming of Chance* (Cambridge: Cambridge University Press, 1990); and Theodore M. Porter, *The Rise of Statistical Thinking, 1820–1900* (Princeton, NJ: Princeton University Press, 1986).

3. "Statistics," *Oxford English Dictionary*, https://www.oed.com/view/Entry /189322?rskey=yxhDA5&result=2&isAdvanced=false#eid (accessed 22 April 2022).

4. A few textbooks make passing (if not fully accurate) reference to this original definition. One for instance notes that statistics "originally meant quantitative information about the government or state." See W. Paul Vogt and R. Burke Johnson, *Dictionary of Statistics and Methodology: A Nontechnical Guide for the Social Sciences* (Thousand Oaks, CA: SAGE, 2011), 380–81. For an excellent work on this original meaning of statistics, see Harm Klueting, *Die Lehre von der Macht der Staaten: Das aussenpolitische Machtproblem in der "politischen Wissenschaft" und in der praktischen Politik im 18. Jahrhundert* (Berlin: Duncker & Humblot, 1986).

5. These examples are taken from M. G. Kendall, "Where Shall the History of Statistics Begin?," in *Studies in the History of Statistics and Probability*, ed. E. S. Pearson and M. G. Kendall (London: Griffin, 1970), 45–46. The view according to which any instance of a government collecting data in order to govern qualifies as "statistics" is not uncommon in contemporary scholarship. On this account, statistics have existed for millennia, they simply took on a more public and large-scale form in the modern era. As I explain in what follows, the word "statistics" is relatively recent and initially meant something far more specific.

6. Kendall, "History of Statistics," 45.
7. Johann Wolfgang Von Goethe, *Italian Journey: 1786–1788*, trans. W. H. Auden and Elizabeth Mayer (London: Penguin, 1992), 37–38.
8. See Keith Tribe, *Governing Economy: The Reformation of German Economic Discourse, 1750–1840* (Cambridge: Cambridge University Press, 1988); and Andre Wakefield, *The Disordered Police State: German Cameralism as Science and Practice* (Chicago: University of Chicago Press, 2009). Keith Tribe's work is particularly interesting, as it explores the decoupling of household rule and national government (for a brief overview, see 21–25), a theme recently explored in international relations; see Patricia Owens, *Economy of Force: Counterinsurgency and the Historical Rise of the Social* (Cambridge: Cambridge University Press, 2015).
9. His *Abriß der neuen Staatswissenschaft der vornehmen Europäischen Reiche und Republiken* (1749) was the first work of this type in German rather than Latin, and therefore helped spread statistics further afield. Alain Desrosières, *The Politics of Large Numbers: A History of Statistical Reasoning*, trans. Camille Naish (Cambridge, MA: Harvard University Press, 2002), 19; Paul F. Lazarsfeld, "Notes on the History of Quantification in Sociology–Trends, Sources, and Problems," *Isis* 52, no. 2 (1961): 284.
10. Klueting, *Macht der Staaten*, 40.
11. Lazarsfeld, "History of Quantification," 292–93.
12. This is often erroneously dated to a work of his "published" in 1589. The problem with this claim is that 1589 is the year of Ghilini's birth. See Kendall, "History of Statistics," 45.
13. Regarding the Venetian tradition, see Johan van der Zande, "Statistik and History in the German Enlightenment," *Journal of the History of Ideas* 71, no. 3 (2010): 412. Another author who published similar "statistical" material is Francesco Sansovino. See Harald Westergaard, *Contributions to the History of Statistics* (London: PSKing, 1932), 4; and Mohammed Rassem and Justin Stagl, eds., "Expose," in *Statistik Und Staatsbeschreibung in Der Neuzeit: Vornehmlich Im 16.–18. Jahrhundert* (Paderborn: Ferdinand Schoningh, 1980), 13. The question of the transfer of Italian thought to Germany is not so well explored, but, regarding Botero's work, one can turn to Michael Stolleis, "Zur Rezeption von Giovanni Botero in Deutschland," in *Botero e La "Ragion Di Stato." Atti Del Convegno in Memoria Di Luigi Firpo*, ed. A. Enzo Baldini (Florence, 1992), 405–16.
14. Even the difference between the earlier work of Germans such as Hermann Conring (1606–1681) and Gottfried Achenwall is striking. While the former was interested in the ends pursued by communities as well as their laws and customs, the latter reduced the purview of statistics to "Land und Leute" (states and peoples). See Guillaume Garner, "Statistique, géographie et savoirs sur l'espace en Allemagne (1780–1820)," *Cybergeo: European Journal of Geography*, no. 433 (November 28, 2008): 2; Zande, "Statistik and History," 415. Achenwall

had been a student at various German universities in the years around 1740, and, as a result, he would have met a widely established tradition of statistical work. Preceding him was a tradition of scholarship initiated in Germany in the lectures of Conring entitled *Notitia rerum publicarum*, which were published in the early eighteenth century. During his stay at the University of Leiden Conring himself came into close contact with members of what Jonathan Israel has termed the "radical enlightenment." See Jonathan I. Israel, *Radical Enlightenment: Philosophy and the Making of Modernity, 1650–1750* (Oxford: Oxford University Press, 2002). Scholars such as Martin Schmeitzel, professor of history and law at the University of Jena and later Halle, continued teaching this subject in the early eighteenth century, as did a string of other academics like Johann Christoph Becmann and Christian Gottfried Hoffmann. See Hans Erich Bödecker, "'Europe' in the Discourse of the Sciences of State in Eighteenth-Century Germany," *Cromohs* 8 (2003): 1; V. John, "The Term 'Statistics,'" *Journal of the Statistical Society of London* 46, no. 4 (1883): 658; and Lazarsfeld, "History of Quantification," 291.

15. Lazarsfeld, 292.

16. Lazarsfeld, 292.

17. Hans Erich Bödecker, "On the Origins of the 'Statistical Gaze': Modes of Perception, Forms of Knowledge, and Ways of Writing in the Early Social Sciences," in *Little Tools of Knowledge: Historical Essays on Academic and Bureaucratic Practices*, ed. Peter Becker and William Clark (Ann Arbor: University of Michigan Press, 2001), 186.

18. Bödecker, "Origins of the 'Statistical Gaze,'" 186–87.

19. On this theme, see Michael Friendly, "The Golden Age of Statistical Graphics," *Statistical Science* 23, no. 4 (2008): 502–35.

20. Garner, "Statistique, géographie et savoirs," 3–9; Bödecker, "Origins of the 'Statistical Gaze,'" 176, 181.

21. John, "Term 'Statistics,'" 670. On Crome's work, see Sybilla Nikolow, "A. F. W. Crome's Measurements of the 'Strength of the State': Statistical Representations in Central Europe Around 1800," *History of Political Economy* 33, no. 5 (2001): 23–56.

22. Zande, "Statistik and History," 420. On the role of A. H. L. Heeren in developing a historical argument about the existence of an 'international system' based on sovereign states, see Edward Keene, *Beyond the Anarchical Society: Grotius, Colonialism, and Order in World Politics* (Cambridge: Cambridge University Press, 2002), chap. 1.

23. Desrosières, *Politics of Large Numbers*, 21–22.

24. Bödecker, "Origins of the 'Statistical Gaze,'" 179.

25. It is therefore rather unsurprising that a historian like A. H. L. Heeren would have been annoyed by this turn of events. See Bödecker, 179.

26. For a similar point about British political arithmetic, see Lazarsfeld, "History of Quantification," 291.

27. Hacking, *Taming of Chance*, 24–25; Zande, "Statistik and History," 418–19.
28. Ted McCormick, *William Petty and the Ambitions of Political Arithmetic* (Oxford: Oxford University Press, 2009), 40–41.
29. John Sinclair cited in Hacking, *Taming of Chance*, 16.
30. McCormick, *William Petty*, 175–85, 300–301.
31. John Campbell, *The Present State of Europe*, 3rd ed. (London: Longman, 1752), chap. 2.
32. On this issue, see Edward Keene, "The Naming of Powers," *Cooperation and Conflict* 48, no. 2 (2013): 268–82.
33. Grete Klingenstein, "Book Review of *Die Lehre von der Macht der Staaten: Das aussenpolitische Machtproblem in der "Politischen Wissenschaft" und in der praktischen Politik im 18. Jahrhundert*, by Harm Klueting, *English Historical Review* 103, no. 406 (1988): 136.
34. H. M. Scott, *The Emergence of the Eastern Powers, 1756–1775* (Cambridge: Cambridge University Press, 2001), 1–10.
35. This omission was based on an agreement with his colleague Johan Stephan Pütter, who taught German Imperial law. See Zande, "Statistik and History," 416–17.
36. Keene, "Naming of Powers," 270; Klueting, *Die Lehre von der Macht der Staaten*.
37. Keene, 274–75.
38. From this perspective, it is also unsurprising that what some see as the ancestor of German statistics developed in the northern Italian cities of the Renaissance. The works of Girolamo Ghilini, Francesco Sansovino, and Giovanni Botero all appeared in an international context that bore some resemblance to the one of late seventeenth- and early eighteenth-century minor German states. See Edward Keene, "International Hierarchy and the Origins of the Modern Practice of Intervention," *Review of International Studies* 39, no. 5 (2013): 1087; Kendall, "History of Statistics," 45; and Harald Westergaard, *Contributions to the History of Statistics* (London: PSKing, 1932), 4.
39. Klueting, *Macht der Staaten*, 56.
40. Martti Koskenniemi, "Into Positivism: Georg Friedrich von Martens (1756–1821) and Modern International Law," *Constellations* 15, no. 2 (2008): 93.
41. Keith Tribe, *Governing Economy: The Reformation of German Economic Discourse, 1750–1840* (Cambridge: Cambridge University Press, 1988), 42. In this book, Tribe explains that cameral sciences were absolutely key in adapting the discourse of natural law to practical issues of government. It should be noted that it was the Protestant universities who were forerunners in this movement, as the Catholic universities were, as Tribe puts it, "moribund" (47).
42. Klueting, *Macht der Staaten*, 40.
43. Koskenniemi, "Into Positivism," 193.
44. Klueting, *Macht der Staaten*, 295–98.

45. Johann Ludwig Klüber, *Acten Des Wiener Congresses, in Den Jahren 1814 und 1815* (Erlangen: J. J. Palm und E. Enke, 1832), 17–23; Klueting, *Macht der Staaten*, 298–300. Interestingly, Pütter also taught law to G. F. von Martens, who would go on to become one of the most important figures in the development of modern international law; see Koskenniemi, "Into Positivism," 193.

46. Heinz Duchhardt, *Gleichgewicht der Kräfte, Convenance, europäisches Konzert : Friedenskongresse u. Friedensschlüsse vom Zeitalter Ludwigs XIV. bis zum Wiener Kongress* (Darmstadt: Wissenschaftliche Buchgesellschaft, 1976), 174; Klueting, *Macht der Staaten*, 299–301.

47. Bödecker, "Origins of the 'Statistical Gaze,'" 189.

48. Hacking, *Taming of Chance*, 20. See also the remarks in Michel Armatte, "Une discipline dans tous ses états: la statistique à travers ses traités (1800–1914)," *Revue de synthèse* 112, no. 2 (April 1991): 168.

49. Nico Randeraad, *States and Statistics in the Nineteenth Century: Europe by Numbers* (Manchester: Manchester University Press, 2010), 72.

50. Bödecker, "Origins of the 'Statistical Gaze,'" 190.

51. Bödecker, 190.

52. Klueting, *Macht der Staaten*, 63–65. To state the obvious, for statistics to become public, some kind of "public sphere" had to exist. Public spheres slowly developed in Europe beginning in the early modern period, notably through journals and periodicals of all sorts. But, as scholars such as Jürgen Habermas and Timothy Blanning have shown, it was in the eighteenth century that the public sphere was really established, notably because of the sheer number of pamphlets and publications of all sorts that emerged. See T. C. W. Blanning, *The Culture of Power and the Power of Culture: Old Regime Europe, 1660–1789* (Oxford: Oxford University Press, 2002); and Jürgen Habermas, *The Structural Transformation of the Public Sphere: An Inquiry into a Category of Bourgeois Society* (Cambridge: Polity, 1989).

53. Klueting, *Macht der Staaten*, 66.

54. Helmut D. Schmidt, "Schlozer on Historiography," *History and Theory* 18, no. 1 (1979): 38.

55. Westergaard, *History of Statistics*, 113.

56. Westergaard, 114–15.

57. Desrosières, *Politics of Large Numbers*, 151.

58. Desrosières, 179.

59. Hacking, *Taming of Chance*, 34; Westergaard, *History of Statistics*, 173.

60. Hacking, *Taming of Chance*, 34.

61. Westergaard, *History of Statistics*, 173.

62. Theodore M. Porter, *Rise of Statistical Thinking, 1820–1900* (Princeton, NJ: Princeton University Press, 1986), 38–39.

63. Randeraad, *States and Statistics*, 112.

64. Klueting, *Macht der Staaten*, 297.

65. The towering figure in Austrian statistics was Carl von Czoernig, who had studied in Vienna, at a university that bore the imprint of the prominent cameralists, Justi and Sonnenfels. See Randeraad, *States and Statistics*, 77.

66. Desrosières, *Politics of Large Numbers*, 167.

67. Westergaard, *History of Statistics*, 119.

68. Desrosières, *Politics of Large Numbers*, 196; Westergaard, *History of Statistics*, 120.

69. Desrosières, 154; Zheng Kang, "La société de statistique de Paris au XIXe siècle: un lieu de savoir social," *Les cahiers du Centre de Recherches Historiques* 9 (1992), http://ccrh.revues.org/2808 (accessed 28 July 2015).

70. Avner Bar-Hen, "Les 150 ans de La Société de Statistique de Paris," CNRS-images des mathématiques, 23 September 2010, http://images.math.cnrs.fr/Les-150-ans-de-la-Societe-de.html#nh3.

71. Desrosières, *Politics of Large Numbers*, 173; Porter, *Rise of Statistical Thinking*, 31.

72. Desrosières, 185.

73. Westergaard, *History of Statistics*, 172.

74. MacKenzie, *Statistics in Britain*, 8.

75. Porter, *Rise of Statistical Thinking*, 35–36.

76. Charles Fenn, *A Compendium of the English and Foreign Funds, and the Principal Joint Stock Companies, Forming an Epitome of the Various Objects of Investment Negotiable in London; with Some Account of the Internal Debt and Revenues of the Foreign States and Tables for Calculating the Value of Different Stocks, Etc.* (London: Sherwood, Gilbert & Piper, 1837).

77. Andrew Odlyzko, "The Collapse of the Railway Mania, the Development of Capital Markets, and Robert Lucas Nash, a Forgotten Pioneer of Accounting and Financial Analysis," SSRN Scholarly Paper, Rochester, New York, 23 January 2011, http://papers.ssrn.com/abstract=1625738, 42–43. Wilson had himself founded a joint stock bank, the Chartered Bank of India, Australia, and China (later Standard Chartered Bank).

78. Odlyzko, "Collapse of the Railway Mania," 42–43. Nash published widely on financial matters. He based one of his most famous books, *A Short Inquiry into the Profitable Nature of our Investments*, on an article on foreign investments by Hyde Clarke (secretary of the Corporation of Foreign Bondholders) in the *Journal of the Statistical Society of London*. It is, however, noteworthy that it contained no information about sovereigns' finances, but only data about bond prices and yields. See Hyde Clarke, "On the Debts of Sovereign and Quasi-Sovereign States, Owing by Foreign Countries," *Journal of the Statistical Society of London* 41, no. 2 (1878), 299–347; and Robert Lucas Nash, *A Short Inquiry into the Profitable Nature of Our Investments: With a Record of Five Hundred of Our Most Important Public Securities During the Ten Years 1870 to 1880* (London: Effingham Wilson, 1880), 2.

79. Marc Flandreau, "Caveat Emptor: Coping with Sovereign Risk Without the Multilaterals" (discussion paper, Centre for Economic Policy Research, London, 1998), http://www.cepr.org/pubs/dps/DP2004.asp (accessed 25 March 2022).

80. Flandreau, "Caveat Emptor," 5.

81. Odlyzko, "Collapse of the Railway Mania," 42–43.

82. Ruth Dudley Edwards, *The Pursuit of Reason: The Economist, 1843–1993* (London: Hamish Hamilton, 1993), 280.

83. André Vanoli, *A History of National Accounting* (Oxford: IOS, 2005), 11. On this issue, see also Paul Studenski's classic *The Income of Nations* (New York: New York University Press, 1958).

84. Vanoli, *History of National Accounting*, 7.

85. M. G. Brock and M. C. Curthoys, eds., *The History of the University of Oxford: Nineteenth-Century Oxford, Pt. 1, Vol. 6* (Oxford: Clarendon, 1997), 499.

86. In Britain and France, manuals of banking and accounting did exist—for instance, James Gilbart's *Practical Treatise* (1827), and John Dalton's *Banker's Clerk* (1843), but these were nothing close to "formal arrangements for tuition." See Edwin Green, *Debtors to Their Profession: A History of the Institute of Bankers, 1879–1979* (London: Methuen, 1979), 5.

87. Eugène Léautey, *L'enseignement commercial et les écoles de commerce en France et dans le monde entier* (Paris: Guillaumin et Cie., 1886), 9–10, 14–41.

88. The École Libre was, of course, not only dedicated to business but also in large part to government. This does not pose a problem for my argument, as we saw that statistics were originally developed out of foreign policy concerns. That it would be transmitted through a school in part dedicated to government makes a great deal of sense.

89. École Libre des Sciences Politiques, *L'École Libre des Sciences Politiques, 1871–1889* (Paris: Typographies Georges Chamerot, 1889), 13–14.

90. École Libre des Sciences Politiques, 66.

91. École Libre des Sciences Politiques, 122–23.

92. Marc Meuleau, "From Inheritors to Managers: The École Des Hautes Etudes Commerciales and Business Firms," in *Management and Business in Britain and France: The Age of the Corporate Economy*, ed. Youssef Cassis, François Crouzet, and Terry Gourvish (Oxford: Oxford University Press, 1995), 134–135.

93. Meuleau, "From Inheritors to Managers," 137.

94. Léautey, *L'enseignement commercial*, 539–40.

95. Green, *Debtors to Their Profession*, 34–36.

96. Studenski, *Income of Nations*, 140. In other words, the men involved in the training of joint stock bankers (not merchant bankers) were very involved in the production of comparative data about states.

97. A. R. Holmes and Edwin Green, *Midland: 150 Years of Banking Business* (London: Batsford, 1986), 134.

98. Holmes and Green, *Midland*, 133. Holden seems to have been particularly pre-occupied with the place of German Jews in international finance. See Yoshiro Kamitake, "Some Notes on the Life and Works of Sir Edward Holden," *Hitotsubashi Journal of Economics* 23, no. 2 (1983): 51–52.

99. On the Institute, see Green, *Debtors to Their Profession*.

100. Green, 47n, 52n.

101. Green, 82.

102. Green, 83.

103. Michael Sanderson, "French Influences on Technical and Managerial Education in England, 1870–1940," in *Management and Business in Britain and France: The Age of the Corporate Economy*, ed. Youssef Cassis, François Crouzet, and Terry Gourvish (Oxford: Oxford University Press, 1995), 119–21.

104. Sanderson, "French Influences," 119–21.

105. Gaëtan Pirou and Charles Rist, eds., *L'enseignement économique en France et à l'étranger* (Paris: Librairie du Recueil Sirey, 1937), 67–69.

106. Alon Kadish and Keith Tribe, "Introduction: The Supply of and Demand for Economic in Late Victorian Britain," in *The Market for Political Economy: The Advent of Economics in British University Culture* (London: Routledge, 1993), 8.

107. Christopher J. Napier, "Accounting and the Absence of a Business Economics Tradition in the United Kingdom," *European Accounting Review* 5, no. 3 (1996): 455–56.

108. H Müller-Merbach, "Management Science in Germany and Its Impact on German Management Practice," *Omega* 16, no. 3 (1988): 197; Pirou and Rist, *L'enseignement économique*, 129.

109. Müller-Merbach, "Management Science in Germany," 197.

110. Hannelore Ludwig, *Die wirtschafts- und sozialwissenschaftliche Lehre in Köln: von 1901 bis 1989/90* (Köln: Böhlau, 1991), 16–17.

111. Pirou and Rist, *L'enseignement économique*, 135.

112. Ludwig, *Die wirtschafts*, 50.

113. Lothar Gall, Gerald D. Feldman, Harold James, Carl-Ludwig Holtfrerich, and Hans E. Büschgen, *The Deutsche Bank, 1870–1995* (London: Weidenfeld & Nicolson, 1995), 113–21.

114. Gall et al., *Deutsche Bank*, 113–21.

115. Behlül Üsdiken, Alfred Kieser, and Peter Kjaer, "Academy, Economy, and Polity: Betriebswirtschaftslehre in Germany, Denmark, and Turkey Before 1945," *Business History* 46, no. 3 (2004): 387.

116. Gall et al., *Deutsche Bank*, 51–52.

117. Kadish and Tribe, "Introduction," 8.

118. W. J. Ashley, "The Universities and Commercial Education," *North American Review* 176, no. 554 (1903): 34.

119. Ashley, "Universities and Commercial Education," 33.

120. Alain Plessis, "The History of Banks in France," in *Handbook on the History of European Banks*, ed. Manfred Pohl and Sabine Freitag (Aldershot: Edward Elgar, 1994), 199–201.

121. Marc Flandreau, "Le service des etudes financières Sous Henri German (1871–1905): une macro-économie d'acteurs," in *Le Crédit Lyonnais, 1863–1986: études historiques*, ed. Bernard Desjardins, Michel Lescure, Roger Nougaret, Alain Plessis, and André Straus (Paris: Droz, 2003), 280.

122. Bertrand de Lafargue, "Henri Germain (1824–1905): un banquier en politique," in *Le Crédit Lyonnais, 1863–1986: études historiques*, ed. Bernard Desjardins, Michel Lescure, Roger Nougaret, Alain Plessis, and André Straus (Paris: Droz, 2003), 59.

123. Lafargue, "Henri Germain," 48.

124. Desrosières, *Politics of Large Numbers*, 154.

125. Flandreau, "Le service des etudes financières," 274.

126. Flandreau, 274–75.

127. Flandreau, 276–77.

128. Flandreau, 281–82.

129. Flandreau, 275–76.

130. Holmes and Green, *Midland*, 134.

131. This is to be contrasted with the output of credit rating agencies, which I shall discuss in the next chapter.

132. Flandreau, "Le service des etudes financières," 278–79.

133. On the link between statistics and public trust see Theodore M. Porter, *Trust in Numbers: The Pursuit of Objectivity in Science and Public Life* (Princeton, NJ: Princeton University Press, 1996).

134. What is perhaps most intriguing is the fact that some financial actors produced ratings of merchants or businesses during the nineteenth century, but never of sovereigns, which goes to show that the move from one to the other was by no means logical. In fact, I would go so far as to say that bankers saw sovereign lending as something qualitatively different from lending to a business or merchant. For comments on the rating of businesses by the Bank of England and the Bank of France, see Marc Flandreau and Stefano Ugolini, "Where It All Began: Lending of Last Resort at the Bank of England Monitoring During the Overend-Gurney Panic of 1866," in *The Origins, History, and Future of the Federal Reserve: A Return to Jekyll Island*, ed. Michael D. Bordo and William Roberds (Cambridge: Cambridge University Press, 2013), 120, 157n16; and Emmanuel Prunaux, "Les comptoirs d'escompte de la Banque de France," *Napoleonica* 6, no. 3 (2009): 49–98. See also Rowena Olegario, *A Culture of Credit: Embedding Trust and Transparency in American Business* (Cambridge, MA: Harvard University Press, 2006).

135. Ian Hacking, *The Emergence of Probability: A Philosophical Study of Early Ideas About Probability, Introduction and Statistical Inference* (Cambridge:

Cambridge University Press, 1984), 5. The statement in this case refers to the emergence of probabilistic statistics and its economic use. But, as we saw here, the development of statistics in the simpler sense of describing states through quantifiable facts was also not well correlated with economic need.

6. THE NEW SOVEREIGN LENDING TRIUMPHS

1. These are the what the Financial Stability Board as well as the Bank for International Settlements refer to as global systemically important financial institutions (G-SIFIs). To quote a prominent economic historian, "At a global level twenty to thirty banks matter." See Adam Tooze, *Crashed: How a Decade of Financial Crises Changed the World* (New York: Viking, 2018), 13.

2. Their emergence, role, and source of authority must be understood as a product of the specific American experience. Two scholars have recently provided a fresh perspective on the emergence of these agencies, arguing that it should not be attributed to the fact that they condensed information in grades and thus reduced transaction costs, or to American judges' particular preference for transparency. Instead, it was due to the specific structure of American banking and its laws, particularly to the fact that, unlike in most European countries, one could not use the price of acceptances as a scale of credit for domestic borrowers, as acceptances were legally hindered from circulating freely and widely across the United States. Thus, the information produced by credit rating agencies became extremely valuable. See Marc Flandreau and Gabriel Geisler Mesevage, "The Separation of Information and Lending and the Rise of Rating Agencies in the United States" (Working Paper 11/2014, Graduate Institute, Geneva, 2014). Nevertheless, it is also true that ratings produced by rating agencies were increasingly used by American courts from the 1900s on, and they were eventually enshrined in regulation in the 1930s. See Marc Flandreau and Joanna Kinga Slawatyniec, "Understanding Rating Addiction: U.S. Courts and the Origins of Rating Agencies' Regulatory License (1900–1940)" (Working Paper 11/2013, Graduate Institute, Geneva, 2013); Timothy J. Sinclair, *The New Masters of Capital: American Bond Rating Agencies and the Politics of Creditworthiness* (Ithaca, NY: Cornell University Press, 2005), 43–44; Richard Sylla, "A Historical Primer on the Business of Credit Rating," in *Ratings, Rating Agencies, and the Global Financial System*, ed. Richard M. Levich, Giovanni Majnoni, and Carmen Reinhart (New York: Springer, 2002)), 37.

3. On the importance of railways for the development of this business see Sylla, "Historical Primer."

4. Sinclair, *New Masters of Capital*, 23–24.

5. Sinclair, 24; Lawrence J. White, "The Credit Rating Industry: An Industrial Organization Analysis," in *Ratings, Rating Agencies, and the Global Financial*

System, ed. Richard M. Levich, Giovanni Majnoni, and Carmen M. Reinhart (New York: Springer, 2002), 8.

6. Sinclair, 24; White, "Credit Rating Industry," 8.

7. Sinclair, 24; White, 8.

8. Sinclair, 26.

9. Herwig Langohr and Patricia Langohr, *The Rating Agencies and Their Credit Ratings: What They Are, How They Work, and Why They Are Relevant* (Hoboken, NJ: John Wiley & Sons, 2009), 411–12.

10. See Youssef Cassis, *Capitals of Capital: The Rise and Fall of International Financial Centres, 1780–2009* (Cambridge: Cambridge University Press, 2010), chap. 4. The phrase ("world's banker") is from Herbert Feis, *Europe: The World's Banker, 1870–1914* (London: Cass, 1961).

11. Norbert Gaillard, *A Century of Sovereign Ratings* (New York: Springer, 2012), 4.

12. Gaillard, 4; Sinclair, *New Masters of Capital*, 24.

13. Flandreau and Kinga Slawatyniec, "Understanding Rating Addiction," 2.

14. Gaillard, *Century of Sovereign Ratings*, 35. On the League of Nations' role in this process, see Patricia Clavin, *Securing the World Economy: The Reinvention of the League of Nations, 1920–1946* (Oxford: Oxford University Press, 2013); and Yann Decorzant, *La Société des Nations et la naissance d'une conception de la régulation économique internationale* (Bruxelles: P.I.E-Peter Lang S.A., 2011).

15. Gaillard, 32.

16. Max Winkler, *Foreign Bonds, an Autopsy: A Study of Defaults and Repudiations of Government Obligations* (Philadelphia: Roland Swain, 1933). See also Max Winkler, *Investments of United States Capital in Latin America* (Boston: World Peace Foundation, 1928).

17. Gaillard, *Century of Sovereign Ratings*, 47–49.

18. Gaillard, 60.

19. Rawi Abdelal, *Capital Rules: The Construction of Global Finance* (Cambridge, MA: Harvard University Press, 2007), 167.

20. Norbert Gaillard, *Les agences de notation* (Paris: La Decouverte, 2010), 48; Standard & Poor's, "Rating Performance 2002: Default, Transition, Recovery, and Spreads," February 2003, https://www4.stat.ncsu.edu/~bloomfld/Ratings Performance.pdf (accessed 28 March 2022), 76. Canada was the only sovereign borrower exempt from the interest equalization tax. See Abdelal, *Capital Rules*, 167.

21. Gaillard, *Les agences de notation*, 48.

22. Clavin, *Securing the World Economy*, 1.

23. Clavin, 1.

24. Clavin, 2.

25. Juan H. Flores Zendejas and Yann Decorzant, "Going Multilateral? Financial Markets' Access and the League of Nations Loans, 1923–28," *Economic History Review* 69, no. 2 (2016): 657.

26. Clavin, *Securing the World Economy*, 6.

27. Clavin, 21–22.

28. Yann Decorzant and Juan H. Flores, "Public Borrowing in Harsh Times : The League of Nations Loans Revisited" (Working Papers in Economic History, Institute of Economics and Econometrics, Geneva School of Economics and Management, University of Geneva, 2012), http://ideas.repec.org/p/cte/whrepe /wp12-07.html (accessed 5 April 2022).

29. Flores Zendejas and Decorzant, "Going Multilateral?," 667.

30. American merchant banks themselves were beginning to change. For instance, in 1923, as it was negotiating a loan for Colombia, Blair & Co. suggested the Colombian government hire a financial expert from the Department of State. See Emily S. Rosenberg, *Financial Missionaries to the World: The Politics and Culture of Dollar Diplomacy, 1900–1930* (Durham, NC: Duke University Press, 2003), 159.

31. Clavin, *Securing the World Economy*, 2; Patricia Clavin and Jens-Wilhelm Wessel, "Transnationalism and the League of Nations: Understanding the Work of Its Economic and Financial Organisation," *Contemporary European History* 14, no. 4 (2005): 465–92; Yann Decorzant, "La Société des Nations et l'apparition d'un nouveau réseau d'expertise économique et financière (1914–1923)," *Critique internationale* 3, no. 52 (2011): 35–50.

32. Clavin, *Securing the World Economy*, 19.

33. Clavin, chap. 10.

34. Clavin, chaps. 8–10.

35. Flores Zendejas and Decorzant, "Going Multilateral?," 2. In a different vein, Julia Gray has recently examined how membership in (regional) economic organizations impacts investors' perceptions of different states. See Julia Gray, *The Company States Keep: International Economic Organizations and Investor Perceptions* (Cambridge: Cambridge University Press, 2013).

36. Clavin, *Securing the World Economy*, 36. I should point out that, for all its efforts, the League never managed to produce fully standardized statistics for central government debt. See Eric Monnet and Blaise Truong-Loï, "The History and Politics of Public Debt Accounting," in *A World of Public Debts: A Political History*, ed. Nicolas Barreyre and Nicolas Delalande (Cham: Palgrave Macmillan, 2020), 481–511.

37. Louis W. Pauly claims that these programs were more intrusive than the contemporary IMF ones. See Louis W. Pauly, "International Financial Institutions and National Economic Governance," in *International Financial History in the Twentieth Century: System and Anarchy*, ed. Marc Flandreau, Carl-Ludwig Holtfrerich, and Harold James (Cambridge: Cambridge University Press, 2002), 247.

38. Clavin, *Securing the World Economy*, 28. Similar commissioners were named in other league-assisted sovereign borrowers—for instance, Hungary. See Flores Zendejas and Decorzant, "Going Multilateral?," 14.

39. Flores Zendejas and Decorzant, 10–17.

40. John Moody, *The Masters of Capital: A Chronicle of Wall Street* (New Haven, CT: Yale University Press, 1919), iv, 4.

41. For a recent exception, see Jerome Roos, *Why Not Default? The Political Economy of Sovereign Debt* (Princeton, NJ: Princeton University Press, 2019), 109–24.

42. Abdelal, *Capital Rules*, 6. On "embedded liberalism," see John G. Ruggie, "International Regimes, Transactions, and Change: Embedded Liberalism in the Postwar Economic Order," *International Organization* 36, no. 2 (1982): 379–415.

43. Michael P. Dooley, "A Retrospective on the Debt Crisis" (Working Paper 4963, National Bureau of Economic Research, Cambridge, MA, December 1994), 3.

44. Vanessa Ogle, "State Rights Against Private Capital: The 'New International Economic Order' and the Struggle over Aid, Trade, and Foreign Investment, 1962–1981," *Humanity* 5, no. 2 (2014): 214. See also the work of Robert Wood, to which she refers. Robert E. Wood, *From Marshall Plan to Debt Crisis: Foreign Aid and Development Choices in the World Economy* (Berkeley: University of California Press, 1986), 83, table 7.

45. For a similar point, see Roos, *Why Not Default?*, 119.

46. Carmen M. Reinhart and M. Belen Sbrancia, "The Liquidation of Government Debt" (Working Paper 16893, National Bureau of Economic Research, Cambridge, MA, March 2011), http://www.nber.org/papers/w16893 (accessed 5 April 2022).

47. Mark Blyth, *Austerity: The History of a Dangerous Idea* (New York: Oxford University Press, 2013), 240. For a good summary of the various mechanisms through which this took place, see Reinhart and Sbrancia, "Liquidation of Government Debt," 3, 6. For the original coining of the term "financial repression," see Ronald I. McKinnon, *Money and Capital in Economic Development* (Washington, DC: Brookings Institution, 1973); and Edward S. Shaw, *Financial Deepening in Economic Development* (New York: Oxford University Press, 1973).

48. Michel Henry Bouchet, Ephraim Clark, and Bertrand Groslambert, *Country Risk Assessment: A Guide to Global Investment Strategy* (Hoboken, NJ: Wiley, 2003), 93. See also Ashok Vir Bhatia, "Sovereign Credit Ratings Methodology: An Evaluation" (working paper, International Monetary Fund, Washington, DC, October 2002), 5.

49. On this key question, see Abdelal, *Capital Rules*; and Eric Helleiner, *States and the Reemergence of Global Finance: From Bretton Woods to the 1990s* (Ithaca, NY: Cornell University Press, 1994). More recently, see also Jeremy Green, "Anglo-American Development, the Euromarkets, and the Deeper Origins of Neoliberal Deregulation," *Review of International Studies* 42, no. 3 (2016): 425–49; and Vanessa Ogle, "Archipelago Capitalism: Tax Havens, Offshore Money, and the State, 1950s–1970s," *American Historical Review* 122, no. 5 (2017): 1431–58.

50. For an excellent account of this development, see Green, "Anglo-American Development."

51. Green, 440. On Siegmund Warburg's remarkably important role, see Niall Ferguson, "Siegmund Warburg, the City of London, and the Financial Roots of European Integration," *Business History* 51, no. 3 (2009): 364–82; and Niall Ferguson, *High Financier: The Lives and Time of Siegmund Warburg* (New York: Penguin, 2010). Another prominent banker in this story is George Bolton. Born in 1900, Bolton had worked at the Société Générale in France, and later on at Helbert Wagg & Co., a London merchant bank that had participated in a number of league loans in the 1920s. In some ways, Bolton illustrates the transition between the old sovereign lending and the new, as his career spanned both types of institutions. See "Bolton, Sir George Lewis French," *Oxford Dictionary of National Biography*, https://www.oxforddnb.com/view/10.1093/ref:odnb /9780198614128.001.0001/odnb-9780198614128-e-46639?rskey=fodjLB&result =1 (accessed 22 April 2022).

52. On the emergence of these markets, see, for instance, Gary Burn, "The State, the City, and the Euromarkets," *Review of International Political Economy* 6, no. 2 (1999): 225–61; Green, "Anglo-American Development"; and Catherine R. Schenk, "The Origins of the Eurodollar Market in London: 1955–1963," *Explorations in Economic History* 35, no. 2 (1998): 221–38. For an excellent—though not wholly academic—introduction, see Ian M. Kerr, *A History of the Eurobond Market: The First 21 Years* (London: Euromoney, 1984).

53. Barbara Stallings, *Banker to the Third World: U.S. Portfolio Investment in Latin America, 1900–1986* (Berkeley: University of California Press, 1987), 90.

54. Green, "Anglo-American Development," 446. A comparison of the main lending syndicate leaders between 1963 and 1983 reveals the rise of joint stock banks and the slow demise of merchant banks. See Kerr, *History of the Eurobond Market*.

55. Geoffrey Jones, *British Multinational Banking, 1830–1990* (Oxford: Clarendon, 1993), 373–76; Green, "Anglo-American Development," 446. The "overseas" banks, formerly involved in banking within the British Empire, engaged in short-term operations abroad but generally refrained from providing long-term finance or merchant banking services, with the exception, perhaps, of HSBC.

56. Lisle-Williams, "Beyond the Market," 244. On the broader shift away from family capitalism in British finance, see also Michael Lisle-Williams, "Merchant Banking Dynasties in the English Class Structure: Ownership, Solidarity, and Kinship in the City of London, 1850–1960," *British Journal of Sociology* 35, no. 3 (1984): 333–62.

57. Pak, *Gentlemen Bankers*, 225.

58. Philip Augar, *The Death of Gentlemanly Capitalism: The Rise and Fall of London's Investment Banks* (London: Penguin, 2008).

59. Green, "Anglo-American Development," 432–33.

60. Green, 446. To get a sense of these developments at the time, see Peter T. Kilborn, "Eurodollar Market Booming in London," *New York Times*, 25 December 1976, https://www.nytimes.com/1976/12/25/archives/eurodollar -market-booming-in-london-international-deals-using-many.html.

61. Blaise Gadanecz, "The Syndicated Loan Market: Structure, Development, and Implications," *BIS Quarterly Review*, December 2004, 75–78. Until the early 1970s, "few developing countries could successfully borrow in financial markets." Bank lending still constituted a very minor part of sovereign lending, the overwhelming majority being provided by official lenders. See Henry J. Bitterman, *The Refunding of International Debt* (Durham, NC: Duke University Press, 1973), 3–36.

62. Yener Altunbas, Blaise Gadanecz, and Alper Kara, "The Evolution of Syndicated Loan Markets," *Service Industries Journal* 26, no. 6 (2006): 691–93.

63. Dooley, "Retrospective on the Debt Crisis," 3–4. Sovereign borrowers also tended to prefer private lenders, as, by comparison with official creditors, there was no strict conditionality involved.

64. Robert E. Weintraub, "International Debt: Crisis and Challenge," *Cato Journal* 4, no. 1 (1984): 33.

65. Reinhart and Sbrancia, "Liquidation of Government Debt," 8.

66. Gerald P. O'Driscoll and Eugenie D. Short, "Safety-Net Mechanisms: The Case of International Lending," *Cato Journal* 4, no. 1 (1984): 189. Sovereign ratings are particularly important, as rating agencies almost never rate domestic firms' foreign currency debt higher than it does its government's. This is the so-called sovereign ceiling. See Abdelal, *Capital Rules*, 162.

67. Raúl L. Madrid, *Overexposed: U.S. Banks Confront the Third World Debt Crisis* (Boulder, CO: Westview, 1992), 62. Walter Wriston is often associated with a famous quip about the fact that "countries don't go bust." On what Wriston really meant, see Alexis Rieffel, *Restructuring Sovereign Debt: The Case for Ad Hoc Machinery* (Washington, DC: Brookings Institution, 2003), 289–294.

68. Madrid, *Overexposed*, 62.

69. Stephen Goodman, "How the Big U.S. Banks Really Evaluate Sovereign Risks," *Euromoney*, February 1977, 105–10.

70. Madrid, *Overexposed*, 64.

71. Goodman, "How the Big U.S. Banks," 105.

72. O'Driscoll and Short, "Safety-Net Mechanisms," 191. On this problem more generally, see the excellent discussion in Monnet and Truong-Loï, "History and Politics."

73. The Group of Ten (G-10) was made up of Belgium, Canada, France, Germany, Italy, Japan, Sweden, Switzerland, the Netherlands, the United Kingdom, and the United States. Luxembourg was an "associate" member because of its monetary union with Belgium. See George Walker, *International Banking Regulation: Law, Policy, and Practice* (London: Kluwer, 2001), 42–43.

74. Basel Committee on Banking Supervision (BCBS), "International Convergence of Capital Measurement and Capital Standards" (Basel, July 1988). See Constantinos Stephanou and Juan Carlos Mendoza, "Credit Risk Measurement Under Basel II: An Overview and Implementation Issues for Developing Countries" (World Bank Policy Research Working Paper 3556, April 2005), 3.
75. For a sense of these discussions, see BCBS, "The Regulatory Treatment of Sovereign Exposures" (Basel, December 2017); and European Systemic Risk Board, "ESRB Report on the Regulatory Treatment of Sovereign Exposures" (Brussels, March 2015).
76. Quentin Bruneau, "In the Club: How and Why Central Bankers Created a Hierarchy of Sovereign Borrowers, c. 1988–2007," *Review of International Political Economy*, (forthcoming).
77. Together, these included: Australia, Australia, Belgium, Canada, Denmark, Finland, France, Germany, Greece, Iceland, Ireland, Italy, Japan, Luxembourg, the Netherlands, New Zealand, Norway, Portugal, Saudi Arabia, Spain, Sweden, Switzerland, Turkey, the United Kingdom, and the United States. The only exception to this rule was that claims on central governments denominated in the local currency were to be considered riskless. The main issue for non-OECD and non-GAB countries was that borrowing in their own currency was difficult, a problem commonly known as the "original sin." See Barry Eichengreen, Ricardo Hausmann, and Ugo Panizza, "Original Sin: The Pain, the Mystery, and the Road to Redemption," Inter-American Development Bank, Washington, DC, 2002. For a recent empirical study of the problem, see Pablo Ottonello and Diego J. Perez, "The Currency Composition of Sovereign Debt," *American Economic Journal: Macroeconomics* 11, no. 3 (2019): 174–208.
78. Abdelal, *Capital Rules*, 88.
79. See BS/88/98, BS/91/94, Bank for International Settlements Archive.
80. See Andrew Cornford, "The Global Implementation of Basel II: Prospects and Outstanding Problems" (Policy Issues in International Trade and Commodities Study Series No. 34, United Nations Conference on Trade and Development, New York and Geneva, 2006). For the European Union directives, see Directive 2006/49/EC of the European Parliament and of the Council of 14 June 2006 on the Capital Adequacy of Investment Firms and Credit Institutions, https://eur-lex.europa.eu/legal-content/EN/TXT/PDF/?uri=CELEX :32006L0049&from=EN (accessed 22 April 2022); and Directive 2006/48/ EC of the European Parliament and of the Council of 14 June 2006 Relating to the Taking Up and Pursuit of the Business of Credit Institutions, https:// eur-lex.europa.eu/legal-content/EN/TXT/PDF/?uri=CELEX:32006L0048 &from=EN (accessed 22 April 2022). For the United States, see Office of the Comptroller of the Currency, Federal Reserve Board, Federal Deposit Insurance Corporation, and Office of Thrift Supervision, "Risk-Based Capital Standards: Advanced Capital Adequacy Framework—Basel II; Final Rule," *Federal Register* 72, no. 235 (2007): 69287–445. Though the United States did

not force all of its banks to comply with it, banks with a large foreign exposure were in fact pushed to adopt the rules. Together, these banks accounted for 99 percent of the foreign assets owned by American banks and two-thirds of all the assets of the country's banks. See Cornford, "Global Implementation of Basel II," 4.

81. BCBS, "International Convergence of Capital Measurement and Capital Standards: A Revised Framework" (Basel, June 2004). On the implementation of Basel II, see Emily Jones and Alexandra O. Zeitz, "The Limits of Globalizing Basel Banking Standards," *Journal of Financial Regulation* 3, no. 1 (2017): 89–124. As Jones and Zeitz note, many non-BCBS members failed to implement Basel II's internal ratings provisions. However, the fact remains that wealth is so unevenly distributed in the global banking sector that adoption among BCBS members states has a disproportionate influence.

82. BCBS, "Basel II," 15–47, 48–112; Bank for International Settlements, "Treatment of Sovereign Risk in the Basel Capital Framework," *BIS Quarterly Review*, December 2013, 10–11; Stijn Claessens and Geert Embrechts, "Basel II, Sovereign Ratings and Transfer Risk External versus Internal Ratings" (paper presented at the Basel II: An Economic Assessment Conference, Bank for International Settlements, Basel, Switzerland, 17–18 May 2002).

83. Ranjit Lall, "From Failure to Failure: The Politics of International Banking Regulation," *Review of International Political Economy* 19, no. 4 (2012): 609–38.

84. "Turmoil Reveals the Inadequacy of Basel II," *Financial Times*, 27 February 2008, https://www.ft.com/content/0e8404a2-e54e-11dc-9334-0000779fd2ac (accessed 22 April 2022).

CONCLUSION

1. John Greenwald, "Greenspan's Rates of Wrath," *Time*, 28 November 1994, http://content.time.com/time/subscriber/article/0,33009,981879,00.html; Robin Wigglesworth, Joe Rennison, Eric Platt, and Colby Smith, "Return of the Bond Vigilantes: Will Inflation Fears Spoil the Post-Pandemic Party?," *Financial Times*, 26 February 2021, https://www.ft.com/content/542d6127-11e7 -47ff-86cb-dd7bd974cda3 (accessed 22 April 2022).

2. Adam Tooze, "Of Bond Vigilantes, Central Bankers, and the Crisis of 2008," in *A World of Public Debts: A Political History*, ed. Nicolas Barreyre and Nicolas Delalande (Cham: Palgrave Macmillan, 2020), 453–56; Ed Yardeni, "A Brief History of Ed Yardeni's 'Bond Vigilante' Model," Business Insider, 13 November 2013, https://www.businessinsider.com/bonds-and-nominal-gdp-2013-11.

3. For an overview, see Basel Committee on Banking Supervision, "The Regulatory Treatment of Sovereign Exposures" (Basel, December 2017); and European Systemic Risk Board, "ESRB Report on the Regulatory Treatment of Sovereign Exposures" (Brussels, March 2015).

4. Quentin Bruneau, "In the Club: How and Why Central Bankers Created a Hierarchy of Sovereign Borrowers, c. 1988–2007," *Review of International Political Economy*, (forthcoming).

5. Cited in Jan Fichtner and Eelke M. Heemskerk, "The New Permanent Universal Owners: Index Funds, Patient Capital, and the Distinction Between Feeble and Forceful Stewardship," *Economy and Society* 49, no. 4 (2020): 499–500.

6. See Fichtner and Heemskerk, "New Permanent Universal Owners"; Benjamin Braun, "Asset Manager Capitalism as a Corporate Governance Regime," in *The American Political Economy: Politics, Markets, and Power*, ed. Jacob S. Hacker, Alexander Hertel-Fernandez, Paul Pierson, and Kathleen Thelen (New York: Cambridge University Press, 2021), 270–94.

7. For a sense of this trend in recent years, see S. M. Ali Abbas, Laura Blattner, Mark De Broeck, Asmaa El-Ganainy, Malin Hu, and Abdelhak S Senhadji, "Sovereign Debt Composition in Advanced Economies: A Historical Perspective" (working paper, International Monetary Fund, Washington, DC, 2014); Serkan Arslanalp and Takahiro Tsuda, "Tracking Global Demand for Advanced Economy Sovereign Debt" (working paper, International Monetary Fund, Washington, DC, 2012); and Alvise Lennkh, Bernhard Bartels, and Thibault Vasse, "The Rise of Central Banks as Sovereign Debt Holders: Implications for Investor Bases" (SUERF Policy Note, European Money and Finance Forum, Vienna, October 2019).

8. For an interesting contrast of the two periods, see Daniela Gabor, "Revolution Without Revolutionaries: Interrogating the Return of Monetary Financing" (paper in the "Transformative Responses to the Crisis" series, Heinrich Böll Stiftung, 2020), https://transformative-responses.org/wp-content/uploads/2021/01/TR_Report_Gabor_FINAL.pdf (accessed 2 May 2022).

9. Joscha Wullweber, *Zentralbankkapitalismus: Transformationen des globalen Finanzsystems in Krisenzeiten* (Berlin: Suhrkamp, 2021), especially chapter 9.

BIBLIOGRAPHY

Abbas, S. M. Ali, Laura Blattner, Mark De Broeck, Asmaa El-Ganainy, and Malin Hu. "Sovereign Debt Composition in Advanced Economies: A Historical Perspective." Working paper, International Monetary Fund, Washington, DC, 2014.

Abdelal, Rawi. *Capital Rules: The Construction of Global Finance.* Cambridge, MA: Harvard University Press, 2007.

Accominotti, Olivier, Marc Flandreau, and Riad Rezzik. "The Spread of Empire: Clio and the Measurement of Colonial Borrowing Costs." *Economic History Review* 64, no. 2 (2011): 385–407.

Ackrill, Margaret, and Leslie Hannah. *Barclays: The Business of Banking, 1690–1996.* Cambridge: Cambridge University Press, 2001.

Adler, Emanuel, and Vincent Pouliot, eds. *International Practices.* Cambridge: Cambridge University Press, 2011.

——. "International Practices: Introduction and Framework." In *International Practices,* edited by Emanuel Adler and Vincent Pouliot, 3–35. Cambridge: Cambridge University Press, 2011.

Aggarwal, Vinod K. *Debt Games: Strategic Interaction in International Debt Rescheduling.* Cambridge: Cambridge University Press, 1996.

Alexandrowicz, Charles H. *An Introduction to the History of the Law of Nations in the East Indies (16th, 17th, and 18th Centuries).* Oxford: Clarendon, 1967.

Allan, Bentley B. "From Subjects to Objects: Knowledge in International Relations Theory." *European Journal of International Relations* 24, no. 4 (2017): 841–64.

——. "Producing the Climate: States, Scientists, and the Constitution of Global Governance Objects." *International Organization* 71, no. 1 (2017): 131–62.

Altunbas, Yener, Blaise Gadanecz, and Alper Kara. "The Evolution of Syndicated Loan Markets." *Service Industries Journal* 26, no. 6 (2006): 689–707.

Anderson, Matthew S. *The Rise of Modern Diplomacy, 1450–1919*. London: Routledge, 1993.

Archives Historiques du Crédit Lyonnais, Paris, France.

Armatte, Michel. "Une discipline dans tous ses états: la statistique à travers ses traités (1800–1914)." *Revue de synthèse* 112, no. 2 (April 1991): 161–206.

Armitage, David. *Foundations of Modern International Thought*. Cambridge: Cambridge University Press, 2012.

Arslanalp, Serkan, and Takahiro Tsuda. "Tracking Global Demand for Advanced Economy Sovereign Debt." Working paper, International Monetary Fund, Washington, DC, 2012.

Ashley, W. J. "The Universities and Commercial Education." *North American Review* 176, no. 554 (1903): 31–38.

Atkin, John. *The Foreign Exchange Market of London: Development Since 1900*. New York: Routledge, 2005.

Augar, Philip. *The Death of Gentlemanly Capitalism: The Rise and Fall of London's Investment Banks*. London: Penguin, 2008.

Ballard-Rosa, Cameron, Layna Mosley, and Rachel L. Wellhausen. "Contingent Advantage? Sovereign Borrowing, Democratic Institutions, and Global Capital Cycles." *British Journal of Political Science* 51, no. 1 (2021): 353–73.

Balogh, Thomas. *Studies in Financial Organization*. Cambridge: Cambridge University Press, 1950.

Balzac, Honoré de. *La Maison Nucingen*. Paris: Gallimard, 1989.

Bank for International Settlements. "Treatment of Sovereign Risk in the Basel Capital Framework." *BIS Quarterly Review*, December 2013, 10–11.

Bank for International Settlement Archives, Basel, Switzerland.

Bar-Hen, Avner. "Les 150 ans de La Société de Statistique de Paris." CNRS-Images des mathématiques, 23 September 2010. http://images.math.cnrs.fr/Les-150-ans-de-la-Societe-de.html#nh3.

Barkin, J. Samuel, and Laura Sjoberg. "Calculating Critique: Thinking Outside the Methods Matching Game." *Millennium—Journal of International Studies* 43, no. 3 (2015): 852–71.

Bartelson, Jens. *A Genealogy of Sovereignty*. Cambridge: Cambridge University Press, 1995.

——. *Visions of World Community*. Cambridge: Cambridge University Press, 2009.

Basel Committee on Banking Supervision. "International Convergence of Capital Measurement and Capital Standards." Basel, July 1988.

——. "International Convergence of Capital Measurement and Capital Standards: A Revised Framework." Basel, June 2004.

——. "The Regulatory Treatment of Sovereign Exposures." Basel, December 2017.

Beasley, Edward. "Marc Flandreau, *Anthropologists in the Stock Exchange*: A Financial History of Victorian Science," *American Historical Review* 123, no. 1 (2018): 306–7.

Beaulieu, Emily, Gary W. Cox, and Sebastian Saiegh. "Sovereign Debt and Regime Type: Reconsidering the Democratic Advantage." *International Organization* 66, no. 4 (October 2012): 709–38.

Bell, Duncan, ed. *Victorian Visions of Global Order: Empire and International Relations in Nineteenth-Century Political Thought.* Cambridge: Cambridge University Press, 2012.

Bergeron, Louis. "Banquiers, négociants et manufacturiers Parisiens du Directoire à l'Empire—Tome I." PhD diss., Paris IV-Sorbonne, 1975.

Bertier de Sauvigny, Guillaume de. *The Bourbon Restoration.* Translated by Lynn M. Case. Philadelphia: University of Pennsylvania Press, 1966.

Bhatia, Ashok Vir. "Sovereign Credit Ratings Methodology: An Evaluation." Working paper, International Monetary Fund, Washington, DC, October 2002.

Bigo, Robert. *Les banques françaises au cours du XIXe siècle.* Paris: Recueil Sirey, 1947.

Bitterman, Henry J. *The Refunding of International Debt.* Durham, NC: Duke University Press, 1973.

Blanning, T. C. W. *The Culture of Power and the Power of Culture: Old Regime Europe, 1660–1789.* Oxford: Oxford University Press, 2002.

Blyth, Mark. *Austerity: The History of a Dangerous Idea.* New York: Oxford University Press, 2013.

Bödecker, Hans Erich. "'Europe' in the Discourse of the Sciences of State in Eighteenth-Century Germany." *Cromohs* 8 (2003): 1–14.

——. "On the Origins of the 'Statistical Gaze': Modes of Perception, Forms of Knowledge, and Ways of Writing in the Early Social Sciences." In *Little Tools of Knowledge: Historical Essays on Academic and Bureaucratic Practices*, edited by Peter Becker and William Clark, 169–96. Ann Arbor: University of Michigan Press, 2001.

Bonin, Hubert. *La banque et les banquiers en france: du Moyen Age à nos jours.* Paris: Larousse, 1992.

——. "The Case of the French Banks." In *International Banking, 1870–1914*, edited by Rondo Cameron and Valerii I. Bovykin, 72–89. Oxford: Oxford University Press, 1991.

——. *Le monde des banquiers français au XXe siècle.* Paris: Editions Complexe, 2000.

Borchard, Edwin. "Foreign Bondholders' Protective Organisations." Faculty Scholarship Series Paper No. 3444, Yale University, 1933. http://digitalcommons.law .yale.edu/fss_papers/3444 (accessed 2 May 2022).

Bordo, Michael D., and Hugh Rockoff. "The Gold Standard as a 'Good Housekeeping Seal of Approval.'" *Journal of Economic History* 56, no. 2 (1996): 389–428.

Born, Karl Erich. *Geld und Banken im 19. und 20. Jahrhundert.* Stuttgart: Kröner, 1977.

Bouchet, Michel Henry, Ephraim Clark, and Bertrand Groslambert. *Country Risk Assessment: A Guide to Global Investment Strategy.* Hoboken, NJ: Wiley, 2003.

Bourdieu, Pierre. *Distinction: A Social Critique of the Judgement of Taste.* New York: Routledge, 2010.

——. *Esquisse d'une theorie de la pratique: précédé de trois études d'ethnologie kabyle.* Paris: Seuil, 2000.

——. *Homo academicus.* Paris: Éditions de Minuit, 1984.

——. *Langage et pouvoir symbolique.* Paris: Seuil, 2001.

——. *La noblesse d'Etat: grandes écoles et esprit de corps.* Paris: Editions de Minuit, 1989.

——. *Le sens pratique.* Paris: Editions de Minuit, 1980.

Bourdieu, Pierre, and Jean-Claude Passeron. *Les héritiers: les étudiants et la culture.* Paris: Editions de Minuit, 1964.

——. *La reproduction: eléments pour une théorie du système d'enseignement.* Paris: Editions de Minuit, 1970.

Bouvier, Jean. *Les Rothschild: histoire d'un capitalisme familial.* Paris: Editions Complexe, 1992.

——. *Un siècle de banque française.* Paris: Hachette, 1973.

Bouwsma, William J. "Lawyers and Early Modern Culture." *American Historical Review* 78, no. 2 (1973): 303–27.

Branch, Jordan. *The Cartographic State: Maps, Territory, and the Origins of Sovereignty.* Cambridge: Cambridge University Press, 2014.

Braun, Benjamin. "Asset Manager Capitalism as a Corporate Governance Regime." In *The American Political Economy: Politics, Markets, and Power,* edited by Jacob S. Hacker, Alexander Hertel-Fernandez, Paul Pierson, and Kathleen Thelen, 270–94. New York: Cambridge University Press, 2021.

Brett, Annabel S. *Changes of State: Nature and the Limits of the City in Early Modern Natural Law.* Princeton, NJ: Princeton University Press, 2014.

Brock, M. G, and M. C. Curthoys, eds. *The History of the University of Oxford: Nineteenth-Century Oxford, Pt. 1, Vol. 6.* Oxford: Clarendon, 1997.

Bruland, Kristine, and Patrick O'Brien. *From Family Firms to Corporate Capitalism: Essays in Business and Industrial History in Honour of Peter Mathias.* Oxford: Clarendon, 1998.

Bruneau, Quentin. "Converging Paths: Bounded Rationality, Practice Theory, and the Study of Change in Historical International Relations." *International Theory* 14, no. 1 (2022): 88–114.

——. "In the Club: How and Why Central Bankers Created a Hierarchy of Sovereign Borrowers, c. 1988–2007." *Review of International Political Economy,* forthcoming.

———. "The Long Nineteenth Century." In *The Oxford Handbook of History and International Relations*, edited by Mlada Bukovansky, Edward Keene, Christian Reus-Smit, and Maja Spanu. Oxford: Oxford University Press, forthcoming.

Bueger, Christian, and Frank Gadinger. *International Practice Theory: New Perspectives*. New York: Palgrave Macmillan, 2014.

Buisseret, David. "The Cartographic Definition of France's Eastern Boundary in the Early Seventeenth Century." *Imago Mundi* 36, no. 1 (1984): 72–80.

Buist, Marten G. *At Spes Non Fracta: Hope & Co., 1770–1815*. The Hague: Nijhoff, 1974.

Bull, Hedley. *The Anarchical Society: A Study of Order in World Politics*. 3rd ed. New York: Columbia University Press, 2002.

Bulle, Nathalie. "Pierre Bourdieu (1930–2002)." *L'année sociologique* 52, no. 2 (2008): 231–37.

Bulow, Jeremy I., and Kenneth Rogoff. "Sovereign Debt: Is to Forgive to Forget?" *American Economic Review* 79, no. 1 (1989): 43–50.

Burk, Kathleen. *Morgan Grenfell, 1838–1988: The Biography of a Merchant Bank*. Oxford: Oxford University Press, 1989.

Burke, Peter. *The Fortunes of the Courtier: The European Reception of Castiglione's Cortegiano*. Cambridge: Polity, 1995.

Burn, Gary. "The State, the City, and the Euromarkets." *Review of International Political Economy* 6, no. 2 (1999): 225–61.

Cain, Peter J., and Antony G. Hopkins. *British Imperialism, 1688–2000*. London: Routledge, 2001.

Callières, François de. *De la manière de négocier avec les souverains: de l'utilité des negociations, du choix des ambassadeurs & des envoyez, & des qualitez nécessaires pour réüssir dans ces emplois*. Amsterdam: La Compagnie, 1715.

———. *De la science du monde, et des connoissances utiles a la conduite de la vie*. Bruxelles: Chez Jean Leonard, 1717.

Cameron, Rondo. *France and the Economic Development of Europe, 1800–1914: Conquests of Peace and Seeds of War*. Princeton, NJ: Princeton University Press, 1961.

———. "Introduction." In *International Banking, 1870–1914*, edited by Rondo Cameron and Valerii I. Bovykin, 3–24. Oxford: Oxford University Press, 1991.

Campbell, John. *The Present State of Europe*. 3rd ed. London: Longman, 1752.

Carey, George G. *A New Guide to the Public Funds: Or, Every Man His Own Stock-Broker*. London: D. B. Woodward, 1825.

Carosso, Vincent. *The Morgans: Private International Bankers, 1854–1913*. Cambridge, MA: Harvard University Press, 1987.

Carosso, Vincent P., and Richard Sylla. "U.S. Banks in International Finance." In *International Banking, 1870–1914*, edited by Rondo Cameron and Valerii I. Bovykin, 48–71. Oxford: Oxford University Press, 1991.

Cassis, Youssef. "Businessmen and the Bourgeoisie in Western Europe." In *Bourgeois Society in Nineteenth-Century Europe*, edited by Jürgen Kocka and Allen Mitchell, 103–24. Oxford: Berg, 1993.

——. *Capitals of Capital: The Rise and Fall of International Financial Centres, 1780–2009*. Cambridge: Cambridge University Press, 2010.

——. *City Bankers, 1890–1914*. Cambridge: Cambridge University Press, 1994.

——. "Le Crédit Lyonnais et ses concurrents européens." In *Le Crédit Lyonnais, 1863–1986: études historiques*, edited by Bernard Desjardins, Michel Lescure, Roger Nougaret, Alain Plessis, and André Straus, 711–23. Paris: Droz, 2003.

Cassis, Youssef, and Eric Bussière. *London and Paris as International Finance Centres in the Twentieth Century*. Oxford: Oxford University Press, 2005.

Cassis, Youssef, and Philip Cottrell, eds. *The World of Private Banking*. Farnham: Ashgate, 2009.

Castiglione, Baldassare. *Il Cortegiano*. Venetia: Nelle case d'Aldo Romano, & d'Andra d'Asola suo suocero, 1528.

——. *The Courtyer of Count Baldessar Castilio: Diuided into Foure Bookes. Very Necessary and Profitable for Yonge Gentilmen and Gentilwomen Abiding in Court, Palaice, or Place, Done into English by Thomas Hoby*. Translated by Sir Thomas Hoby. London: By Wyllyam Seres at the Signe of the Hedghogge, 1561.

Certeau, Michel de. *L'invention du quotidien, tome 1: arts de faire*. Paris: Gallimard, 1990.

Chapman, Stanley D. "The International Houses: The Continental Contribution to British Commerce, 1800–1860." *Journal of European Economic History* 6, no. 1 (1977): 5–48.

——. *The Rise of Merchant Banking*. London: Allen & Unwin, 1984.

Chester, Sir Norman. *Economics, Politics, and Social Studies in Oxford, 1900–85*. London: Globe Education, 1986.

Chwieroth, Jeffrey M. *Capital Ideas: The IMF and the Rise of Financial Liberalization*. Princeton, NJ: Princeton University Press, 2010.

Claessens, Stijn, and Geert Embrechts. "Basel II, Sovereign Ratings and Transfer Risk External Versus Internal Ratings." Paper presented at the Basel II: An Economic Assessment Conference, Bank for International Settlements, Basel, 17–18 May 2002.

Clarke, Hyde. "On the Debts of Sovereign and Quasi-Sovereign States, Owing by Foreign Countries." *Journal of the Statistical Society of London* 41, no. 2 (1878): 299–347.

Clavin, Patricia. *Securing the World Economy: The Reinvention of the League of Nations, 1920–1946*. Oxford: Oxford University Press, 2013.

Clavin, Patricia, and Jens-Wilhelm Wessel. "Transnationalism and the League of Nations: Understanding the Work of Its Economic and Financial Organisation." *Contemporary European History* 14, no. 4 (2005): 465–92.

Cohn, Bernard S. *Colonialism and Its Forms of Knowledge: The British in India*. Princeton, NJ: Princeton University Press, 1996.

Collini, Stefan. "The Idea of 'Character' in Victorian Political Thought." *Transactions of the Royal Historical Society* 35 (1985): 29–50.

Cooke, Colin Arthur. *Corporation, Trust, and Company: An Essay in Legal History*. Manchester: Manchester University Press, 1950.

Cooley, Alexander, and Jack Snyder, eds. *Ranking the World: Grading States as a Tool of Global Governance*. Cambridge: Cambridge University Press, 2015.

Cornford, Andrew. "The Global Implementation of Basel II: Prospects and Outstanding Problems." Policy Issues in International Trade and Commodities Study Series No. 34., United Nations Conference on Trade and Development, New York and Geneva, 2006.

Coss, Peter R., and Maurice H. Keen. *Heraldry, Pageantry, and Social Display in Medieval England*. London: Boydell, 2002.

Cottrell, Philip. "Great Britain." In *International Banking, 1870–1914*, edited by Rondo Cameron and Valerii I. Bovykin, 25–47. Oxford: Oxford University Press, 1991.

——. "London's First 'Big Bang?' Institutional Change in the City, 1858–1883." In *The World of Private Banking*, edited by Youssef Cassis and Philip Cottrell, 61–98. London: Ashgate, 2009.

——. "United Kingdom." In *Handbook on the History of European Banks*, edited by Manfred Pohl and Sabine Freitag, 1135–1274. Aldershot: Edward Elgar, 1994.

Cox, Gary W., and Sebastian M. Saiegh. "Executive Constraint and Sovereign Debt: Quasi-Experimental Evidence from Argentina During the Baring Crisis." *Comparative Political Studies* 51, no. 11 (2018): 1504–25.

Crook, J. Mordaunt. *The Rise of the Nouveaux Riches: Style and Status in Victorian and Edwardian Architecture*. London: John Murray, 1999.

Cross, Mai'a K Davis. *The European Diplomatic Corps: Diplomats and International Cooperation from Westphalia to Maastricht*. Basingstoke: Palgrave Macmillan, 2008.

——. "Rethinking Epistemic Communities Twenty Years Later." *Review of International Studies* 39, no. 1 (2013): 137–60.

Davis, Kevin, Angelina Fisher, Benedict Kingsbury, and Sally Engle Merry, eds. *Governance by Indicators: Global Power Through Quantification and Rankings*. Oxford: Oxford University Press, 2012.

Davis, Lance Edwin, and Robert A. Huttenback. *Mammon and the Pursuit of Empire: The Political Economy of British Imperialism, 1860–1912*. Cambridge: Cambridge University Press, 1986.

Dayer, Roberta A. *Finance and Empire: Sir Charles Addis, 1861–1945*. Basingstoke: Macmillan, 1988.

De Cecco, Marcello. *Money and Empire: The International Gold Standard, 1890–1914*. Oxford: Blackwell, 1974.

Decorzant, Yann. "La Société des Nations et l'apparition d'un nouveau réseau d'expertise économique et financière (1914–1923)." *Critique internationale* 3, no. 52 (2011): 35–50.

——. *La Société des Nations et la naissance d'une conception de la régulation économique internationale*. Brussels: PIE-Peter Lang, 2011.

Decorzant, Yann, and Juan H. Flores. "Public Borrowing in Harsh Times: The League of Nations Loans Revisited." Working Papers in Economic History, Institute of Economics and Econometrics, Geneva School of Economics and Management, University of Geneva, 2012. http://ideas.repec.org/p/cte/whrepe /wp12-07.html (accessed 5 April 2022).

Deringer, William. *Calculated Values: Finance, Politics, and the Quantitative Age.* Cambridge, MA: Harvard University Press, 2018.

Desjardins, Bernard, and Alain Plessis. "L'entreprise, ses hommes, ses métiers." In *Le Credit Lyonnais, 1863–1986: études historiques*, edited by Bernard Desjardins, Michel Lescure, Roger Nougaret, Alain Plessis, and André Straus, 23–32. Paris: Droz, 2003.

Desrosières, Alain. *The Politics of Large Numbers: A History of Statistical Reasoning.* Translated by Camille Naish. Cambridge, MA: Harvard University Press, 2002.

Desrosieres, Alain, and Emmanuel Didier. *Prouver et gouverner.* Paris: La Découverte, 2014.

Dezalay, Yves, and Bryant G. Garth. *Dealing in Virtue: International Commercial Arbitration and the Construction of a Transnational Legal Order.* Chicago: University of Chicago Press, 1998.

——. *The Internationalization of Palace Wars: Lawyers, Economists, and the Contest to Transform Latin American States.* Chicago: University Of Chicago Press, 2002.

Dickson, Peter George Muir. *The Financial Revolution in England: A Study in the Development of Public Credit, 1688–1756.* London: Macmillan, 1967.

Dilley, Andrew Richard. "Gentlemanly Capitalism and the Dominions: London Finance, Australia, and Canada, 1900–14." PhD diss., University of Oxford, 2006.

Directive 2006/48/EC of the European Parliament and of the Council of 14 June 2006 Relating to the Taking Up and Pursuit of the Business of Credit Institutions. https://eur-lex.europa.eu/legal-content/EN/TXT/PDF/?uri=CELEX:32006 L0048&from=EN (accessed 22 April 2022).

Directive 2006/49/EC of the European Parliament and of the Council of 14 June 2006 on the Capital Adequacy of Investment Firms and Credit Institutions. https://eur-lex.europa.eu/legal-content/EN/TXT/PDF/?uri=CELEX:32006 L0049&from=EN (accessed 22 April 2022).

Disraeli, Benjamin. *Coningsby or, The New Generation.* Leipzig: Berhn. Tauchnitz, 1844.

Dooley, Michael P. "A Retrospective on the Debt Crisis." NBER Working Paper 4963, National Bureau of Economic Research, Cambridge, MA, December 1994.

Duchhardt, Heinz. *Gleichgewicht der Kräfte, Convenance, europäisches Konzert : Friedenskongresse u. Friedensschlüsse vom Zeitalter Ludwigs XIV. bis zum Wiener Kongress.* Darmstadt: Wissenschaftliche Buchgesellschaft, 1976.

Duindam, Jeroen F. J. *Dynasties: A Global History of Power, 1300–1800*. Cambridge: Cambridge University Press, 2015.

——. *Vienna and Versailles: The Courts of Europe's Major Dynastic Rivals, 1550–1780*. Cambridge: Cambridge University Press, 2003.

École Libre des Sciences Politiques. *L'École Libre des Sciences Politiques, 1871–1889*. Paris: Typographies Georges Chamerot, 1889.

Edwards, Ruth Dudley. *The Pursuit of Reason: The* Economist, *1843–1993*. London: Hamish Hamilton, 1993.

Ehrenberg, Richard. *Capital and Finance in the Age of the Renaissance: A Study of the Fuggers and Their Connections*. New York: Augustus M. Kelley, 1963.

Eichengreen, Barry, Ricardo Hausmann, and Ugo Panizza. "Original Sin: The Pain, the Mystery, and the Road to Redemption." Inter-American Development Bank, Washington, DC, 2002.

Elias, Norbert. *The Civilizing Process*. Oxford: Blackwell, 1994.

——. *The Civilizing Process*. 2nd ed. Oxford: Blackwell, 2000.

Endelman, Todd M. *The Jews of Britain, 1656 to 2000*. Berkeley: University of California Press, 2002.

Esteves, Rui Pedro. "The Bondholder, the Sovereign, and the Banker: Sovereign Debt and Bondholders' Protection before 1914." *European Review of Economic History* 17, no. 4 (2013): 389–407.

——. "Quis Custodiet Quem? Sovereign Debt and Bondholders' Protection Before 1914." Discussion Paper 323, University of Oxford, April 2007. http://www .economics.ox.ac.uk/department-of-economics-discussion-paper-series/quis -custodiet-quem-sovereign-debt-and-bondholders-protection-before-1914 (accessed 5 April 2022).

European Systemic Risk Board. "ESRB Report on the Regulatory Treatment of Sovereign Exposures." Brussels, March 2015.

Feis, Herbert. *Europe: The World's Banker, 1870–1914*. London: Cass, 1961.

Fenn, Charles. *A Compendium of the English and Foreign Funds, and the Principal Joint Stock Companies, Forming an Epitome of the Various Objects of Investment Negotiable in London; with Some Account of the Internal Debt and Revenues of the Foreign States and Tables for Calculating the Value of Different Stocks, Etc.* London: Sherwood, Gilbert & Piper, 1837.

Ferguson, Niall. *High Financier: The Lives and Time of Siegmund Warburg*. New York: Penguin, 2010.

——. *The House of Rothschild: Money's Prophets, 1798–1848*. London: Penguin, 1998.

——. *The House of Rothschild: The World's Banker, 1849–1999*. London: Penguin, 2000.

——. "The Rise of the Rothschilds: The Family Firm as Multinational." In *The World of Private Banking*, edited by Youssef Cassis and Philip Cottrell, 1–30. Farnham: Ashgate, 2009.

——. "Siegmund Warburg, the City of London, and the Financial Roots of European Integration." *Business History* 51, no. 3 (2009): 364–82.

Ferguson, Niall, and Moritz Schularick. "The Empire Effect: The Determinants of Country Risk in the First Age of Globalization, 1880–1913." *Journal of Economic History* 66, no. 2 (2006): 283–312.

Fichtner, Jan, and Eelke M. Heemskerk. "The New Permanent Universal Owners: Index Funds, Patient Capital, and the Distinction Between Feeble and Forceful Stewardship." *Economy and Society* 49, no. 4 (2020): 493–515.

Finnemore, Martha. *The Purpose of Intervention: Changing Beliefs About the Use of Force*. Ithaca, NY: Cornell University Press, 2004.

Flandreau, Marc. "Anatomy of Regime Change: Underwriters' Reputation, New Deal Financial Acts and the Collapse of International Capital Markets (1920–1935)." Draft, Graduate Institute of International Studies and Development, Geneva, 18 August 2011. http://econ.as.nyu.edu/docs/IO/21858/Flandreau_10142011.pdf.

——. *Anthropologists in the Stock Exchange: A Financial History of Victorian Science*. Chicago: University of Chicago Press, 2016.

——. "Caveat Emptor: Coping with Sovereign Risk Without the Multilaterals." Discussion paper, Centre for Economic Policy Research, London, 1998. https://cepr.org/active/publications/discussion_papers/dp.php?dpno=2004# (accessed 29 April 2022).

——. "Le service des études financières sous Henri Germain (1871–1905): une macro-économie d'acteurs." In *Le Crédit Lyonnais, 1863–1986: études historiques*, 271–302. Paris: Droz, 2003.

——. *The Glitter of Gold: France, Bimetallism, and the Emergence of the International Gold Standard, 1848–1873*. Oxford: Oxford University Press, 2004.

Flandreau, Marc, and Frederic Zumer. *The Making of Global Finance, 1880–1913*. Paris: Organization for Economic Cooperation & Development, 2004.

Flandreau, Marc, and Gabriel Geisler Mesevage. "The Separation of Information and Lending and the Rise of Rating Agencies in the United States." Working Paper 11/2014, Graduate Institute of International Studies, Geneva, 2014.

Flandreau, Marc, and Juan H. Flores. "Bonds and Brands: Foundations of Sovereign Debt Markets, 1820–1830." *Journal of Economic History* 69, no. 3 (2009): 646–84.

——. "The Peaceful Conspiracy: Bond Markets and International Relations During the Pax Britannica." *International Organization* 66, no. 2 (2012): 211–41.

Flandreau, Marc, Juan H. Flores, Norbert Gaillard, and Sebastián Nieto-Parra. "The End of Gatekeeping: Underwriters and the Quality of Sovereign Bond Markets, 1815–2007." NBER Working Paper 15128, National Bureau of Economic Research, Chicago, 2010. http://www.nber.org/papers/w15128 (accessed 5 April 2022).

Flandreau, Marc, Juan Flores, and Sebastiàn Nieto-Parra. "The Changing Role of Global Financial Brands in the Underwriting of Foreign Government Debt (1815–2010)." Working Paper 15/2011, Graduate Institute of International Studies, Geneva, 2011. http://ideas.repec.org/p/gii/giihei/heidwp15-2011.html (accessed 5 April 2022).

Flandreau, Marc, and Joanna Kinga Slawatyniec. "Understanding Rating Addiction: U.S. Courts and the Origins of Rating Agencies' Regulatory License (1900–1940)." Working Paper 11/2013, Graduate Institute of International Studies, Geneva, 2013. https://www.econstor.eu/bitstream/10419/122121/1/787563811.pdf (accessed 29 April 2022).

Flandreau, Marc, and Stefano Ugolini. "Where It All Began: Lending of Last Resort at the Bank of England Monitoring During the Overend-Gurney Panic of 1866." In *The Origins, History, and Future of the Federal Reserve: A Return to Jekyll Island*, edited by Michael D. Bordo and William Roberds, 113–61. Cambridge: Cambridge University Press, 2013.

Flores Zendejas, Juan H., and Yann Decorzant. "Going Multilateral? Financial Markets' Access and the League of Nations Loans, 1923–28." *Economic History Review* 69, no. 2 (2016): 653–78.

Fohlin, Caroline. "The History of Corporate Ownership and Control in Germany." In *A History of Corporate Governance Around the World: Family Business Groups to Professional Managers*, edited by Randall K. Morck, 223–82. Chicago: University of Chicago Press, 2005.

Fontaine, Laurence. *The Moral Economy: Poverty, Credit, and Trust in Early Modern Europe*. Cambridge: Cambridge University Press, 2014.

Fortune, Thomas. *Fortune's Epitome of the Stocks and Public Funds, Containing Every Necessary Information for Perfectly Understanding the Nature of Those Securities and the Mode of Doing Business Therein: With a Full Acount of All the Foreign Funds and Loans*. 13th ed. London: J. J. Secretan, 1833.

Foucaud, David. "The Impact of the Companies Act of 1862." *Revue économique* 62, no. 5 (2011): 867–97.

Foucault, Michel. *Histoire de la folie à l'âge classique*. Paris: Gallimard, 1999.

——. *Les mots et les choses: une archéologie des sciences humaines*. Paris: Gallimard, 1966.

——. *Sécurité, territoire, population: cours au Collège de France, 1977–1978*. Paris: Seuil, 2004.

——. *Surveiller et punir: naissance de la prison*. Paris: Gallimard, 1993.

Fraser, Nancy. "A Triple Movement? Parsing the Politics of Crisis After Polanyi." *New Left Review* 81 (2013): 119–32.

Friendly, Michael. "The Golden Age of Statistical Graphics." *Statistical Science* 23, no. 4 (2008): 502–35.

Gabor, Daniela. "Revolution Without Revolutionaries: Interrogating the Return of Monetary Financing." Paper, "Transformative Responses to the Crisis" series, Heinrich Böll Stiftung, 2020. https://transformative-responses.org/wp-content/uploads/2021/01/TR_Report_Gabor_FINAL.pdf (accessed 2 May 2022).

Gadanecz, Blaise. "The Syndicated Loan Market: Structure, Development, and Implications." *BIS Quarterly Review*, December 2004, 75–89.

Gaillard, Norbert. *A Century of Sovereign Ratings*. New York: Springer, 2012.

——. *Les agences de notation*. Paris: La Decouverte, 2010.

Gall, Lothar, Gerald D. Feldman, Harold James, Carl-Ludwig Holtfrerich, and Hans E. Büschgen. *The Deutsche Bank, 1870–1995*. London: Weidenfeld & Nicolson, 1995.

Garner, Guillaume. "Statistique, géographie et savoirs sur l'espace en Allemagne (1780–1820)." *Cybergeo: European Journal of Geography*, no. 433 (November 28, 2008): 1–18.

Geisst, Charles R. *Wall Street: A History*. Oxford: Oxford University Press, 2012.

Gerschenkron, Alexander. *Economic Backwardness in Historical Perspective: A Book of Essays*. Cambridge, MA: Belknap Press of Harvard University Press, 1962.

Getachew, Adom. *Worldmaking After Empire: The Rise and Fall of Self-Determination*. Princeton, NJ: Princeton University Press, 2019.

Gille, Bertrand. *La banque en France au XIXe siècle: recherches historiques*. Paris: Droz, 1970.

——. *Histoire de la maison Rothschild*. 2 vols. Geneva: Droz, 1965.

Gilpin, Robert. *War and Change in World Politics*. Cambridge: Cambridge University Press, 1981.

Girouard, Mark. *The Return to Camelot: Chivalry and the English Gentleman*. New Haven, CT: Yale University Press, 1985.

Goethe, Johann Wolfgang Von. *Italian Journey: 1786–1788*. Translated by W. H. Auden and Elizabeth Mayer. London: Penguin, 1992.

Gong, Gerrit W. *The Standard of "Civilization" in International Society*. Oxford: Clarendon, 1984.

Goodman, Stephen. "How the Big U.S. Banks Really Evaluate Sovereign Risks." *Euromoney*, February 1977, 105–10.

Gray, Julia. *The Company States Keep: International Economic Organizations and Investor Perceptions*. Cambridge: Cambridge University Press, 2013.

Green, Edwin. *Debtors to Their Profession: A History of the Institute of Bankers, 1879–1979*. London: Methuen, 1979.

Green, Jeremy. "Anglo-American Development, the Euromarkets, and the Deeper Origins of Neoliberal Deregulation." *Review of International Studies* 42, no. 3 (2016): 425–49.

——. *The Political Economy of the Special Relationship: Anglo-American Development from the Gold Standard to the Financial Crisis*. Princeton, NJ: Princeton University Press, 2020.

Greenwald, John. "Greenspan's Rates of Wrath." *Time*, 28 November 1994. http://content.time.com/time/subscriber/article/0,33009,981879,00.html.

Grittersová, Jana. *Borrowing Credibility: Global Banks and Monetary Regimes*. Ann Arbor: University of Michigan Press, 2017.

Guinnane, Timothy W. "Delegated Monitors, Large and Small: Germany's Banking System, 1800–1914." *Journal of Economic Literature* 40, no. 1 (2002): 73–124.

Haas, Peter M. "Introduction: Epistemic Communities and International Policy Coordination." *International Organization* 46, no. 1 (1992): 1–35.

Häberlein, Mark. *The Fuggers of Augsburg: Pursuing Wealth and Honor in Renaissance Germany.* Charlottesville: University of Virginia Press, 2012.

Habermas, Jürgen. *The Structural Transformation of the Public Sphere: An Inquiry into a Category of Bourgeois Society.* Cambridge: Polity, 1989.

Hacking, Ian. *The Emergence of Probability: A Philosophical Study of Early Ideas About Probability, Introduction, and Statistical Inference.* Cambridge: Cambridge University Press, 1984.

——. *Historical Ontology.* Cambridge, MA: Harvard University Press, 2002.

——. *The Taming of Chance.* Cambridge: Cambridge University Press, 1990.

Haldén, Peter. "A Non-Sovereign Modernity: Attempts to Engineer Stability in the Balkans 1820–90." *Review of International Studies* 39, no. 2 (April 2013): 337–59.

Hannah, Leslie. "What Did Morgan's Men Really Do?" Paper presented at the Business History Conference, Cleveland, Ohio, 2007. https://www.researchgate.net/profile/Leslie_Hannah2/publication/24135378_What_did_Morgan's_Men_really_do/links/0a85e537b748780abb000000.pdf (accessed 29 April 2022).

Heine, Heinrich. *Heine's Wit, Wisdom and Pathos.* 2nd ed. Translated by J. Snodgrass. London: Alexander Gardner, 1888.

Helleiner, Eric. *States and the Reemergence of Global Finance: From Bretton Woods to the 1990s.* Ithaca, NY: Cornell University Press, 1994.

Hennessy, Elizabeth. "The Governors, Directors, and Management of the Bank of England." In *The Bank of England: Money, Power, and Influence, 1694–1994,* edited by David Kynaston and Richard Roberts, 85–207. Oxford: Oxford University Press, 1995.

Hirschman, Albert O. *The Passions and the Interests: Political Arguments for Capitalism Before Its Triumph.* Princeton, NJ: Princeton University Press, 2013.

Holmes, A. R., and Edwin Green. *Midland: 150 Years of Banking Business.* London: Batsford, 1986.

Hopf, Ted. "The Logic of Habit in International Relations." *European Journal of International Relations* 16, no. 4 (2010): 539–61.

Horwitz, Morton J. *The Transformation of American Law, 1870–1960: The Crisis of Legal Orthodoxy.* Oxford: Oxford University Press, 1992.

Hudson, Peter James. *Bankers and Empire: How Wall Street Colonized the Caribbean.* Chicago: University of Chicago Press, 2017.

Huertas, Thomas F. "U.S. Multinational Banking: History and Prospects." In *Banks as Multinationals,* edited by Geoffrey Jones, 248–67. London: Routledge, 1990.

Hutchings, Kimberly, Jens Bartelson, Edward Keene, Lea Ypi, Helen M. Kinsella, and David Armitage. "Foundations of Modern International Theory." *Contemporary Political Theory* 13, no. 4 (2014): 387–418.

Israel, Jonathan I. *Radical Enlightenment: Philosophy and the Making of Modernity, 1650–1750.* Oxford: Oxford University Press, 2002.

Jackson, Peter. "Pierre Bourdieu, the 'Cultural Turn,' and the Practice of International History." *Review of International Studies* 34, no. 1 (2008): 155–81.

Jaeger, C. Stephen. *The Origins of Courtliness: Civilizing Trends and the Formation of Courtly Ideals, 939–1210*. Philadelphia: University of Pennsylvania Press, 1985.

James, Harold. *Family Capitalism: Wendels, Haniels, Falcks, and the Continental European Model*. London: Belknap Press of Harvard University Press, 2006.

John, V. "The Term 'Statistics.'" *Journal of the Statistical Society of London* 46, no. 4 (1883): 656–79.

Jones, Charles A. *International Business in the Nineteenth Century: The Rise and Fall of a Cosmopolitan Bourgeoisie*. New York: New York University Press, 1987.

Jones, Emily, and Alexandra O. Zeitz. "The Limits of Globalizing Basel Banking Standards." *Journal of Financial Regulation* 3, no. 1 (2017): 89–124.

Jones, Geoffrey. *British Multinational Banking, 1830–1990*. Oxford: Clarendon, 1993.

Kadish, Alon, and Keith Tribe. "Introduction: The Supply of and Demand for Economics in Late Victorian Britain." In *The Market for Political Economy: The Advent of Economics in British University Culture*, 1–19. London: Routledge, 1993.

Kamitake, Yoshiro. "Some Notes on the Life and Works of Sir Edward Holden." *Hitotsubashi Journal of Economics* 23, no. 2 (1983): 48–56.

Kang, Zheng. "La société de statistique de Paris au XIXe siècle: un lieu de savoir social." *Les cahiers du Centre de Recherches Historiques—archives*, no. 9 (1992). http://ccrh.revues.org/2808 (accessed 5 April 2022).

Kayaoglu, Turan. *Legal Imperialism: Sovereignty and Extraterritoriality in Japan, the Ottoman Empire, and China*. Cambridge: Cambridge University Press, 2014.

Keen, Maurice. *Chivalry*. New Haven, CT: Yale University Press, 1984.

——. *Origins of the English Gentleman: Heraldry, Chivalry, and Gentility in Medieval England, c.1300–c.1500*. Stroud: Tempus, 2002.

Keene, Edward. "The Age of Grotius." In *Routledge Handbook of International Law*, edited by David Armstrong, 126–40. London: Routledge, 2009.

——. *Beyond the Anarchical Society: Grotius, Colonialism, and Order in World Politics*. Cambridge: Cambridge University Press, 2002.

——. "The English School and British Historians." *Millennium—Journal of International Studies* 37, no. 2 (2008): 381–93.

——. "International Hierarchy and the Origins of the Modern Practice of Intervention." *Review of International Studies* 39, no. 5 (2013): 1077–90.

——. "International Intellectual History and International Relations: Contexts, Canons, and Mediocrities." *International Relations* 31, no. 3 (2017): 341–56.

——. *International Political Thought: A Historical Introduction*. Cambridge: Polity, 2005.

——. "The Naming of Powers." *Cooperation and Conflict* 48, no. 2 (2013): 268–82.

Keens-Soper, H. M. A. "The French Political Academy, 1712: A School for Ambassadors." *European History Quarterly* 2, no. 4 (1972): 329–55.

Kendall, M. G. "Where Shall the History of Statistics Begin?" In *Studies in the History of Statistics and Probability*, edited by E. S. Pearson and M. G. Kendall, 45–46. London: Griffin, 1970.

Kerr, Ian M. *A History of the Eurobond Market: The First 21 Years*. London: Euromoney, 1984.

Kindleberger, Charles P. *A Financial History of Western Europe*. London: Routledge, 2006.

King, Frank H. H. *History of the Hongkong and Shanghai Banking Corporation*. 4 vols. Cambridge: Cambridge University Press, 1987.

King, Gary, Robert O. Keohane, and Sidney Verba. *Designing Social Inquiry: Scientific Inference in Qualitative Research*. Princeton, NJ: Princeton University Press, 1994.

Kirshner, Jonathan. *Appeasing Bankers: Financial Caution on the Road to War*. Princeton, NJ: Princeton University Press, 2007.

Kleeberg, John Martin. "The Disconto-Gesellschaft and German Industrialization: A Critical Examination of the Career of a German Universal Bank, 1851–1914." PhD diss., University of Oxford, 1988.

Klingenstein, Grete. "Book Review of *Die Lehre von Der Macht Der Staaten: Das Aussenpolitische Machtproblem in Der 'politischen Wissenschaft' Und in Der Praktischen Politik Im 18. Jahrhundert*, by Harm Klueting." *English Historical Review* 103, no. 406 (1988): 134–38.

Klüber, Johann Ludwig. *Acten Des Wiener Congresses, in Den Jahren 1814 Und 1815*. Erlangen: J. J. Palm und E. Enke, 1832.

Klueting, Harm. *Die Lehre von der Macht der Staaten: Das aussenpolitische Machtproblem in der "politischen Wissenschaft" und in der praktischen Politik im 18. Jahrhundert*. Berlin: Duncker & Humblot, 1986.

Konvitz, Josef. *Cartography in France, 1660–1848: Science, Engineering, and Statecraft*. Chicago: University of Chicago Press, 1987.

Koskenniemi, Martti. *The Gentle Civilizer of Nations: The Rise and Fall of International Law, 1870–1960*. Cambridge: Cambridge University Press, 2004.

——. "Into Positivism: Georg Friedrich von Martens (1756–1821) and Modern International Law." *Constellations* 15, no. 2 (2008): 189–207.

Krasner, Stephen D. *Sovereignty: Organized Hypocrisy*. Princeton, NJ: Princeton University Press, 1999.

Kugeler, Heidrun. "Le Parfait Ambassadeur: The Theory and Practice of Diplomacy in the Century Following the Peace of Westphalia." PhD diss., University of Oxford, 2006.

Kuhn, Thomas S. *The Structure of Scientific Revolutions*. Chicago: University of Chicago Press, 1996.

Kynaston, David. *Till Time's Last Sand: A History of the Bank of England, 1694–2013*. London: Bloomsbury, 2020.

Lafargue, Bertrand de. "Henri Germain (1824–1905): un banquier en politique." In *Le Crédit Lyonnais, 1863–1986: études historiques*, edited by Bernard Desjardins, Michel Lescure, Roger Nougaret, Alain Plessis, and André Straus, 33–60. Paris: Droz, 2003.

Lahire, Bernard. *L'homme pluriel*. Paris: Hachette, 2006.

Lall, Ranjit. "From Failure to Failure: The Politics of International Banking Regulation." *Review of International Political Economy* 19, no. 4 (2012): 609–38.

Landes, David S. *Bankers and Pashas: International Finance and Economic Imperialism in Egypt.* London: Heinemann, 1958.

——. "Vieille banque et banque nouvelle: la révolution financière du dix-neuvième siècle." *Revue d'histoire moderne et contemporaine* 3, no. 3 (1956): 204–22.

Langohr, Herwig, and Patricia Langohr. *The Rating Agencies and Their Credit Ratings: What They Are, How They Work, and Why They Are Relevant.* Hoboken, NJ: John Wiley & Sons, 2009.

Lawson, John, and Harold Silver. *A Social History of Education in England.* London: Routledge, 2013.

Lazarsfeld, Paul F. "Notes on the History of Quantification in Sociology—Trends, Sources, and Problems." *Isis* 52, no. 2 (1961): 277–333.

Learoyd, Arthur. "Configurations of Semi-Sovereignty in the Nineteenth Century." In *De-Centering State Making: Comparative and International Perspectives*, edited by Jens Bartelson, Martin Hall, and Jan Teorell, 155–74. Cheltenham: Edward Elgar, 2018.

——. "Semi-Sovereignty and Relationships of Hierarchy." PhD diss., University of Oxford, 2017.

Léautey, Eugène. *L'enseignement commercial et les écoles de commerce en France et dans le monde entier.* Paris: Guillaumin et Cie., 1886.

Lechner, Silviya, and Mervyn Frost. *Practice Theory and International Relations.* Cambridge: Cambridge University Press, 2018.

Leedham-Green, E. S. *A Concise History of the University of Cambridge.* Cambridge: Cambridge University Press, 1996.

Lemarchand, Yann. " 'A la conquête de la science des comptes.' Variations autour de quelques manuels de comptabilité des XVIIe et XVIIIe siècles." In *Ecrire, compter, mesurer /2 : vers une histoire des rationalités pratiques*, edited by Natacha Coquery, François Menant, and Florence Weber, 34–65. Paris: Editions Rue d'Ulm, 2013.

Lennkh, Alvise, Bernhard Bartels, and Thibault Vasse. "The Rise of Central Banks as Sovereign Debt Holders: Implications for Investor Bases." SUERF Policy Note, European Money and Finance Forum, Vienna, October 2019.

Lienau, Odette. *Rethinking Sovereign Debt: Politics, Reputation, and Legitimacy in Modern Finance.* Cambridge, MA: Harvard University Press, 2014.

Lipson, Charles. *Standing Guard: Protecting Foreign Capital in the Nineteenth and Twentieth Centuries.* Berkeley: University of California Press, 1985.

Lisle-Williams, Michael. "Beyond the Market: The Survival of Family Capitalism in the English Merchant Banks." *British Journal of Sociology* 35, no. 2 (1984): 241–71.

——. "Merchant Banking Dynasties in the English Class Structure: Ownership, Solidarity, and Kinship in the City of London, 1850–1960." *British Journal of Sociology* 35, no. 3 (1984): 333–62.

Lord Byron. *Don Juan*. London: Penguin, 2004.

Loubère, Simon de la. *Du royaume de Siam*. Amsterdam: Chez Abraham Wolfgang près de la Bourse, 1691.

Ludwig, Hannelore. *Die wirtschafts- und sozialwissenschaftliche Lehre in Köln: von 1901 bis 1989/90*. Köln: Böhlau, 1991.

Lünig, Johann Christian. *Theatrum Ceremoniale Historico-Politicum, Oder Historisch- Und Politischer Schau-Platz Aller Ceremonien*. 2 vols. Leipzig, 1720.

MacKenzie, Donald. *An Engine, Not a Camera: How Financial Models Shape Markets*. Cambridge, MA: MIT Press, 2008.

——. *Statistics in Britain, 1865–1930: The Social Construction of Scientific Knowledge*. Edinburgh: Edinburgh University Press, 1981.

Madrid, Raúl L. *Overexposed: U.S. Banks Confront the Third World Debt Crisis*. Boulder, CO: Westview, 1992.

Malik, Hassan. *Bankers and Bolsheviks: International Finance and the Russian Revolution*. Princeton, NJ: Princeton University Press, 2020.

Marken, Bernard van, and Piet A. Geljon. "La banque de crédit et de dépôt des Pays-Bas (Nederlandsche Credit en Deposito Bank): aux origines de la Banque de Paris et des Pays-Bas, 1863–1872." *Histoire, économie et société* 32, no. 1 (2013): 19–43.

Mauro, Paolo, Nathan Sussman, and Yishay Yafeh. *Emerging Markets and Financial Globalization: Sovereign Bond Spreads in 1870–1913 and Today*. Oxford: Oxford University Press, 2006.

McCormick, Ted. *William Petty and the Ambitions of Political Arithmetic*. Oxford: Oxford University Press, 2009.

McKinnon, Ronald I. *Money and Capital in Economic Development*. Washington, DC: Brookings Institution, 1973.

Merry, Sally Engle, Kevin E. Davis, and Benedict Kingsbury, eds. *The Quiet Power of Indicators*. Cambridge: Cambridge University Press, 2015.

Meuleau, Marc. "From Inheritors to Managers: The École Des Hautes Études Commerciales and Business Firms." In *Management and Business in Britain and France: The Age of the Corporate Economy*, edited by Youssef Cassis, François Crouzet, and Terry Gourvish, 128–46. Oxford: Oxford University Press, 1995.

Michie, R. C. *The Global Securities Market: A History*. Oxford: Oxford University Press, 2006.

Micklethwait, John, and Adrian Wooldridge. *The Company: A Short History of a Revolutionary Idea*. London: Weidenfeld & Nicolson, 2003.

Mikkelsen, Anders L. "Dealing with Risk: Underwriting Sovereign Bond Issues in London 1870–1914." EABH Paper No. 14–06, June 2014. http://www.eabh. info/fileadmin/user_upload/documents/eabhpapers14_06.pdf (accessed 4 April 2022).

Mitchell, Timothy. *Rule of Experts: Egypt, Techno-Politics, Modernity*. Berkeley: University of California Press, 2002.

Money Trust Investigation: Investigation of Financial and Monetary Conditions in the United States Under House Resolutions 429 and 504 Before a Subcommittee of the Committee on Banking and Currency, Parts 1–29. Washington, DC: Government Printing Office, 1913.

Monnet, Eric, and Blaise Truong-Loï. "The History and Politics of Public Debt Accounting." In *A World of Public Debts: A Political History*, edited by Nicolas Barreyre and Nicolas Delalande, 481–511. Cham: Palgrave Macmillan, 2020.

Moody, John. *The Masters of Capital: A Chronicle of Wall Street*. New Haven, CT: Yale University Press, 1919.

Mosley, Layna. *Global Capital and National Governments*. Cambridge: Cambridge University Press, 2003.

Mösslang, Markus, and Torsten Riotte, eds. *The Diplomats' World: The Cultural History of Diplomacy, 1815–1914*. Oxford: Oxford University Press, 2008.

Muchlinski, Peter. "The Development of German Corporate Law to 1990: An Historical Reappraisal." *German Law Journal* 14, no. 2 (2013): 339–79.

Muldoon, James. *Empire and Order: The Concept of Empire, 800–1800*. New York: Palgrave Macmillan, 1999.

Müller-Merbach, H. "Management Science in Germany and Its Impact on German Management Practice." *Omega* 16, no. 3 (1988): 197–202.

Munck, Ronaldo. "Globalization and Democracy: A New 'Great Transformation?'" *Annals of the American Academy of Political and Social Science* 581, no. 1 (2002): 10–21.

Munn, Charles W. "The Emergence of Joint-Stock Banking in the British Isles: A Comparative Approach." *Business History* 30, no. 1 (1988): 69–83.

Napier, Christopher J. "Accounting and the Absence of a Business Economics Tradition in the United Kingdom." *European Accounting Review* 5, no. 3 (January 1, 1996): 449–81.

Nash, Robert Lucas. *A Short Inquiry into the Profitable Nature of Our Investments: With a Record of Five Hundred of Our Most Important Public Securities During the Ten Years 1870 to 1880*. London: Effingham Wilson, 1880.

Neumann, Iver B. "The English School on Diplomacy: Scholarly Promise Unfulfilled." *International Relations* 17, no. 3 (2003): 341–69.

——. "Returning Practice to the Linguistic Turn: The Case of Diplomacy." *Millennium—Journal of International Studies* 31, no. 3 (2002): 627–51.

Nexon, Daniel H. *The Struggle for Power in Early Modern Europe: Religious Conflict, Dynastic Empires, and International Change*. Princeton, NJ: Princeton University Press, 2009.

Nikolow, Sybilla. "A. F. W. Crome's Measurements of the 'Strength of the State': Statistical Representations in Central Europe Around 1800." *History of Political Economy* 33, no. 5 (2001): 23–56.

North, Douglass C., and Barry R. Weingast. "Constitutions and Commitment: The Evolution of Institutional Governing Public Choice in Seventeenth-Century England." *Journal of Economic History* 49, no. 4 (1989): 803–32.

Obstfeld, Maurice, and Alan M. Taylor. "Sovereign Risk, Credibility, and the Gold Standard: 1870–1913 Versus 1925–31." *Economic Journal* 113, no. 487 (2003): 241–75.

Odlyzko, Andrew. "The Collapse of the Railway Mania, the Development of Capital Markets, and Robert Lucas Nash, a Forgotten Pioneer of Accounting and Financial Analysis." SSRN Scholarly Paper, Rochester, New York, 23 January 2011. http://papers.ssrn.com/abstract=1625738.

O'Driscoll, Gerald P., and Eugenie D. Short. "Safety-Net Mechanisms: The Case of International Lending." *Cato Journal* 4, no. 1 (1984): 185–204.

Office of the Comptroller of the Currency, Federal Reserve Board, Federal Deposit Insurance Corporation, and Office of Thrift Supervision. "Risk-Based Capital Standards: Advanced Capital Adequacy Framework—Basel II." *Federal Register* 72, no. 235 (2007). https://www.federalregister.gov/documents/2007/12/07/07 -5729/risk-based-capital-standards-advanced-capital-adequacy-framework-- -basel-ii (accessed 22 April 2022).

Ogle, Vanessa. "Archipelago Capitalism: Tax Havens, Offshore Money, and the State, 1950s–1970s." *American Historical Review* 122, no. 5 (2017): 1431–58.

——. "State Rights Against Private Capital: The 'New International Economic Order' and the Struggle over Aid, Trade, and Foreign Investment, 1962–1981." *Humanity* 5, no. 2 (2014): 211–34.

Olegario, Rowena. *A Culture of Credit: Embedding Trust and Transparency in American Business.* Cambridge, MA: Harvard University Press, 2006.

Orbell, John. "Private Banks and International Finance in the Light of the Archives of Baring Brothers." In *The World of Private Banking*, edited by Youssef Cassis and Philip Cottrell, 141–58. London: Ashgate, 2009.

Osiander, Andreas. *Before the State: Systemic Political Change in the West from the Greeks to the French Revolution.* Oxford: Oxford University Press, 2007.

——. "Sovereignty, International Relations, and the Westphalian Myth." *International Organization* 55, no. 2 (2001): 251–87.

Ottonello, Pablo, and Diego J. Perez. "The Currency Composition of Sovereign Debt." *American Economic Journal: Macroeconomics* 11, no. 3 (2019): 174–208.

Owens, Patricia. *Economy of Force: Counterinsurgency and the Historical Rise of the Social.* Cambridge: Cambridge University Press, 2015.

Owens, Patricia, and Katharina Rietzler, eds. *Women's International Thought: A New History.* Cambridge: Cambridge University Press, 2021.

Pak, Susie J. *Gentlemen Bankers: The World of J. P. Morgan.* Cambridge, MA: Harvard University Press, 2013.

Parkin, Frank. *Marxism and Class Theory: A Bourgeois Critique.* New York: Taylor & Francis, 1979.

Paudyn, Bartholomew. *Credit Ratings and Sovereign Debt: The Political Economy of Creditworthiness Through Risk and Uncertainty.* New York: Palgrave Macmillan, 2014.

Pauly, Louis W. "International Financial Institutions and National Economic Governance." In *International Financial History in the Twentieth Century: System and Anarchy*, edited by Marc Flandreau, Carl-Ludwig Holtfrerich, and Harold James, 239–64. Cambridge: Cambridge University Press, 2002.

——. *Who Elected the Bankers? Surveillance and Control in the World Economy.* Ithaca, NY: Cornell University Press, 1997.

Peuchet, Jacques. *Manuel du banquier, de l'agent de change et du courtier: contenant les lois et réglemens qui s'y rapportent, les diverses opérations de change, courtage et négociations des effets à la Bourse.* Paris: Roret, 1829.

Phillips, Andrew, and Jason Sharman. *International Order in Diversity: War, Trade, and Rule in the Indian Ocean.* Cambridge: Cambridge University Press, 2015.

——. *Outsourcing Empire: How Company-States Made the Modern World.* Princeton, NJ: Princeton University Press, 2020.

Philpott, Daniel. *Revolutions in Sovereignty: How Ideas Shaped Modern International Relations.* Princeton, NJ: Princeton University Press, 2001.

Pistor, Katharina, Yoram Keinan, Jan Kleinheisterkamp, and Mark D. West. "Evolution of Corporate Law: A Cross-Country Comparison." *University of Pennsylvania Journal of International Law* 23, no. 4 (2002): 791–871.

Pitts, Jennifer. *Boundaries of the International: Law and Empire.* Cambridge, MA: Harvard University Press, 2018.

——. *A Turn to Empire: The Rise of Imperial Liberalism in Britain and France.* Princeton, NJ: Princeton University Press, 2006.

Plessis, Alain. "The History of Banks in France." In *Handbook on the History of European Banks*, edited by Manfred Pohl and Sabine Freitag, 185–296. Aldershot: Edward Elgar, 1994.

——. "The Parisian 'Haute Banque' and the International Economy in the Nineteenth and Early Twentieth Centuries." In *The World of Private Banking*, edited by Youssef Cassis and Philip Cottrell, 127–40. Farnham: Ashgate, 2009.

——. *Régents et gouverneurs de la Banque de France sous le Second Empire.* Paris: Droz, 1985.

Pohl, Manfred. *Entstehung und Entwicklung des Universalbankensystems: Konzentration und Krise als wichtige Faktoren.* Frankfurt am Main: F. Knapp, 1986.

Pohle Fraser, Monika. "Personal and Impersonal Exchange—The Role of Reputation in Banking: Some Evidence from Nineteenth- and Early Twentieth-Century Banks' Archives." In *Centres and Peripheries in Banking: The Historical Development of Financial Markets*, edited by Philip Cottrell, Even Lange, and Ulf Olsson, 177–96. Aldershot: Ashgate, 2007.

Polanyi, Karl. *The Great Transformation: The Political and Economic Origins of Our Time.* 2nd ed. Boston: Beacon, 2001.

"The Politics of Numbers." Special issue, *Review of International Studies* 41, no. 5 (2015).

Porter, Theodore M. *The Rise of Statistical Thinking, 1820–1900.* Princeton, NJ: Princeton University Press, 1986.

———. *Trust in Numbers: The Pursuit of Objectivity in Science and Public Life*. Princeton, NJ: Princeton University Press, 1996.

Pouliot, Vincent. *International Security in Practice: The Politics of NATO-Russia Diplomacy*. Cambridge: Cambridge University Press, 2010.

———. "The Logic of Practicality: A Theory of Practice of Security Communities." *International Organization* 62, no. 2 (2008): 257–88.

———. " 'Sobjectivism': Toward a Constructivist Methodology." *International Studies Quarterly* 51, no. 2 (2007): 359–84.

Prunaux, Emmanuel. "Les comptoirs d'escompte de la Banque de France." *Napoleonica* 6, no. 3 (2009): 49–98.

Randeraad, Nico. *States and Statistics in the Nineteenth Century: Europe by Numbers*. Manchester: Manchester University Press, 2010.

Rassem, Mohammed, and Justin Stagl, eds. "Expose." In *Statistik Und Staatsbeschreibung in Der Neuzeit: Vornehmlich Im 16.–18. Jahrhundert*, edited by Mohammed Rassem and Justin Stagl, 11–16. Paderborn: Ferdinand Schoningh, 1980.

Redlich, Fritz. "Jacques Lafitte and the Beginnings of Investment Banking in France." *Bulletin of the Business Historical Society* 22, nos. 4–6 (1948): 137–61.

Reinhart, Carmen M., and M. Belen Sbrancia. "The Liquidation of Government Debt." NBER Working Paper 16893, National Bureau of Economic Research, Cambridge, MA, March 2011. http://www.nber.org/papers/w16893 (accessed 5 April 2022).

Reus-Smit, Christian. *The Moral Purpose of the State: Culture, Social Identity, and Institutional Rationality in International Relations*. Princeton, NJ: Princeton University Press, 1999.

Pirou, Gaëtan, and Charles Rist. *L'enseignement économique en France et à l'étranger*. Paris: Librairie du Recueil Sirey, 1937.

Rieffel, Alexis. *Restructuring Sovereign Debt: The Case for Ad Hoc Machinery*. Washington, DC: Brookings Institution, 2003.

Riley, James. *International Government Finance and the Amsterdam Capital Market, 1740–1815*. Cambridge: Cambridge University Press, 2009.

Ringmar, Erik. "The Search for Dialogue as a Hindrance to Understanding: Practices as Inter-Paradigmatic Research Program." *International Theory* 6, no. 1 (2014): 1–27.

Roberts, Richard. "What's in a Name? Merchants, Merchant Bankers, Accepting Houses, Issuing Houses, Industrial Bankers, and Investment Bankers." *Business History* 35, no. 3 (1993): 22–38.

Roos, Jerome. *Why Not Default? The Political Economy of Sovereign Debt*. Princeton, NJ: Princeton University Press, 2019.

Roosen, William J. "Early Modern Diplomatic Ceremonial: A Systems Approach." *Journal of Modern History* 52, no. 3 (1980): 452–76.

Rosenbaum, Eduard, and A. J Sherman. *M. M. Warburg & Co., 1798–1938: Merchant Bankers of Hamburg*. London: C. Hurst, 1979.

Rosenberg, Emily S. *Financial Missionaries to the World: The Politics and Culture of Dollar Diplomacy, 1900–1930*. Durham, NC: Duke University Press, 2003.

Rottenburg, Richard, Sally E. Merry, Sung-Joon Park, and Johanna Mugler, eds. *The World of Indicators: The Making of Governmental Knowledge Through Quantification*. Cambridge: Cambridge University Press, 2015.

Ruggie, John Gerard. "International Regimes, Transactions, and Change: Embedded Liberalism in the Postwar Economic Order." *International Organization* 36, no. 2 (1982): 379–415.

——. "Territoriality and Beyond: Problematizing Modernity in International Relations." *International Organization* 47, no. 1 (1993): 139–74.

Saiegh, Sebastian M. "Do Countries Have a 'Democratic Advantage'? Political Institutions, Multilateral Agencies, and Sovereign Borrowing." *Comparative Political Studies* 38, no. 4 (2005): 366–87.

Sanderson, Michael. "French Influences on Technical and Managerial Education in England, 1870–1940." In *Management and Business in Britain and France: The Age of the Corporate Economy*, edited by Youssef Cassis, François Crouzet, and Terry Gourvish, 111–27. Oxford: Oxford University Press, 1995.

Saul, Samir. "Banking Alliances and International Issues on the Paris Capital Market, 1890–1914." In *London and Paris as International Financial Centres in the Twentieth Century*, edited by Eric Bussière and Youssef Cassis, 119–50. Oxford: Oxford University Press, 2005.

Scaglione, Aldo. *Knights at Court: Courtliness, Chivalry, and Courtesy from Ottonian Germany to the Italian Renaissance*. Berkeley: University of California Press, 1992.

Schenk, Catherine R. "The Origins of the Eurodollar Market in London: 1955–1963." *Explorations in Economic History* 35, no. 2 (1998): 221–38.

Schmidt, Helmut D. "Schlözer on Historiography." *History and Theory* 18, no. 1 (1979): 37–40.

Schmitt, Hans A. "From Sovereign States to Prussian Provinces: Hanover and Hesse-Nassau, 1866–1871." *Journal of Modern History* 57, no. 1 (1985): 24–56.

Schultz, Kenneth A., and Barry R. Weingast. "The Democratic Advantage: Institutional Foundations of Financial Power in International Competition." *International Organization* 57, no. 1 (2003): 3–42.

Scott, H. M. *The Emergence of the Eastern Powers, 1756–1775*. Cambridge: Cambridge University Press, 2001.

Scott, James. *Seeing Like a State: How Certain Schemes to Improve the Human Condition Have Failed*. New Haven, CT: Yale University Press, 1999.

Selwyn, Ben. "Trotsky, Gerschenkron, and the Political Economy of Late Capitalist Development." *Economy and Society* 40, no. 3 (2011): 421–50.

Shaw, Edward S. *Financial Deepening in Economic Development*. New York: Oxford University Press, 1973.

Siegel, Jerold. *Modernity and Bourgeois Life*. Cambridge: Cambridge University Press, 2012.

Sinclair, David. *The Land That Never Was: Sir Gregor MacGregor and the Most Audacious Fraud in History*. London: Headline, 2003.

Sinclair, Timothy J. *The New Masters of Capital: American Bond Rating Agencies and the Politics of Creditworthiness*. Ithaca, NY: Cornell University Press, 2005.

Skinner, Quentin. *The Foundations of Modern Political Thought*: vol. 2, *The Age of Reformation*. Cambridge: Cambridge University Press, 1978.

——. *Visions of Politics*, vol. 2: *Renaissance Virtues*. Cambridge: Cambridge University Press, 2002.

Slobodian, Quinn. "World Maps for the Debt Paradigm: Risk Ranking the Poorer Nations in the 1970s." *Critical Historical Studies* 8, no. 1 (2021): 1–22.

Spruyt, Hendrik. *The Sovereign State and Its Competitors: An Analysis of Systems Change*. Princeton, NJ: Princeton University Press, 1996.

Stallings, Barbara. *Banker to the Third World: U.S. Portfolio Investment in Latin America, 1900–1986*. Berkeley: University of California Press, 1987.

Standard & Poor's. "Rating Performance 2002: Default, Transition, Recovery, and Spreads." February 2003. https://www4.stat.ncsu.edu/~bloomfld/Ratings Performance.pdf (accessed 28 March 2022).

Stasavage, David. *Public Debt and the Birth of the Democratic State: France and Great Britain 1688–1789*. Cambridge: Cambridge University Press, 2008.

——. *States of Credit: Size, Power, and the Development of European Polities*. Princeton, NJ: Princeton University Press, 2011.

Stephanou, Constantinos, and Juan Carlos Mendoza. "Credit Risk Measurement Under Basel II: An Overview and Implementation Issues for Developing Countries." World Bank Policy Research Working Paper 3556, April 2005.

Stern, Fritz. *Gold and Iron: Bismarck, Bleichröder, and the Building of the German Empire*. New York: Vintage, 1979.

Stolleis, Michael. "Zur Rezeption von Giovanni Botero in Deutschland." In *Botero e La "Ragion Di Stato." Atti Del Convegno in Memoria Di Luigi Firpo*, edited by A.Enzo Baldini, 405–16. Florence: Olschki, 1992.

Stoskopf, Nicolas. "La fondation du comptoir national d'escompte de Paris, banque révolutionnaire (1848)." *Histoire, économie et société* 21, no. 3 (2002): 395–411.

——. "Qu'est-ce que la haute banque Parisienne au XIXe siècle?" In *Journée d'études sur l'histoire de la haute banque*, 2000. https://hal.archives-ouvertes.fr/hal -00431248/document (accessed 5 April 2022).

Studenski, Paul. *The Income of Nations*. New York: New York University Press, 1958.

Stürmer, Michael, Gabriele Teichmann, and Wilhelm Treue. *Striking the Balance: Sal. Oppenheim Jr. & Cie—A Family and a Bank*. Translated by Ewald Osers. London: Weidenfeld & Nicolson, 1994.

Subrahmanyam, Sanjay. *Courtly Encounters: Translating Courtliness and Violence in Early Modern Eurasia*. Cambridge, MA: Harvard University Press, 2012.

Sullivan, Arthur, and William S. Gilbert. *Utopia Limited, Or, The Flowers of Progress: An Original Comic Opera in Two Acts*. London: Chappell, 1893.

Sunderland, David. *Managing the British Empire: The Crown Agents, 1833–1914*. Woodgate: Boydell & Brewer, 2004.

Suzuki, Toshio. *Japanese Government Loan Issues on the London Capital Market, 1870–1913*. London: Athlone, 1994.

Sylla, Richard. "A Historical Primer on the Business of Credit Rating." In *Ratings, Rating Agencies, and the Global Financial System*, edited by Richard M. Levich, Giovanni Majnoni, and Carmen Reinhart, 19–40. Boston: Kluwer, 2002.

Szramkiewicz, Romuald. *Les régents et censeurs de la Banque de France nommés sous le Consulat et l'Empire*. Paris: Droz, 1974.

Terpstra, Nicholas. *Religious Refugees in the Early Modern World*. Cambridge: Cambridge University Press, 2015.

Teschke, Benno. *The Myth of 1648: Class, Geopolitics, and the Making of Modern International Relations*. 2nd ed. London: Verso, 2009.

Tilly, Charles. *Coercion, Capital and European States, A.D. 990—1992*. Cambridge, MA: Basil Blackwell, 1990.

Tilly, Richard. "Germany." In *Handbook on the History of European Banks*, edited by Manfred Pohl and Sabine Freitag, 299–489. Aldershot: Edward Elgar, 1994.

——. "International Aspects of the Development of German Banking." In *International Banking 1870–1914*, edited by Rondo Cameron and Valerii I. Bovykin, 90–112. Oxford: Oxford University Press, 1991.

Todd, David. "Republican Capitalism: The Political Economy of French Capital Exports in the Nineteenth Century." Working paper, King's College, London, 2015.

Tomz, Michael. *Reputation and International Cooperation: Sovereign Debt Across Three Centuries*. Princeton, NJ: Princeton University Press, 2007.

Tooze, Adam. *Crashed: How a Decade of Financial Crises Changed the World*. New York: Viking, 2018.

——. *The Deluge: The Great War, America, and the Remaking of the Global Order, 1916–1931*. New York: Penguin, 2015.

——. "Of Bond Vigilantes, Central Bankers, and the Crisis of 2008." In *A World of Public Debts: A Political History*, edited by Nicolas Barreyre and Nicolas Delalande, 453–78. Cham: Palgrave Macmillan, 2020.

——. *Statistics and the German State, 1900–1945: The Making of Modern Economic Knowledge*. Cambridge: Cambridge University Press, 2001.

Tribe, Keith. *Governing Economy: The Reformation of German Economic Discourse, 1750–1840*. Cambridge: Cambridge University Press, 1988.

Üsdiken, Behlül, Alfred Kieser, and Peter Kjaer. "Academy, Economy, and Polity: Betriebswirtschaftslehre in Germany, Denmark, and Turkey Before 1945." *Business History* 46, no. 3 (2004): 381–406.

Vanoli, André. *A History of National Accounting*. Oxford: IOS, 2005.

Veblen, Thorstein. *The Theory of the Leisure Class*. New York: Penguin, 1994.

Vec, Miloš. *Zeremonialwissenschaft im Fürstenstaat: Studien zur juristischen und politischen Theorie absolutistischer Herrschaftsrepräsentation.* Frankfurt am Main: Klostermann, 1998.

Vergerio, Claire. "Context, Reception, and the Study of Great Thinkers in International Relations." *International Theory* 11, no. 1 (2019): 110–37.

Vogt, W. Paul, and R. Burke Johnson. *Dictionary of Statistics & Methodology: A Nontechnical Guide for the Social Sciences.* Thousand Oaks, CA: SAGE, 2011.

Waibel, Michael. *Sovereign Defaults Before International Courts and Tribunals.* Cambridge: Cambridge University Press, 2011.

Wake, Jehanne. *Kleinwort, Benson: The History of Two Families in Banking.* Oxford: Oxford University Press, 1997.

Wakefield, Andre. *The Disordered Police State: German Cameralism as Science and Practice.* Chicago: University of Chicago Press, 2009.

Walker, George. *International Banking Regulation: Law, Policy, and Practice.* London: Kluwer, 2001.

Wallenius, Tomas. "The Case for a History of Global Legal Practices." *European Journal of International Relations* 25, no. 1 (2019): 108–30.

Walter, Andrew. *World Power and World Money: The Role of Hegemony and International Monetary Order.* New York: Harvester Wheatsheaf, 1993.

Watt, Donald Cameron. *Succeeding John Bull: America in Britain's Place, 1900–1975.* Cambridge: Cambridge University Press, 1984.

——. *What About the People? Abstraction and Reality in History and the Social Sciences: An Inaugural Lecture.* London: London School of Economics and Political Science, 1983.

Weber, Max. *Economy and Society: An Outline of Interpretive Sociology.* Edited by Guenther Roth and Claus Wittich. Berkeley: University of California Press, 1978.

Wechsberg, Joseph. *The Merchant Bankers.* London: Weidenfeld & Nicolson, 1967.

Weintraub, Robert E. "International Debt: Crisis and Challenge." *Cato Journal* 4, no. 1 (1984): 21–61.

Wenger, Etienne. *Communities of Practice: Learning, Meaning, and Identity.* Cambridge: Cambridge University Press, 1999.

Westergaard, Harald. *Contributions to the History of Statistics.* London: PSKing, 1932.

Whale, P. Barrett. *Joint Stock Banking in Germany: A Study of the German Credit-banks Before and After the War.* London: Cass, 1968.

White, Lawrence J. "The Credit Rating Industry: An Industrial Organization Analysis." In *Ratings, Rating Agencies, and the Global Financial System*, edited by Richard M. Levich, Giovanni Majnoni, and Carmen M. Reinhart, 41–63. New York: Springer, 2002.

Wicquefort, Abraham de. *L'ambassadeur et ses fonctions.* La Haye: Chez Jean & Daniel Steucker, 1681.

Wigglesworth, Robin, Joe Rennison, Eric Platt, and Colby Smith. "Return of the Bond Vigilantes: Will Inflation Fears Spoil the Post-Pandemic Party?" *Financial Times*, 26 February 2021. https://www.ft.com/content/542d6127-11e7-47ff -86cb-dd7bd974cda3.

Wight, Martin. *Power Politics*. London: Leicester University Press, 1995.

Wilkins, Mira. "Foreign Investment in the U.S. Economy Before 1914." *Annals of the American Academy of Political and Social Science* 516, no. 1 (1991): 9–21.

——. *The History of Foreign Investment in the United States to 1914*. Cambridge, MA: Harvard University Press, 1989.

Wilson, Peter. "The English School Meets the Chicago School: The Case for a Grounded Theory of International Institutions." *International Studies Review* 14, no. 4 (2012): 567–90.

Winkler, Max. *Foreign Bonds, an Autopsy: A Study of Defaults and Repudiations of Government Obligations*. Philadelphia: Roland Swain, 1933.

——. *Investments of United States Capital in Latin America*. Boston: World Peace Foundation, 1928.

Wood, Ellen Meiksins. *The Pristine Culture of Capitalism: A Historical Essay on Old Regimes and Modern States*. London: Verso, 1991.

Wood, Robert E. *From Marshall Plan to Debt Crisis: Foreign Aid and Development Choices in the World Economy*. Berkeley: University of California Press, 1986.

Wullweber, Joscha. *Zentralbankkapitalismus: Transformationen des globalen Finanzsystems in Krisenzeiten*. Berlin: Suhrkamp, 2021.

Yardeni, Ed. "A Brief History of Ed Yardeni's 'Bond Vigilante' Model." *Business Insider*, November 13, 2013. https://www.businessinsider.com/bonds-and-nominal -gdp-2013-11.

Zande, Johan van der. "Statistik and History in the German Enlightenment." *Journal of the History of Ideas* 71, no. 3 (2010): 411–32.

Ziegler, Philip. *The Sixth Great Power: Barings, 1765–1929*. London: Collins, 1988.

Zincone, Giovanna, and John Agnew. "The Second Great Transformation: The Politics of Globalisation in the Global North." *Space and Polity* 4, no. 1 (2000): 5–21.

Zucker, Stanley. *Ludwig Bamberger: German Liberal Political and Social Critic, 1823–1899*. Pittsburgh: University of Pittsburgh Press, 1975.

INDEX

GPSR Authorized Representative: Easy Access System Europe, Mustamäe tee
50, 10621 Tallinn, Estonia, gpsr.requests@easproject.com

www.ingramcontent.com/pod-product-compliance
Lightning Source LLC
Chambersburg PA
CBHW032131020426
42334CB00016B/1120

9 780231 204699